NORTH AFRICAN WOMEN IN FRANCE

CAITLIN KILLIAN

North African Women in France

Gender, Culture, and Identity

STANFORD UNIVERSITY PRESS

STANFORD, CALIFORNIA 2006

Library of Congress Cataloging-in-Publication Data
Killian, Caitlin.
    North African women in France : gender,
culture, and identity / Caitlin Killian.
        p.   cm.
    Includes bibliographical references and index.
    ISBN-13: 978-0-8047-5420-0 (cloth : alk. paper)
    ISBN-10: 0-8047-5420-9 (cloth : alk. paper)
    ISBN-13: 978-0-8047-5421-7 (pbk. : alk. paper)
    ISBN-10: 0-8047-5421-7 (pbk. : alk. paper)
        1. Muslim women — France. 2. North
Africans — France. 3. Women immigrants —
France. I. Title.
    HQ1170.K36   2006
    305.48'6970944 — dc22   2006005158

Typeset by BookMatters in 10/14 Janson

For my parents, Sylvia and Larry Killian

Contents

Acknowledgments

A book is rarely a lone endeavor, and I wish to thank several people who have contributed to this book's fruition. Timothy Dowd, Nancy Eiesland, Jen'nan Ghazal Read, Carrie Wickham, and three anonymous reviewers devoted time to reading and commenting on different versions of this work. Paul Silverstein's thoughtful comments improved the historical framing of the book and introduced me to valuable sources. In addition to spending many hours with the text, Cathryn Johnson provided encouragement and mentorship. Karen Hegtvedt's expert editorial eye was a great asset, but I am also grateful for her advice on academia and life in general. My editor at Stanford, Kate Wahl, has believed in this project through thick and thin. The final product has benefited enormously from all of their valuable suggestions.

My initial fieldwork was supported by funds from the graduate school at Emory University. Drew University provided release time to work on the manuscript and financial support for a later trip to consult recent sources and statistical data. My colleagues in the Sociology Department and friends in other departments at Drew have provided a rich and supportive environment since I joined the faculty. My student research assistant, Diane Kaminskas, helped me compile the index.

Several people facilitated my research in France, and I am indebted to them all, including those I am unable to list here. Camille Lacoste-Dujardin shared with me her experiences interviewing Kabyle women in Algeria and girls of North African origin in Paris. Mohamed Salemkour reviewed my interview guide. Patrice Coulon, from the journal *Hommes & Migrations*, kindly sent me a long list of both professional and personal contacts. Radwane Souir helped me recruit participants, as did two French-language and literacy teachers who will remain anonymous in order to protect the confidentiality of their students.

This research, of course, would not have been possible without all of the respondents who agreed to be interviewed and who not only made this study illuminating but also enjoyable. For taking the time to talk with me, and for sharing so much, from the pain of hurtful experiences to the joys of food, I am grateful to them.

Finally, I want to thank my husband, André Benhaïm. From debating ideas to taking care of our son on countless early mornings, it is his support that has allowed me to finish the book in a (relatively) timely manner.

A shorter version of Chapter 3 entitled "Culture on the Weekend: Maghrebin Women's Adaptation in France" was published in the *International Journal of Sociology and Social Policy* 22, no. 1–3 (2002).

NORTH AFRICAN WOMEN IN FRANCE

Introduction

Fouzia was born in a village in southern Morocco, the daughter of an Arab father and a Berber mother. At age 17 she married a man 10 years older than herself. He worked in Paris and left her for a year at his parents in Morocco before bringing her to France. At 19, she had her first child; now she has seven. She was never sent to school and is illiterate. As the oldest child in her family, her mother had kept her at home to help with the chores and her brothers and sisters. At her arrival in France, she did not speak a word of French. Now, 24 years later, she is taking a literacy class and says that she likes life in France and is glad to be living with her husband. She has never worked, other than occasionally babysitting some of her friends' children, but she would like to look for a part-time job after she finishes her class. Even what she considers her husband's well-paying job is not enough to support a wife and seven children in France. She wants to be able to pay for the family's annual month-long summer vacation to Morocco. Although they drive to Spain and take the boat rather than fly, the voyage is still expensive. When asked if she plans to return to Morocco, she says she will do whatever her husband wants, but that they cannot move to Morocco definitively because her children wish to remain in France. She has a permanent resident card but never asked for citizenship — "What's the point now?" she says. She is very religious. She celebrates all the holidays, does not consume pork or alcohol, and prays five times a day. She wears a veil, although she has given up the traditional djellaba (loose-fitting, long-sleeved garment) for long skirts and long-sleeved, oversized sweaters. She speaks to her children in Arabic, although some speak it better than others, and she tries to transmit her religious values to them. It is very important to her that her daughters marry Muslims, although she says her sons can marry whomever they choose. Although she loves her children, she admits that her days are very hard. She is up until midnight every night, often doing the family's ironing. At 43, she feels old and tired.

1

Malika is from an urban area of Tunisia. Her father is Tunisian, and her mother was born and raised in France, the child of an Italian mother and a Tunisian father. Malika grew up speaking French and was sent to a French school in Tunisia. At age 18, after passing her baccalaureate, she wanted to come to France, but her parents would not let her go. After finishing a master's degree, she came to Paris to continue her studies at the age of 22. She says that as a young woman she rejected everything Tunisian and used the excuse of studies to get away from her country and her family. In France she first worked as an au pair, and then took a series of part-time jobs to work her way through school. For years she lied to her father about her relationship with a young French man. She finally admitted to him that she wished to marry her non-Muslim boyfriend despite her fear that she would be disowned. To her great surprise, he responded that she was old enough to decide what she wanted. The relationship with the young man did not last, however. She recognizes that she has problems with relationships because she feels like she should marry a Muslim, and yet she has only dated French men. At 38 she remains single. She is not religious; she does not practice Islam and labels herself an atheist. She drinks alcohol and eats pork. Nevertheless, she has issues with clothing. As a teenager in Tunisia she was scolded for wearing miniskirts. Only recently has she felt comfortable wearing short skirts in France, and she continues to wear pants every year when she visits Tunisia for a week. She says she has few North African friends, but that if she ever has children, she would like to try to teach them some Arabic. When asked if she plans to stay in France permanently, she says that she probably will, but that she could just as easily travel to the United States or return to Tunisia. She says that she had to fight very hard to make it in France and believes that things would have been much easier for her in Tunisia. Although she received French nationality after one year, thanks to her mother's French citizenship, she suffered financially and from the coldness of the people in France. She believes now she has become cold like the French. Today she is a successful executive producer at a production house.

Deha is from Algiers, the capital of Algeria. Her father is an Algerian Muslim, her mother an Algerian Jew with Spanish origins. As a teenager she was labeled "the French one" because of her behavior and liberal attitudes. She admits she liked to provoke people by wearing short dresses, drinking alcohol, and not fasting during Ramadan. At 17, she moved out of her parents' home and began working to support herself. She went to college for two years and eventually became a reporter. She married her husband because she was already pregnant and because they wanted to live together, something impossible for an unmarried couple in Algeria. With the rise of Islamic fundamentalism and the political problems in Algeria in the early 1990s, it became harder and harder for her husband to continue working in the French-language publishing industry. After being arrested by the military for a story she had aired, she found that other journalists were too afraid to support her. Only one spoke up for her, and he was assassinated. She got out of jail after hiring an internationally known lawyer and drawing a great deal of public attention to her case. Although she wanted to stay and help her country, friends of hers were also murdered, and she finally decided to move to France in 1995 at age 31. Because all Algerian Jews automatically had French citizenship, she was able to be naturalized thanks to her mother. However, she had difficulty obtaining papers for her husband and son and only succeeded after two years of legal battles, during which time her husband was not allowed to work. She and her husband speak French at home, and her eight-year-old son no longer speaks Arabic. They do not celebrate any Muslim holidays and instead celebrate Christmas and Easter. She notes that they still cook almost exclusively Algerian food, however. Since her arrival in France, she has been unable to break into the world of French journalism. She works sporadically through a temp agency doing office work. She also volunteers for an Algerian association in Paris and has been back to Algeria four times in three and a half years. She laughs about being called "the French one" in Algeria, and says that in France she stands out as a North African.

Fouzia, Malika, and Deha are all Maghrebin immigrants to France, and yet their lives are very different.[1] Edwige Rude-Antoine (1997:104) writes that "the paradox of immigration" is that it is "at the same time destructuring and restructuring. These families do not all live in an identical manner in the host society. They accept, reject, transform their cultural heritage" (translation mine). This book will explore some key questions about the experiences of North African female immigrants. What do they keep from the country of origin and what do they decide to embrace in the new country? How do Muslim women immigrants construct and manage their identities in the midst of a foreign culture? What challenges do these women face, and why do some cope better than others?

Primarily as a result of immigration, there are approximately 5 million Muslims in France out of a total population of around 60 million, making Islam the country's second largest religion and France the European nation with the highest concentration of Muslims. With a growing, visible minority population, France, like other western countries, has been grappling with questions of adaptation and integration. The public debate and eventual passage of the law banning Muslim headscarves in French schools is evidence of the weight these issues carry for France as a nation. Until recently in the United States, what immigrants took from U.S. culture and kept from their own, how they viewed their position here, whether they felt American or remained tied to an ethnic or other national identity, were largely questions for the immigrants themselves to resolve. Since September 11, 2001, however, there is increasing recognition that these questions are important for society in general. Looking at how Muslim immigrant groups are faring in another western society and getting a perspective into how these immigrants view their own lives allow us to see how the processes of incorporation and acculturation can be compromised for certain groups and that the societal context immigrants find themselves in matters.

In his book on *La nouvelle islamophobie* (*Islamophobia in France*), Vincent Geisser (2003:115) argues that in the current fervor about Muslims living in western countries, security experts and media commentators who hold a monopoly on the cultural representations of Muslim immigrants have lost sight of "ordinary Muslims. . . . *lived Islam* does not interest them" (translation mine). Similarly, Catherine Raissiguier (2003:3) writes that in France, the "hyper-visibility of immigrant women (especially those from the African continent) in political discourse and media representations interestingly is accompanied by a real paucity of (scholarly) knowledge about them." Although there are several academic studies that examine the history of French immigration policies and the status of Islam in France, few researchers talk directly to first-generation North African immigrant women about their actual lived experience.[2] Thus, rather than beginning with structural-level questions, I chose to take a "grounded theory" approach (Glaser and Strauss 1967; Blumer 1969). In this book, I attempt to add to our knowledge of acculturation processes by looking for patterns of cultural choices and how these decisions affect identity. From a social psychological perspective, I seek to extend identity theory by looking at the case of immigrant women. People who are multiply marginalized (female, immigrant, and racial and religious minority) and in a situation of profound change, both social and personal, are exemplary candidates for studying identity negotiation. Several respondents' statements complicate the idea that minority women automatically suffer more than men. Additionally, the fact that some participants reject certain common labels highlights the need to look not only at self-identifications, but also at self-disidentifications and the consequences they have for both individuals and society.

There are potential practical ramifications of this research. In trying to understand how North African women are managing their lives in France, I examine factors that facilitate or hinder their adaptation and affect their well-being. This study looks at why some women are better than others at adapting to life in a foreign country and what can be done to help those who are struggling with acculturative stress and marginalization.

In order to frame this study, I provide some background on challenges that immigrants encounter and the factors that mediate acculturative stress, and I discuss the immigration literature and debates about assimilation. Recognizing the differences in the experiences of visible minority ethnics from previous white immigrant groups, recent theorists have nuanced our understanding of acculturation and incorporation processes, but this approach is still relatively new and needs further exploration. In addition, relatively little attention has been paid to immigrant women, and yet their experiences differ in many ways from those of immigrant men. Muslim women are a particularly misunderstood group, and interviewing them not only sheds light on the key questions of this study, but also serves to clear up common misperceptions about their status, roles in their families, and feelings about their lives. At the same time, the 45 women I interviewed are not a monolithic group. I do not seek to take away from the heterogeneity of their experiences or to make sweeping generalizations, but rather to highlight the patterns that emerge from the data (see Appendix 1 for the research methodology).[3] In the next section, I provide a brief introduction to the identity issues that immigrants face to set the stage for the themes of the book.

Immigration Contexts and Processes

Immigrants face both structural and cultural challenges upon arrival in the host nation. In general, even well-educated immigrants with professions experience downward social and occupational mobility. Immigrants must adapt to a combination of new language, climate, food, customs, and laws. They experience discrimination due to their accents, dress, and other cultural behaviors, as well as their resident alien status. This discrimination is only heightened when the immigrants are also a racial minority in the host country. In addition, immigrants are likely to be missing family members left behind in the country of emigration, and thus it is not only the societal structure, but also the family structure that undergoes radical changes.

Adaptation to a new country causes stress and feelings of marginalization. The mental health effects of immigration depend on a number of factors, including human capital, social support, socioeconomic status, material resources, problem-solving skills, health, positive attitude, bicultural orientation, and control over life events/choices (Kim and Berry 1986; Portes and Rumbaut 1996). Early immigration researchers noted that rural, poorly educated, economically disadvantaged immigrants fare worse in terms of mental health than their urban, well-educated, middle-class counterparts. Srole et al. (1962) pointed out that the former traveled greater social distance than geographical distance in arriving in industrialized New York City at the turn of the century. They therefore had to make greater adjustments than well-off immigrants who experienced less social disparity.

Recent work by Portes and Rumbaut (1996) focuses less on social distance and more on contexts of exit and reception. The conditions under which an immigrant leaves (a chosen, well-planned exit, or a forced, last-minute escape) and the conditions upon arrival (such as community networks or isolation and discrimination) affect the psychological well-being of immigrants. Refugees, for instance, score higher on measures of acculturative stress than do other immigrants. Having coethnic friends and relatives nearby reduces levels of stress and depression, "underscoring the buffering effects of co-ethnic social support" (Portes and Rumbaut 1996:171). The political and social climate of a country helps determine the context of reception. Like earlier work, Portes and Rumbaut (1996) find that lower status immigrants feel more alienated and powerless and experience more psychological problems than those who are better educated and wealthier.

How do immigrants become a part of the host society? Do they inevitably assimilate, or are other patterns possible? The literal meaning of assimilation is "making alike," and it originally had a biological meaning (Joppke 1998). "Assimilation refers to the adoption by the immigrant of the mannerisms, language, traditions, cultural mores, and values of the host society. Over a period of time the immigrant becomes indistinguishable from the members of the host society" (Bhatnagar 1981:14). "Straight-line assimilation" theorists like Gordon (1964) see the process beginning with cultural adaptation and ending with "identificational assimilation" as American with no hyphenated identity (Gordon 1964; Rumbaut 1994). Structural assimilation, meaning entering into the majority group's networks and institutions, and intermarriage facilitate this process (Gordon 1964; Rumbaut 1994).[4]

This model, however, is based on white European immigrants to the United States in the early twentieth century. The more racially varied immigration in the second half of the century has forced theorists and government officials alike to rethink their conception of assimilation. Despite attempts by Alba and Nee (1997) to resurrect the term, it has been largely replaced by other words that carry a less negative, ethnocentric association and/or complicate the traditional pattern proposed by straight-line assimilation theorists.[5] Visibility and discrimination often prevent modern immigrants from reaching identificational assimilation, whether they desire it or not. When lower-status groups are blocked from achieving higher status because of discrimination, they take on behaviors of the host society, but at the same time recommit to their ethnic (Mexican, Cambodian) or panethnic (Latino, Asian) identities rather than identifying assimilatively (Yinger 1981). Researchers refer to this model as segmented assimilation (Portes and Zhou 1993) or sometimes nonlinear or bumpy-line assimilation (Gans 1992). According to this perspective, contextual factors, such as discrimination or lack of it, determine identification (Portes and Zhou 1993). Segmented assimilation can be caused by visible ethnic minority status, geographic location (including percentage of coethnics), and changing labor markets (Portes and Rumbaut 1996). Thus, under some conditions, straight-line assimilation will occur, and under others, ethnic identity will remain primary (Rumbaut 1994).

In many references to immigrants' interactions with members of the host society and changes in behavior today, the word *acculturation* has replaced *assimilation*. However, various writers' reasons for using the term *acculturation* vary. Some authors simply use *acculturation* as a synonym for cultural assimilation (Yinger 1981; Portes and Rumbaut 1996); "acculturation is the first step of the adaptation process and is defined by different patterns of learning the language and culture of the host country. The final stage of this same process can be labeled assimilation" (Portes and Rumbaut 1996:247).

Yet acculturation differs from assimilation because it implies becoming competent in the ways of the host society while continuing to be identified by others as a member of a minority group — in other words assimilating culturally but not being socially and/or economically assimilated into the host country's institutions (LaFromboise et al. 1993; Gans 1999).[6] Used this way, acculturation reads much like segmented assimilation.

For others, acculturation implies changes in the cultural patterns of either or both the immigrant group and the host society, and therefore is not necessarily unidirectional, but rather depends on the context, so that in conformist societies, acculturation equals assimilation but in those societies fostering multiculturalism, acculturation occurs on both sides (Redfield et al. 1936, cited in Berry 1986; Naidoo 1986; Phinney and Rotherman 1987). When acculturation is used to focus on the cultural maintenance that accompanies cultural change and thus prevents true assimilation, it is called *selective* acculturation. Selective acculturation occurs when learning the ways of the country of residence is combined with strong ties to the ethnic community and its norms (Portes and Rumbaut 1996).

Even if selective acculturation is a more conscious, individually controlled process, some level of acculturation is involuntary because immigrants must learn the new culture in order to survive economically (LaFromboise et al. 1993). This can lead to acculturative stress, the psychological distress and dysfunction caused by the process of acculturation (Berry and Annis 1974). Acculturation is particularly stressful when it is truly a unilateral process on the part of the minority group; the mental health of immigrants tends to be better in multicultural societies (Murphy 1973). In their psychological work on racial and ethnic minorities and biculturalism, LaFromboise et al. (1993) introduce the alternation model. The alternation model differs from assimilation and some definitions of acculturation in that it is bidirectional and does not presuppose a hierarchy between the cultures involved.[7] In this model, individuals are biculturally competent, maintain a cultural identity, and are not forced to choose categorically between cultures; instead, they alternate back and forth between modes of behavior appropriate to the respective culture in a given situation.

In addition to immigration specialists and psychologists, cultural theorists are also interested in questions of immigrant adaptation. Swidler (1986), for instance, conceptualizes culture as a "toolkit" of "strategies of action" that people use to reach goals. Actors thus have a variety of cultural elements from which to choose when constructing modes of action, and during unsettled periods, such as immigration, new strategies of action can arise. Swidler explicitly calls on researchers to examine "what aspects of a cultural heritage have enduring effects on action" (1986:284). Although some work has examined this question, "[r]esearch into immigration, ethnicity and identity has tended to take the experiences of immigrant and 'second generation' men as paradigmatic of the experiences of immigrants more generally" (Freedman and Tarr 2000:vii). "Only a few scholars have attempted to outline the dimensions of assimilation, acculturation, and cultural change for immigrant women" (Gabaccia 1989:157).

North African Women Immigrants

The process of acculturation is especially complex when dealing with cultures as disparate as Catholic France and Muslim North Africa, particularly in regard to the role of women. As Prieto (1992:186) notes, "When socially constructed ideas about gender confront a totally different environment (as happens with migration), migrant men and women may resist, change, or adapt their old beliefs to the new situation." In this study, I explore the acculturation of North African women immigrants in France, looking at what cultural choices they make and why, and the consequences of these choices for their identities. Muslim, Maghrebin women suffer from multiple layers of oppression, as Muslims, as North Africans, as immigrants, and as women. Recent research on female immigrants builds on the work of Deborah King (1989), Kimberlé Crenshaw (1989), Patricia Hill Collins (1991), and other African American feminist scholars who theorize the intersectionality of race and gender. In their work on Asians in the United States, Espiritu (1997) states that minority women are caught in a bind in which they are forced to choose to identify with only one aspect of their identity at a time, minority member or female, and Pyke and Johnson (2003:36) argue that negative images of nonwhite femininity take away minority women's "power of self identification." How individual women and different groups of women react to identity pressures remains a crucial question.

Muslim women suffer from particularly weighty historical representations and derogatory images. Westerners typically view Muslim women as the ultimate "other" because they are of a different nationality, race, and religion, and because they are female. During the past two centuries, Muslims and non-Muslims both have manipulated images of Muslim women and deprived the women themselves of voice. Recently, some researchers have acknowledged that all Muslims are not alike. Often they look to regional and religious differences, but continue to ignore gender. Others recognize the importance of studying women, but fall into the trap of confusing Muslims from different national and socioeconomic origins.[8]

Writers often portray women as being affected by society and not the other way around. Although colonizers viewed Arab women as holding back their men by hanging onto traditional ways, they also clung to the somewhat contradictory, yet practically universally held "false notion that the world of Islam is a world created by men for men rather than the joint creation of men and women" (Mahdi, foreword to Fernea and Bezirgan 1978:xi). Because women were rarely seen and seemingly ill-treated, most westerners assumed that they had no control or power in shaping their own societies. "Ignorance of the real condition of women . . . stems partly from the general attitude which, until very recently, regarded the roles that women assume as being unimportant, or at best marginal, to an understanding of the working of the social order under study" (Rassam in UNESCO 1984:1–2).

Given that women did not count, they did not need to be studied. Research on Arab women did not really begin in earnest until the 1960s (Altorki and El-Sohl 1988), and until the 1990s, research on immigrants focused primarily on men.[9] According to Freedman and Tarr (2000:2), "Whilst they make up very nearly half of the populations of immigrant origin in France, within dominant representations women of immigrant origin are more often than not either ignored or represented in stereotyped categories." They continue, "Given the way in which the dominant culture excludes, marginalizes or stereotypes immigrant women and their daughters, it is important to find a way of narrating and visualizing their own attitudes and experiences" (6).[10] North-African and sub-Saharan immigrant women and their daughters are generating attention in France, but almost always around controversial and stereotypical issues that are sensationalized such as clitoral excision, polygamy, and veiling, issues that serve to further exoticize them. Rarely are the more mundane and constant issues they face, such as discrimination at work or which language to speak to their children, studied. The recent interest by government officials and the French public in the integration of the second generation has led to a surge in recent studies looking at girls born in France, but the first generation remains seriously neglected.[11]

This is pressing because women's situation differs in significant ways from that of their male counterparts and leads to several key questions: How do female immigrants deal with challenges that fall disproportionately on them, in particular combining child care (without the aid of relatives left behind) and paid labor? What are the effects of women's work and strategies in the host country on the balance of power in the home (Foner 1986; Kibria 1994)? Is work a means to independence for immigrant women or another form of exploitation (Grasmuck and Pessar 1991; Espiritu 1997)? What other new roles, besides paid labor, do immigrant women assume in their families and communities (Andezian 1986; Hondagneu-Sotelo 1994)? Do women immigrants benefit as much and in the same ways as men from ethnic resources and social networks (Zhou and Logan 1989; Hagan 1998)? Can patriarchal values be good for women (Fernandez-Kelly and Garcia 1990)? How can traditional and modern values coexist in the lives of female immigrants (Naidoo 1986; Bhachu 1986; Kibria 1994)? And finally, because women are viewed as the primary socialization agents for children, where do they fall on the line of preserving culture or integrating children into the new society (Deutsch 1987; Kibria 1994; Karakasidou 1996)?

Kibria (1994:248) notes that immigrant women have been viewed in two different lights, either as "barriers to assimilation" because of their determination to cling to traditional ways, or alternatively, as "vehicles of integration into dominant society" (citing Deutsch 1987:719–20). Graham-Brown (1988:17–18) notes that because Arab women are seen as the guardians of culture and are thus "portrayed as the repository of traditional ways and values," colonists and nationalists fought each other in an effort to control them and further their group's interest until the Arab countries gained independence. These depictions of Maghrebin women — as simultaneously "keepers of 'traditions'" and as an integrating/assimilating force," particularly for the latter in the case of girls born in France — remain prevalent today (Raissiguier 1999:451).[12] The headscarf controversy is a telling contemporary example of how various societal groups continue to use women in battles over culture and identity and how Muslim women in particular bear the brunt of fears about the "other."[13] The 2004 law banning the headscarf in French schools is a symbolic solution to the problems of violence and integration of Muslim immigrants in France, and, importantly, it is enacted on women's bodies.

Identity Negotiation

Immigrants have three distinct identities: immigrant, ethnic, and national/ host country. But these three are complicated by status and/or visibility of their ethnic immigrant group in the country, by religion, by race, and by gender. The influence and interplay of each of these identities differs given the specific context. Clearly, the identity issues faced by a white, male, Catholic Italian immigrant to France will not be the same as for an Arab, female, Muslim Moroccan immigrant. North African women immigrants can rarely hide their "stigma" (Goffman 1963); even if they do not wear traditional Maghrebin dress or have regional tattoos, the majority of Arab and Berber women are identifiable by their hair type and/or skin color. The fact that North Africans are a visible minority means that other people are likely to treat them according to one aspect of their identity at the expense of others.

Maghrebin women in France are low status in terms of gender, ethnicity, and immigrant status. This poses problems because individuals need to feel positively about both their personal and group identities (Tajfel 1981; Snow and Anderson 1987; Swann et al. 1987). Consequently, members of low status groups are likely to engage in "identity work," attempting "to create, present, and sustain personal identities that are congruent with and supportive of the self-concept" (Snow and Anderson 1987:1348). Because people want consistency between how they see themselves and how they think others view them, stress results when comments or behavior by others do not match an individual's own conception of his or her identity (Burke 1991).

In this book, I examine Maghrebin women's self-perceptions, including whether or not they have changed over time. I also ask how immigrant women believe they are viewed by others (meta-perceptions) in order to explore any tension between self- and meta-perceptions (Lalonde et al. 1992). My findings complicate Burke's (1991) original identity-control model by revealing that the level of stress experienced in the long term depends on women's ability to confront misperceptions, but not necessarily on the success of those confrontations. I therefore challenge the notion that misperceptions must be corrected in order to mitigate stress. Finally, I highlight not only positive identity claims but also self-disidentifications as the latter are a particularly important form of reactive identity work (McCall

2003). Learning how participants creatively manage identities in various contexts to feel positively about themselves, including by resisting certain labels that seem self-evident and nonnegotiable, not only informs our understanding of the interactions between the self and society, but also has important implications for immigrant adaptation.

Plan of the Book

In order to situate the context in which the participants live and construct their present selves, Chapter 1 provides some background and history on French–North African relations and Maghrebin immigration to France and details the participants' characteristics. Chapter 2 analyzes the way that gender conditions North African women's lives growing up in the Maghreb, immigrating, and adapting in France. It examines the responsibilities and restraints placed on North African women and how these gender norms often change in France as immigrants take on new roles and renegotiate family relations. Although westerners frequently view North Africa as a bastion of patriarchal values, Algerian, Moroccan, and Tunisian women compare and contrast sexism in both the Maghreb and in France. They also highlight interesting differences between their experiences as women and those of male Muslim immigrants.

Immigrants are confronted with multiple models of behavior in the host country, and Chapter 3 explores the cultural choices that they make in terms of values and comportments including cooking, dress, language use, and religious practices. Structural constraints on religious practices result in transformations of women's beliefs about what it means to be Muslim in France. This chapter also focuses on boundary work, what women prefer and dislike in the Maghreb and in France, and how they feel about their own acculturation and that of others. Chapter 4 discusses identity negotiation: how North African women construct their self-concepts and respond to the perceptions of others, what labels they accept or reject, and their situated identities in relation to other groups: nonemigrants from the Maghreb, the French, Arab/Berbers, and members of the second generation.

Chapter 5 describes the structural problems and relational problems that Maghrebin immigrants face in France. These include finding suitable apartments and jobs, negotiating the bureaucracies that deal with immigrants, living with language difficulties, and combating social isolation. The last chapter, Chapter 6, looks toward the future, concentrating on women's relationships to their children. Many women who planned to return to North Africa upon their own and/or their husband's retirement find that returning to the Maghreb would mean leaving their adult children behind in France. They struggle with the question of how to raise second-generation children to be successful in France yet maintain certain cultural traditions. This frequently leads to interesting, and often promising, compromises.

ONE

North Africans in France

Identities are created and change in context, and the responses of participants clearly demonstrate the interplay of the social structure and individual psychological processes. Therefore, to begin to understand the experiences of Maghrebin women in France, it is necessary to start with some historical, political, and social background on immigration to France and North African/French relations.

Historical Background of Immigration in France

> *T:* I'd say the French don't like foreigners in general. They don't accept
> strangers, even between themselves, Europeans. They don't like to see
> the foreigner take their place. . . . When I go do interviews and they hire
> French people before me, I won't say no, but that they see a foreigner
> working and hold it against him, that I don't understand.

> *H:*   All the unappreciated work, it's immigrants. Who built France?
>
> *T:*   They like immigrants doing dirty jobs, but they don't like seeing a
> foreigner work as an engineer.
>
>

— TINHINAN, 34-YEAR-OLD ALGERIAN;

HOURIYA, 34-YEAR-OLD ALGERIAN
>

Before 1914, movement of people into and out of France was unregulated, and there were no regulations on labor (Wihtol de Wenden 1984). Belgians, Swiss, Germans, Italians, and Spaniards regularly came to work in French factories and fields (Weil 1991). During World War I, France requisitioned more workers, including thousands from their colonies and protectorates in North Africa, to replace battle casualties, and even to fight alongside the French (Khellil 1991; Stora 2001). The numbers of immigrants continued to grow after the war, but with increasing unemployment in the 1930s, provisions were passed to protect French workers, and the settlement of foreigners was discouraged (Wihtol de Wenden 1984). Eastern Europeans, especially Poles, were forcibly repatriated during the 1930s (Weil 2005). After World War II, France again induced foreigners to come to work in jobs left vacant by war casualties, as poorly paid manual laborers, and in socially unacceptable occupations. Free circulation between colonial Algeria and France permitted large numbers of immigrants to enter the country. Many of these migrants were young men who worked for a period of time and then returned home.

France, unlike its neighbors, had demographic goals as well as economic ones, and thus passed legislation as early as 1945 to allow family reunification (Kennedy-Brenner 1979; Weil 1991, 2005). French politicians encouraged settlement of European workers, which also aided certain industries that wanted a stable foreign labor force (Weil 1991; Raissiguier 1999). North and sub-Saharan Africans were much less welcome on a permanent basis.[1] French people, including government officials, saw Arabs and black Africans as a source of temporary labor, but not as future citizens.[2] Although French law prohibited national origin quotas, immigration offices were more prevalent in some countries than others, and in the late 1950s, boarding houses for immigrant workers were built expressly to keep Algerian men from bringing their families (Weil 2005). During the economic boom of the 1960s immigration continued to expand rapidly; Tunisian immigration began in earnest in 1956, and Moroccan immigration swelled in the 1960s (Rude-Antoine 1997). Numerous workers without papers were tolerated by the government, but after Algeria's independence, an agreement was passed in 1968 to supervise the emigration of workers from Algeria and to monitor them upon arrival (Rude-Antoine 1997).

Given their opposing goals, at times the French ministries worked against one another; some furthered the goal of controlling the labor market by raising or lowering the number of work permits issued, and others tried to create social policies aimed at those who would stay permanently and assimilate (Kennedy-Brenner 1979). Following a downturn of the economy in the early 1970s, the French government temporarily suspended the entry of foreign workers in 1974. In the late 1970s, legislators passed measures aimed at curbing illegal employment, and President Giscard D'Estaing sought unsuccessfully to repatriate 500,000 North Africans, predominately Algerians, but also Moroccans and Tunisians, in the early 1980s (Weil 1991).

At the same time, however, French policy changed once again to facilitate family reunification for migrant workers. The first general decree recognizing the right to family reunification was announced in 1976, and the necessary conditions an immigrant had to meet to take advantage of the law were relaxed in legislation in 1984 (Rude-Antoine 1997). Thus although the entry of male workers slowed, the entry of their wives and children climbed exponentially.[3] In order to bring his family, an immigrant must prove that he has the funds to support them and lodging large enough to meet the standards set by the government for the number of people in his family.[4] Many immigrants cannot meet these requirements. In fact, between 20 and 30 percent of requests for family reunification have been denied over the past decade because of the inability of the petitioner to meet the housing size requirement (Quiminal 1997). This does not prevent women and children from coming, however. Wives often come with tourist visas and then stay illegally. This places them in a precarious situation in which they have trouble finding work and live in constant fear of being caught and deported (Quiminal 1997). Thus, new arrivals continued in the 1980s and 1990s as a result of legal family reunification, illegal immigration, and refugees. In 1999, France had over 4 million immigrants, representing 7.4 percent of the total population (INSEE 2000a).[5]

France is often called a *terre d'accueil*, a welcoming country, because it has traditionally been more open to immigrants than many other European nations. However, the French do not see themselves as a people of immigrants the way Americans do (Horowitz 1998). Immigrants in France are expected to become French and not cling to hyphenated identities like Irish Americans and Italian Americans. The French method of integration implies a loss of ethnic identity and pressure to conform to civic and cultural norms. Current President Jacques Chirac has said in the past, "We cannot accept that France becomes a pluricultural society in which our historical heritage would be placed on the same level as this or that other recently imported culture" (cited in Rude-Antoine 1997:89). Yet the increasing numbers of non-European immigrants are challenging this model, and in doing so, they have provoked new fears about immigration in the rest of Europe and the United States. Auslander (2000:305) argues that

> France has, in fact, always demanded conformity to French norms of its citizens; it has never understood itself to be a hybrid culture and earlier immigrants were treated badly until they assimilated. But the immigrants of the 1880s through the 1950s were not immigrants with a colonial past, they were not immigrants understood to be racially marked, and they were not living in a France with a weak economy and a strong but threatened state.[6]

Kastoryano (2002:10) points out that the French rhetoric of antimulticulturalism is often at odds with practical, "applied multiculturalism," the many measures the government has adopted to deal with others' differences, such as providing Muslim worship spaces. She also notes that despite a republican model that ostensibly recognizes only individuals and not ethnic groups, the word *community* ("Muslim community," "Algerian community") is frequently used in political discourse (34). Amselle (2003) argues that beginning in the 1970s, the French state worked to accommodate French Muslims by instituting Arabic classes in schools and providing cultural television programs in Arabic. However, these initiatives can be seen as part of a policy aimed at encouraging North African immigrants to remain connected to their countries of origin so that they would eventually return home. These concessions were also made to the Maghrebin countries in exchange for a reduction in the number of people North African states allowed to emigrate to France (Amselle 2003). Thus these measures were more self-serving than in the interest of immigrants' welfare or in the name of multiculturalism.

French officials, realizing that the majority of immigrants will not repatriate, continue to promote policies that focus on integration as assimilation, despite the assumptions that North and sub-Saharan Africans will never truly fit in France. Césari (2000:93) writes that France's assimilation model

> insists that if immigrants seek to become French citizens, they must eschew their foreign cultural, religious, political and ideological alliances. In other words, they must accept the already existing consensus of reality and polity of the prevailing system and assimilate into it, shedding all alien characteristics. The French policy of Gallicization sees the end result of integration as the privatization of religious practice, with the Muslim individuals becoming socially and economically assimilated.[7]

However, given the discrimination that Maghrebin immigrants face in employment, housing, education, and social relations, the obstacles to integration are numerous.[8]

Schain (1988) argues that, by acknowledging nonwhite immigration as a problem in France, the once powerful Communist Party (PCF) legitimized an anti-immigrant discourse that took a more central stage as the extremist right-wing party, the Front National (FN), gained power in French politics. The FN has always stood on a racist anti-immigration platform, arguing that the unemployment crisis would be resolved if immigrants were deported. They focus their efforts specifically on black and Arab immigrants. Before the 1980s, however, the FN was rarely taken seriously because it gained few votes and occupied a marginalized status. Today, however, a few French cities have FN mayors, and the FN candidate, Jean-Marie Le Pen, placed second in the last presidential elections, with 18 percent of the final vote. FN voters cite problems of immigration and law and order as their primary concerns (Schain 1988).

In order to compete with the rising power of the FN, centrist right parties have been forced to discuss the immigrant problem, and even though the PCF reversed itself on immigration, the left is still dealing with the fallout (Schain 1988). As the FN's racist rhetoric sways more people, other politicians are forced to reify immigration as a political problem.[9] Wihtol de Wenden (1984) characterizes the immigration theme as a commodity in French politics. Changes in the law in response to European Union policies and the Pasqua and Debré laws of the 1980s and 1990s made life harder for immigrants, most notably by creating situations in which people who had been living in France legally suddenly found themselves in an irregular situation as a result of new laws applied retroactively.[10] Although laws regarding children born in France have been eased in the last few years, overall, the Sarkozy and Villepin laws of 2003 have continued to make it more difficult for immigrants to get residency or to bring family members to France (Weil 2005). Recent scholarly works in France, responding to increasing public concerns and legislation aimed at immigrants, study the transformation in the meaning of French nationality over time (Weil 2002), question France's "Republican model of integration" (Wieviorka 1996), compare the French state's policies and attitudes toward its immigrants to those of other western countries (Kastoryano 1996, 2002), and examine the treatment of nondocumented immigrants and refugees (Noiriel 1998; Fassin et al. 1997).

The French have no racially based affirmative action policies and exclude foreigners from civil service employment and membership in the professions (such as doctors and lawyers) (Horowitz 1998). The creation of the European Union has led to two classes of immigrants: those from member states and those from elsewhere. One of the disparities is that members may travel unrestricted to other participating nations, but non-European legal residents of member states are required to declare themselves upon arrival at the border of another European country.[11] North and sub-Saharan African immigrants are also more likely to be arbitrarily stopped and checked by the police in France, and deportations can happen quickly.[12] Immigrants themselves lack the right to vote, but they mobilize around forced deportations and labor strikes (Fassin et al. 1997). Immigrant aid associations continue to defend the rights of immigrants, and the children of immigrants born in France are also speaking out.

During discussions about integration, politicians and scholars alike worry that the second generation of North African immigrants is turning toward religion as a way to express their identity and find purpose in their lives.[13] Warner and Wittner (1998) point out that in the United States, immigrants actively cling to religious traditions because religion is the one cultural aspect in which they are not expected to assimilate. Parents may also emphasize religion in their children's training because they view language and other cultural behaviors as already lost (Warner and Wittner 1998). In France, Maghrebin immigrants are also likely to place great emphasis on religion, but unlike the Americans, the French are less encouraging of religious difference and expect religious expression to be confined to the home and places of worship.

One example in particular is extremely telling about French attitudes toward cultural differences. In 1989, three high school students provoked a controversy by deciding to wear the veil at school despite French authorities' insistence that religion has no place in schools. They were prevented from attending school for a time, but the girls eventually took off their veils and were readmitted. In 1994, a similar situation reemerged and spread until school officials refused to allow more than 100 Muslim girls to attend public school. These events became a national scandal hotly debated in the newspapers and by the various political parties. Some took the view that these girls needed to be saved from their families by the French educational system, and many believed that the girls had been coopted by extremist Islamic political groups (Begag 1990; Khosrokhavar 1997). Politicians assert that banning the headscarf in school will help students get along with one another and ease ethnic tensions.

Weil (2001) points out that unlike in the United States, where citizenship is based on place of birth, or Germany, where citizenship is based on ethnicity, in France, citizenship comes from being socialized in France and taking on the norms of the Republic. The two historical forces responsible for the French socialization of immigrant children are the army and the French public school. Thus, in addition to the "headscarf affair" being a battle over secularism (*laïcité*), it is also about maintaining the school's role as French socialization agent. We see this in statements made by former Prime Minister Alain Juppé: "[I]ntegration which confers rights, all the rights of the French, of course, with naturalization, also implies accepting a certain number of rules for common life, in particular performing national [military] service for France, when one wants to be French; accepting the role of the school as integrator and not multicultural . . . ; and finally, accepting certain modes of social and family organization" (cited in Rude-Antoine 1997:93). It is important to note that at this time the cross and the Jewish *kippah* were frequently tolerated in French public schools. Auslander (2000:291) argues that "it is likely that the everyday signs of religious adherence to Christianity or Judaism have not been understood to threaten the foundations of the French nation because they are not associated with immigration (or racial difference)." At one point during the headscarf affair, François Bayrou, the minister of education in 1994, declared that "France is a Judeo-Christian country," despite the fact that the girls were being excluded from school in the name of *laïcité*.

In the midst of the turbulent voicing of opinions by school and government officials, few bothered to talk to the girls directly and admit a more nuanced view of their motivations. Gaspard and Khosrokhavar (1995) spoke with more than 100 girls at the center of the debate and found that their explanations were at odds with the media depictions of the reasons for their behavior. Although they had different views of the veil, only one girl had any ties to political Islamic fundamentalism. The majority of adolescents and preadolescents who veiled did so because of family pressure. Girls who were older, between 18 and 22, were more likely to adopt the veil out of personal religious conviction, or as a symbol of difference and pride in their ethnic identity. For several of the girls interviewed, the veil was a way to negotiate between the community of their parents and the French society in which they are immersed. These young women reject what they view as a devaluation of their parents' culture and an emphasis on assimilation.

Venel's (1999) study of second-generation North African university students who veil echoes Gaspard and Khosrokhavar's (1995) findings that women of this age have deliberately chosen to veil out of personal religious conviction and that they are trying to reconcile identity issues. When questioned about their identity, of Venel's 12 respondents, 6 self-identified as Muslim first, but 3 picked French first, 5 placed French in second position, and 1 person ranked French third. Only two respondents did not list French in their top three, and only one of the 12 ranked herself as of Moroccan heritage in third place; none of the others rated their heritage highly for their identities. The women therefore see themselves as French Muslims and are committed to this identity and expression of their faith while at the same time acknowledging that wearing a headscarf is likely to make it difficult for them to find employment that matches their level of education.

Despite the progress these veiled students are making toward advanced degrees, many non-Muslims continue to assume that veiling and education for women are automatically contradictory. Conditioned by stereotypes, they have a difficult time recognizing that certain cultural behaviors do not always entail a whole set of other specific ideas or acts. Donning the veil thus does not necessarily equal a lesser commitment to education, although by forcing veiled students to leave school, French authorities put them in a difficult position.[14] The French government passed a law in February 2004 banning headscarves, Jewish *kippot*, and large Christian crosses in school starting with the 2004–2005 school year. This law was passed after a series of debates in 2003 even though in 2002, only 150 cases of veiled girls in school had to be resolved by calling in a mediator. This was half the number of such cases in 1994 (Geisser 2003). The symbol of the headscarf has clearly taken on such enormous meaning in popular opinion that it must be legislated against even when the number of girls wearing it is dropping. Geisser (2003:11) believes that "the defensive and punitive policies toward all visible signs of *Islamity*" are a response to fears of an "Arabo-Muslim menace" (translation mine). Auslander (2000) argues that public reaction against the veil is a way to reassert national identity at a time when France is feeling threatened by globalization, the European Union, and immigration. Critics also assert that the addition of the large crosses and Jewish *kippot* in the law is simply to prevent charges that the government is being racist toward Muslims (Stroobants 2003).[15] The effects of this law on the North African community and their French-born children remain to be seen.

French–North African Relations

At the beginning of the nineteenth century, much of North Africa was part of the Ottoman Empire. Algeria was first invaded by the French in 1830; it remained a French colony until 1962. Tunisia and Morocco were not colonies but rather protectorates of France, and became so later, Tunisia in 1881, and Morocco in 1912. In the mid-1800s, the French were interested in Algeria for the land and the settling of French citizens, including political instigators, landless peasants, and even displaced Alsatians who fled to Paris to escape the Prussian army. By the time the French took control of Tunisia and Morocco, there was less demographic and political pressure in France (Stora 2001; Lacoste 2004). Tunisia was seen as a strategic outpost for controlling Algeria, and Morocco was attractive for its mines (Lacoste 2004). With the complicity of indigenous leaders who were compensated by the French, these two conquests were accomplished more quickly than in Algeria. In Morocco, the sultan capitulated in part because he could exact taxes from renegade tribes with the aid of the French (Lacoste 2004). Land ownership by the French in both Tunisia and Morocco was much more limited than in Algeria, and both countries were granted independence with relatively little bloodshed in 1955–1956.

Although they share religion (Maliki Sunni Islam), language, and a similar cultural history, Algeria, Morocco, and Tunisia developed different types of government after decolonization.[16] From its independence until the 1990s, Algeria was controlled by a single dictatorial, socialist-leaning political party that increasingly accommodated Islamist demands. Morocco is ruled by a king who is also the religious leader. Tunisia is the most secular and the most progressive in terms of women's rights, but its heads of state have also repressed the opposition. Despite a successful 1987 coup against the elderly, ailing President Bourguiba in Tunisia, and two failed assassination attempts against the Moroccan King Hassan II, today, both Tunisia and Morocco have relatively stable governments under President Zine El Abidine Ben Ali and King Mohammed VI (Hassan II's son). Both nations enjoy good relations with France and are prime vacation destinations for European tourists.

Algerian-French relations are much more strained. Unlike more distant and less settled colonies and protectorates, the French viewed Algeria as an integral part of France. Numerous French colonists, many of whom had lived in Algeria for many generations, as well as French officials who were interested in newly discovered oil reserves and the possibility of nuclear testing in the Sahara, were staunchly opposed to giving it up (Stora 2001). Algeria finally gained its independence in 1962 after seven and a half years of war. This war was not officially designated as such by the French until 1999. Stora (2005) notes that in 2000, a series of media reports and public confessions about the French atrocities and use of torture during the Algerian war surfaced. These were part of popular and political discourse in the 1950s, but after Algeria's independence, they disappeared from the public realm for 40 years. Decades later, this part of France's history is still raw. Millions of French people and Algerians, both in Algeria and in France, were directly affected by the war: approximately 9 million Muslim Algerians who fought in or lived through the war, including 100,000 *harkis* (Algerians who fought for or supported the French side), 2 million French soldiers, 1 million former colonists, 150,000 Jews who grew up in Algeria, and the children of all these groups (Stora 2001, 2005). The February 2005 law recognizing "repatriated" French citizens and Algerian soldiers who served alongside the French has only fanned the fires in France and Algeria by stating that school curricula must recognize the "positive role of the French presence" in Algeria, Morocco, Tunisia, and Indochina.

As the twentieth century progressed, the Maghreb strained under the ever-increasing demands of a growing population and the difficult transition from agriculture to manufacturing. Between 1962 and the end of the century, the Algerian population increased from 11 million to more than 32 million, the Moroccan population went from 12 to 31 million, and Tunisians saw their country grow from 4 to 10 million (Lacoste 2004).[17] Many peasants left their villages for the large cities in search of work, only to find harder lives than those they had left behind. This prompted North African governments to encourage emigration of male workers. Given colonial ties, Algeria has sent the greatest number of immigrants of the three countries, followed by Morocco, which not only has a larger population than Tunisia but also a lower standard of living.

This pattern of migration fits Portes and Rumbaut's (1996) "structural imbalancing of peripheral societies" model of immigration. They argue that immigration is not simply determined by "push-pull" or "cost-benefit" models, but rather that immigrants move to countries that have historical ties to their own nations and have in the past induced outmigration. Thus, given the history of colonization, North African immigrants are more likely to go to France than to other European countries with equally high standards of living.[18] The political violence in Algeria in the 1990s has caused a new type of immigration to France and exacerbated the old colonial French stereotypes of Arabs as violent and fanatic.

FROM THE ALGERIAN WAR OF INDEPENDENCE
TO THE CURRENT ALGERIAN CIVIL WAR

I have the feeling that, well, France colonized Algeria for a long time. . . . I don't want to say that [France] is responsible for all that is happening to [Algeria], but it is partially responsible. I can't put a number on it and say this or that percentage, I can't say that, but [France] had something to do with it. Because if Algerians are ignorant, what's causing the sociocultural problems? All this in Algeria, it's ignorance. It's education, ignorance, religions, all that, and France is responsible. France prevented Algerians from going to school, getting properly educated, it taught them what it wanted to put in their heads. So [France] made them ignorant, workers for the French on their own lands. And now this is the result. And we're constrained, those of us born after independence, they call us the children of the independence, indirectly we're forced to live the side effects.

And then when we come to France they don't want us. Um, it's a feeling that revolts me. I say to myself, I say, my parents lived the war, they didn't have the chance to go to school, they didn't have the chance to live their adolescence, their childhood normally, like the French. Because me, my parents, they lost their own parents during the war. They worked small jobs; they couldn't go to school because it was wartime. They're ignorant. And, um, you can't transmit to your children what you don't have. Luckily Algeria gave us the chance to go to school for free. There's that. But, um, the French are also responsible for what's happening to us.

— HOURIYA

In the mid-1950s, there were 1 million people of European origin in Algeria, or approximately 10 percent of the total population, and many families had lived there for four or five generations (Stora 2001).[19] They were the *pieds noirs*. Although their standard of living was lower than in France and many of them were relatively poor, colonists' gross income was still 28 times that of Algerian Muslims, and they owned 38 percent of the crop-growing farmland (Stora 2001; Lacoste 2004). All European colonists, regardless of origins, could become French citizens, as were all Jews living in Algeria after the Crémieux decree in 1870. In contrast, for Muslim Algerians to become French, they had to give up Muslim law. Because of this restriction, only 2,500 Algerians applied to become French citizens between 1865 and 1934, and most of these were Berber schoolmasters (Mansell 1961). The Blum-Violette plan of 1936 would have provided easier access to citizenship to Algerians without calling on them to give up Muslim law. Vigorous efforts by colonists, however, led to the defeat of this bill (Mansell 1961). Finally, in 1947, 10 years after the proposed Blum-Violette plan, all Algerians were declared automatic French citizens.

Mansell (1961) argues that the original defeat of the Blum-Violette plan can be seen as the true beginning of the Algerian nationalist movement that had seen undercurrents forming, especially among Algerian emigrants in France, since the late 1920s. Despite the promises of 1947, the new "Algerian assembly" was divided into two separate colleges, one for Muslims and one for Europeans whose votes were worth seven Algerian votes, and its elections were fixed to ensure that only a few members of nationalist parties won seats (Stora 2001). This move only served to radicalize many moderate

Algerians (Stora 2001). Tunisians and Moroccans were simultaneously calling for independence, and in May 1954, the French empire in Indochina suffered a crushing military defeat. The armed insurrection against the French by the Algerian Front de Libération Nationale (FLN) began only six months later, in November 1954. Within a few years, nationalist revolutionaries had generated extensive support among the popular masses, the millions of displaced peasants and those who were living in increasingly overcrowded city slums. Extreme tactics, including bombings, massacres, and torture, were used by both sides and drew international attention to the Algerian cause. After several changes of administration in France in four years that ultimately ended in the fall of the Fourth Republic, World War II hero General Charles de Gaulle became president in 1958. Although de Gaulle was initially supported by the colonists, he soon began calling for peace negotiations that led the army and the colonists to turn against him despite his continued military strikes against Algeria in 1959. On December 8, 1960, Muslim crowds descended on the streets of Algiers carrying FLN flags. A month later, a referendum on decolonization passed both in France and in Algeria. In April 1961, French army generals in Algeria attempted a coup d'état against de Gaulle but surrendered within a few days. The cease-fire agreed to at the Evian peace accords began on March 19, 1962. On July 1, 1962, Algerians voted 5,975,581 to 16,534 for independence (Ruedy 1992).

At least 500,000 people died during the war, with Algerians putting the casualties at 1 million (Stora 2001). Internal political violence, which had already killed almost 10,000 Algerians during the war, continued after independence (Stora 2001). Thousands of *harkis* who fought on the French side were massacred, Berber groups fought Arabs for their autonomy, and various political factions battled for control of the government.[20] During the first 30 years of Algeria's independence, the country was controlled by one party, the FLN. Over time, more and more Algerians demanded a multiparty system. An Islamic movement, calling for a religious government, had been on the rise throughout the 1970s and 1980s, owing largely to the state of the economy. The mass emigration of the colonists left Algeria, already with a poor standard of living, in an even worse state. Practically overnight, the country lost much of its professional and technical expertise. Fleeing colonists also destroyed factories, hospitals, schools, and libraries, and carried much Algerian capital out with them (Ruedy 1992). The struggling new state's economic problems were exacerbated as oil prices fell in the mid-1980s. Much of the Algerian population was disillusioned with the socialist government's promises given inflation and an unemployment rate that by 1989 had reached 25 percent overall, and double that number for the almost half of the population under 24 years old (Ruedy 1992; Silverstein 2002a, 2004). The fall of the communist bloc further undermined the credibility of the socialist government (Martinez 2000). Islamist leaders encouraged an open market to provide equal opportunities and better the standard of living (Martinez 2000; Stora 2001). The morality they urged was especially welcome given the corruption of previous FLN leaders. The Islamists worked to win the hearts of the populace by distributing food, clothing, and financial aid for medical care and funerals, and by promising jobs to the increasing numbers of students educated only in Arabic who faced hiring discrimination because they could not speak French well enough (Stone 1997; Martinez 2000). These fundamentalists called for legislation based on the moral code (*Shari'a*) and renewed Muslim solidarity.

After bloody popular demonstrations and rioting in late 1988, the government took steps toward liberalization by legalizing other political parties. The Islamist party, the Front Islamique du Salut (FIS), won overwhelmingly in the June 1990 municipal elections and the first round of legislative elections in December 1991. These results were as much an anti-FLN vote as an endorsement of Islamist principles (Stone 1997; Martinez 2000).[21] In January 1992, the military government annulled the results and fought to stay in power. Algeria was a divided nation. Secularists were split between those who wished to keep an FLN-type government and those who wanted true democratization. Islamists and their sympathizers, primarily disillusioned young men who were new to the cities and felt let down by the socialist government, were powerful and had popular support, but the military ran the government. Between 1992 and 1996 the country dissolved into civil war marked by bombings, assassinations, and random killings. Foreigners, who had fled the country en masse, were specifically targeted by the FIS's military wing, the Armée Islamique du Salut (AIS), and journalists have been the victims of both the Islamists and the government. As suspicions and countermeasures, including the use of torture, increased, more and more civilians lost their lives.

The Algerian government became multiparty again in 1996, with the exclusion of Islamic parties, but, under this "pseudo-democracy," elections continued to be fixed by the military elites (Volpi 2003:121). Violence escalated in 1997 with the slaughter of hundreds of men, women, and children in various villages in the Mitidja plain outside of Algiers. Algerians worldwide are still debating whether the massacres were the work of Islamists or government security forces (Silverstein 2002a).

Intellectuals, among the first targets of the FIS, have sought refuge in France. As the violence escalated, however, the response of the French government in 1994 was to tighten restrictions on visas. After a wave of bombings in France in 1995 by terrorists linked to Algeria, border controls were further strengthened. Out of 2.2 million visa requests for France throughout the world in 1996, only 405,000 people (18.4 percent) received visas (Gourévitch 1998). According to French government statistics, in 1998, only 56 Algerian refugees and 8 members of their families were admitted to France.[22] Yet Islamists continued to assassinate political opponents and civilians, and Algerian security forces have allegedly "disappeared" as many as 22,000 people (Silverstein 2002a). The total death count is now over 100,000 people. The FIS's power gradually waned as a result of rivalries among various Islamist groups and an erosion of popular support. Its military wing disbanded in 1999 after an amnesty, but remnants of the smaller Groupes Islamique Armées (GIA) continue to be active. In September 2005, Algerians approved President Bouteflika's Charter for Peace and National Reconciliation, but shootings and a roadside bombing occurred prior to the vote indicating that the violence is not over.

BERBERS

Even among us, they forbid us to marry, for example, I'd say personally for me, it was forbidden to marry an Arab. Since they always separated us into Arab/Kabyle in Algeria, it's not allowed to marry an Arab. Before it was out of the question to marry an Arab.

— TINHINAN

I'm definitely Arab, but, um, I know that in our family there are a lot of Berbers. And I think all of Algeria is like that because, I believe that, well the Arabs, when they invaded Algeria, they came without wives, so I think they married Berbers and everything. So I think we're all, um, a little bit Berber.

— AMEL, 26-YEAR-OLD ALGERIAN

It's funny, we say Kabyle, Berber, equals Berber, but we never talk about Chaouis or other Berbers in Algeria.

— NEDJMA, 52-YEAR-OLD TUNISIAN

The Berbers were early inhabitants of North Africa and belong to various groups that still populate the central Maghreb today. Many live in mountainous regions, but others, including the often nomadic Touaregs, live in the desert. The Berbers resisted rule by the Phoenicians, Romans, Byzantines, Vandals, Arabs, Turks, and French. Indeed, the Berbers of the central Maghreb managed to continue the fight against the Arab invaders in the seventh century for 35 years, longer than anywhere else in the Maghreb. Although most of the Berbers converted to Islam by the eighth century, this did not cause them to accept the Arab conquerors, and in 740, the successful Khariji rebellion drove the invaders out of all of Morocco and the majority of Algeria (Ruedy 1992). Given centuries of intermarriage, many people in the North Africa are descendants of both Berbers and Arabs; but for a general idea of the population, region of origin and language are the best approximations. Although only a very small percentage of Tunisians are from the Berber-speaking regions, approximately one-fourth of Algerians and more than one-third of Moroccans are Berber speakers (Lacoste 2004; Tribalat 1996). The majority of Berber speakers in North Africa today also speak the local Arabic. Many Algerian Berbers are from the Djurdjura mountain range in the Kabylia region, and hence are called Kabyles.

During colonization, French people held specific stereotypes about Arabs and about Kabyles — stereotypes that continue to have repercussions on the Algerian population in France today. The common view was that Kabyles were smarter, harder workers, more practical, and more rational because they were less influenced by Islam than the Algerian Arabs.[23] French colonial officials, geographers, and ethnographers, including Alexis de Toqueville, proliferated the idea that Arab tribes were lazy nomads who shared territory collectively, but that Kabyles were rooted to privately owned land on which they toiled diligently (Silverstein 2002b). Arabs were painted as patriarchal oppressors of women and dependent on absolute authority, whereas Kabyles were described as respectful of women and craving democracy (Silverstein 2002b). According to Silverstein (2002b:142), "[i]n this way, colonial scholars drew on economic, religious, and political comparisons to argue that the Kabyles were the exact cultural opposites of the Arabs. Rather than a single people united by religion, the Algerian natives were deemed to constitute in fact two peoples divided by a primordial hate."

Although this division of the Algerian population into different groups is clearly a divide-and-conquer technique, it also played into the French myth of assimilation. Certain French scholars believed that the Kabyles would eventually fuse together with the French people, a thought less often extended to include the Arabs (Silverstein 2002b; Amselle 2003). The French spent more energy on evangelization and education in the Kabylia region than elsewhere in Algeria, and they held the Kabyle language and culture in higher esteem than those of the Arabs (Ruedy 1992). However, the Arabs and Kabyles were not as diametrically opposed as the French implied, and European colonists also had a stake in keeping the Kabyles below them. Consequently, this group never fused with the French. As Tinhinan's quote demonstrates, in marriage patterns in France, Berbers are actually more endogamous than Arabs (Tribalat 1996). Even today, many Berbers continue to identify according to their home villages more than with the capitals where they often go to find work.

The Islamists' insistence on Arabness has kept many Berbers from being caught up in this movement.[24] After the Algerian war of independence, it was the Berbers who made sure that the term used was Algerian and not Arab (Ruedy 1992). In 1962, between July and September, hundreds of Algerians were killed because of political infighting and Berber and Arab disputes, and the Kabyle political party Front des Forces Socialistes (FFS) was established in 1963. The FFS and another secular Berber party formed in 1989, the Rassemblement pour la Culture et la Démocratie (RCD), have been fighting the Islamists' takeover. In response to the push for Arabicization in 1979 and 1980, the Mouvement Culturel Berbère (MCB), originally created in 1968, has been calling for the official recognition of Berber language, Tamazight, and for its use in schools (Stone 1997).[25] Berber organizing is extremely strong in Kabylia, and rallies have drawn tens of thousands, although the Chaouis in the Aurès mountain range and the Berbers of the south Saharan desert have not been as politically active (Simon 1994). The political involvement in the 1960s and 1970s, as well as public demonstrations in Kabylia in 1980, referred to as the "Berber Spring," helped lay the groundwork for rapid mobilization when politics opened up at the end of the 1980s. The FFS won more seats than the FLN in the 1991 legislative elections. During the 1990s, several high-profile Kabyles, including popular writers and singers, were assassinated by Islamist groups angered by their insistence on a non-Arab identity and language (Stone 1997). At the same time, Kabyles demonstrated against the government in 1998 after Kabyle singer Lounès Matoub's murder and again in 1999 after the election of the military-backed president Abdelaziz Bouteflika.[26] In 2001 massive protests occurred in both Kabylia and Algiers after a boy was killed by a police officer. Riots during these demonstrations ultimately undermined the political clout of the FFS and the RCD, who were unable to control the demonstrators and their demands (Volpi 2003). Although the vote-getting power of Berber political parties is necessarily limited by their regional heritage, the Berber activists continue to be key players in an Algeria torn between the military-backed government and the Islamists.

WOMEN'S STATUS

Sometimes you find that in a couple it's the woman who makes everything work, everything. It's she who has everything, the economic power, and everything, in the family. And sometimes it's the opposite. She has no power, she is subservient. She has no rights with her husband; she's mistreated. She's sometimes beaten too.

— LEILA, 43-YEAR-OLD TUNISIAN

My mother took my brothers to school, but us girls, they said girls will get married, stay at home. [In Morocco] now, happily, there are women in offices too.

— FATIMA, 54-YEAR-OLD MOROCCAN

[In Tunisia] women have the same legal rights as men . . . but it's not because the law allows something that mentalities allow it, and it's not because a small number of women have power, have access to instruction, knowledge, that it's the lot of all women. The problem is that there's a wide gap, for example, between a [well-educated] girl like me, you see, and a girl from the Tunisian countryside.

— MALIKA

In many interpretations of Islam, differences between the sexes are seen as inherent, and women's primary role is that of wife and mother. Not only religious writing, but also government legislation often reflects this view of

Muslim women. However, the way Islam is practiced and the options available to women differ from country to country, among social classes, and between rural peasants and urban residents. Cultural traditions from various regions are mixed with Islam. Thus Islamic dress, when observed, varies not only from Asia to Africa to the Middle East but within these regions. Clitoridectomy, while not a part of Islam, and not practiced in North Africa, has been closely linked to it in some Muslim countries, predominately in sub-Saharan Africa. Several Muslim governments rely primarily on *Shari'a*, Islamic personal or family law dictating morality, to shape their codes of law. Others, particularly Turkey and Tunisia, although still influenced by Islam, are more secular in orientation.

Differences in the treatment of women are apparent within the countries of the Maghreb. Tunisia is the most liberal Muslim country, with the highest participation of women in the workforce and in politics (Moghadam 1993).[27] Islamic fundamentalists, who hold a strict interpretation of what is appropriate for women, have made far fewer gains in Tunisia than in Algeria. Importantly, although Islamist political parties are officially banned in both Tunisia and Morocco, the monarchy of Morocco is also a religious power, and the state is more reliant on traditional *Shari'a* for interpretations of women's rights than in Tunisia (Lacoste 2004; Lacoste-Dujardin 2004b).

Charrad (2001) argues that the level of postindependence alliances with tribal kin groups in the three countries of the Maghreb influenced their level of conservatism or liberalism in terms of women's rights. Legislating Islamic family law helped placate strong tribal kin groups and was a symbolic way to create a national identity. Thus Morocco, with strong tribal kin groups, remained traditional, whereas Tunisia, whose newly formed state was largely independent of such tribal-based communities and eager to further weaken them and pan-Islamist factions in general, adopted a progressive approach. The first Tunisian president, Habib Bourgiba, advocated the primacy of the conjugal unit and encouraged marriages between people of different villages, chiefly to undo tribal kin structures and modernize his country. Algeria fell somewhere in between the two, with partial alliances and consequently vacillated back and forth before adopting a strict family code in 1984 in an attempt to shore up Islamist support at a time when the government was weakened by the growing Berber movement.

Algerian and Moroccan codes of law stipulate matrimonial guardians for women and allow polygamy and repudiation (albeit with some restrictions), whereas Tunisia's personal statute code abolished these practices.[28] Tunisian woman have been able to initiate divorce without restrictions since 1956, may marry non-Muslims, and have had access to legal and free abortions since 1973 (Turki 1998; Lacoste-Dujardin 2004b). Tunisia has more liberal inheritance laws for women and more custody rights for divorced mothers. Unlike in other North African countries, a Tunisian woman with means is obligated to contribute to the support of the household (Charrad 2001; Lacoste-Dujardin 2004b). Algerian women have much lower levels of employment than Tunisian women as a result of more cultural conservatism, development strategies, and the general high unemployment rate (Moghadam 1993). This is also true of Moroccan women, although conservative family law policy in Morocco began to ease with reforms in 2004 under the new king, Mohamed VI (Lacoste-Dujardin 2004b). Despite the important and celebrated role of women in the war for independence, women's rights in Algeria went progressively downhill under mounting Islamist pressure.

In 1981, Algerian women managed to fight off a family code heavily reliant on Islamic *Shari'a*, but by 1984, there was little resistance and much government support for the fundamentalists' proposals. After the Islamists' success at the polls in late 1991, women not dressed modestly experienced more and more harassment in the streets, and some women who refused to veil have even been murdered (Ghiles 1994). Khalida Messaoudi, a leader of the Mouvement pour la République, who has organized countless protests against the family code, is on the FIS's widely publicized hit list (Schem 1994). Other female leaders and writers have sought refuge in France.

The Maghrebin Population in France

According to the French census, there were 1,298,273 Maghrebin immigrants living in France in 1999 out of a total immigrant population of 4,306,094 (30 percent). The census lists 574,208 Algerian, 522,504 Moroccan, and 201,561 Tunisian immigrants (INSEE 2000a).[29] Unofficial numbers put the total much higher. In the mid-1990s there were some 800,000 Algerians living in France, and possibly as many as 1.5 million if those who have French citizenship are included (Stone 1997; Kastoryano 2002; Silverstein 2004). The French census and most other government sur-

veys, in addition to being dependent on respondents' willingness to participate, do not include questions about race, religion, or ethnic origin, so there
are no official numbers for determining the number of children of immigrants born in France, including second-generation North Africans, referred
to as *les Beurs*.[30] Early immigration to France was skewed in favor of Kabyles
as a result of colonial practices that favored them and the French land grab
that displaced peasants in the fertile Kabyle region, but this demographic
advantage has disappeared over time. Whereas in the 1950s, over 60 percent
of Algerian immigrants to France were from Kabylia, by 1992, Berbers made
up only 28 percent of Algerians in France, which represents approximately
their percentage of the population in Algeria (Tribalat 1996; Silverstein
2004).[31] Berbers are less well represented in Moroccan immigration, 21.5
percent of immigrants compared with 40 percent in Morocco. Twenty-six
percent of Algerians claim Berber, Berber-Arabic, or Berber-French as their
maternal language, compared with 50 percent Arabic, 19 percent French-
Arabic, and 4 percent French. For Moroccans, the numbers are 21 percent
for Berber or a Berber combination, and 55 percent Arabic, 18 percent
French-Arabic, and 5 percent French (Tribalat 1996).

After Algerian independence, the French placed certain restrictions on
Algerians. In 1973, a year before the French suspended the entry of foreign
workers in an effort to curb unemployment, the Algerian government had
stopped new emigration in response to attacks on Algerian citizens living in
France. In 1973–1974, the number of female Algerian immigrants surpassed
that of males and has remained higher as a result of family reunification laws.
The average date of entry for immigrants with children in school in France
between the ages of 2 and 25 in 1992 was 1964 for Algerian men, 1972 for
Algerian women and Moroccan and Tunisian men, and 1977 for Moroccan
and Tunisian women (INSEE 1997). Four-fifths of women who immigrated
were married, and many brought children with them (Tribalat 1996).
Between 1968 and 1982, the Algerian female population in France increased
fourfold (Raissiguier 1994). The 1999 census revealed that 42.5 percent of
Tunisians, 44 percent of Algerians, and 46 percent of Moroccans in France
are female.

On the basis of her work among Mexican immigrants to the United
States, Pierette Hondagneu-Sotelo (1994) argues that women's presence in
the immigrant population contributes to settlement in numerous ways.

When men come alone, they are more likely to be sojourners who participate in circular migration, returning to the home country to see their families or when seasonal work ends. When women also migrate, families form,
and families become "enmeshed" in community institutions. Once families
become enmeshed, they are less likely to return to the home country permanently.[32] Despite choosing to remain in France, the majority of North
African immigrants are permanent residents and do not apply for citizenship
(Lebon 1998).[33]

The majority of Maghrebins live in large cities, particularly Paris and
Marseilles.[34] According to an important study of immigrants in France
(Tribalat 1995, 1996), Maghrebins are poorly educated and occupy the bottom rungs of the social structure.[35] Although the levels of education and pro-
fessionalism are lower among all groups of immigrants in France, North
Africans are behind European immigrants. Thirty-one percent of Algerian
men and 25 percent of Moroccan men never went to school; for women, the
figures are 32 percent and 36 percent. For Maghrebin parents of children in
school between the ages of 2 and 25 in 1992, three-fourths did not have a
high school diploma (INSEE 1997). The majority, 64 percent of Algerians
and 52 percent of Moroccans, come from rural regions where most were
agricultural workers. The next most common employment before immigration was blue collar work. In France, North African men are especially likely
to hold manual jobs in factories or construction. Early labor recruiters targeted Maghrebin men for work in mines and especially in car factories where
they were rarely able to rise above the level of unskilled worker, despite years
of experience (Sayad 2004).[36] Women are less likely to work, and when they
do, they often engage in paid domestic work, cleaning, and child care.[37]
Almost 77 percent of Algerians and 82 percent of Moroccans in France are
either construction workers or low-level employees. Only 4.3 percent of
Algerians and 5.5 percent of Moroccans are professionals or top-level management (INSEE 1997).

The education and social origin of all immigrants has increased since
1974 as a result of laws that excluded laborers and favored people moving to
France for educational or familial reasons.[38] Immigrants since 1974 have also
come mainly from urban centers. In 1998, 37,058 Maghrebins arrived in
France: 15,346 Algerians, 16,763 Moroccans, and 4,949 Tunisians.[39] Of
these new immigrants, only 923 came as permanent laborers; 11,987 came
for family reunification, and 6,476 came as the spouse of a French person

(INSEE 2000b).[40] Nevertheless, immigrants of Maghrebin origin remain behind immigrants from Europe in terms of education and employment.

As members of the secondary labor market, Maghrebin immigrants and their children are caught up in the tide of rising unemployment. In 1990, the unemployment rate for French people was 9 percent. In 1995, 27 percent of Algerian men, 28 percent of Tunisian men, and 29 percent of Moroccan men were unemployed. The figures for women were 36, 39, and 43 percent (INSEE 1997).[41] By 1996, the unemployment rate had climbed to 12 percent for French people, 24 percent for immigrants, and 32.3 percent for non-European immigrants (Gourévitch 1998). Female North Africans had an unemployment rate of 40 percent compared with 10.7 percent for French women (Gourévitch 1998). In 1997, 63 percent of Algerians, 58 percent of Moroccans, and 39 percent of Tunisians looking for work were female (Lebon 1998). Gaspard (1998) points out that female immigrants have less access than men to higher-paying jobs and that the French generally prohibit employing noncitizens in public functions (an area of the job market that favors women), which further reduces immigrant women's employment possibilities. The declared income of immigrant families is 20 percent lower than the national average (Gourévitch 1998). In 1990, 41 percent of Algerians, 39 percent of Moroccans, and 30 percent of Tunisians lived in public housing; compared with a national percentage of 14.5 percent (INSEE 1990).

Particularly disturbing is the fact that 20.7 percent of naturalized French citizens of Algerian origin were unemployed in the 1990s (Taïeb 1998). The second generation continues to be at a disadvantage in looking for work, especially in the private sector, despite being educated in France and having French citizenship. Youth of Algerian origin were unemployed at a rate almost triple that of youth of Portuguese descent in 1990, and a study of job applications mailed with the same educational degree and skills revealed that those with a North African name were substantially less likely to be called for an interview than applicants who are not identified as Arab (Weil 2005).

According to Césari (2000:97), "[I]t is difficult (if not impossible) for North Africans to assimilate because the majority in the receiving country discriminates against them: for example, in France they are considered more visible and more 'problematic' than other equally 'exotic' migrants." Noiriel (2001) points out, for instance, that there has been relatively little xenophobia toward blacks in France, whether from the Americas or from Africa.

Opinion polls showed that until the 1950s, Germans were the group most hated by French people. This changed with the Algerian war, and today French racism is primarily directed at Maghrebins (Noiriel 2001).

Khellil (1991) explains that for many ordinary French citizens, immigrant now automatically equals Arab. Some authors and politicians worry that anti-Arab sentiment is conflated with anti-Muslim sentiment as a result of stereotypes of fundamentalist terrorists and perceptions of insecurity and violence in largely immigrant suburbs (Geisser 2003). Many North Africans in France live in a situation analogous to poor blacks in the United States, trapped in public housing projects where unemployment and crime rates are high.[42] The November 2005 riots in French suburbs are an expression of the frustration felt by many dispossessed members of the second and third generation and highlight the stark realities that belie French belief in color-blind integration into the Republic.[43]

A 2005 poll of 1,000 people by the Commission Nationale Consultative des Droits de l'Homme (CNCDH) found that one out of three French people surveyed labeled themselves racist (Zappi 2005). Documented acts of racism, which had dropped some in the late 1990s, have been on the rise in the past few years in response to the increasing tensions in the Middle East, particularly between Palestinians and Israelis, and also in response to September 11, 2001, and the war in Iraq. Jews are the most common victims of racist acts in France (often perpetrated by people of North African descent), but Maghrebins are the second most frequent target (CNCDH 2004; Zappi 2004). In a 2003 poll of 1,052 people, the CNCDH found that almost a quarter of French people, 23 percent, asserted that French Muslims are not like other French people, 39 percent believed that there were too many Muslims in France, and 41 percent said that there were too many immigrants in general in France (CNCDH 2004; Zappi 2004). This last number grew to 56 percent in the 2005 CNCDH poll conducted after the November riots (Zappi 2005).

Given the decade of strife in Algeria and several bombing incidents in France, the French fear that militant Islamist groups are becoming more prevalent in their own country is not a new one after September 11.[44] It is difficult to measure how many immigrants and members of the second generation are truly involved in political/religious terrorist organizations or other types of crime, and the media contributes to an exaggerated picture of these activities (Geisser 2003).

Maghrebin women and men are both affected by the social climate in France, but they differ on characteristics that influence their adaptation. Women are less likely than men to be educated or employed. North African women are also less likely to be working or looking for work than other immigrant or French women. In 1999, the level of activity for Maghrebins between the ages of 25 and 59 was 83.7 percent for Algerian men, 87.4 percent for Moroccan men, and 91.1 percent for Tunisian men.[45] The figures for women were 47.7, 40.4, and 41.6 percent, respectively. The French activity rate was 91.5 percent for men and 75.7 percent for women (INSEE 2000b).

Maghrebin women have different patterns not only of work, but also of marriage. Whereas 30 percent of Algerian men and 22 percent of Moroccan men in France live with a French woman, only 11 percent of Algerian women and 8 percent of Moroccan women live with a French man (Tribalat 1996). Mixed marriages have more than doubled between 1981 and 1992, and although women who came to France at a young age or were born in France are more likely to be involved with French men than the previous generation, North African men are still twice as likely to make exogamous unions. More than half of Algerian and Moroccan women in France had an arranged marriage, often to a cousin. For women who entered France already married, the numbers climb to between 60 and 70 percent. In the majority of these cases the woman was asked for her consent, although 20 percent of Algerian women were married without their consent (Tribalat 1996). These matrimonial practices are increasingly rare among the second generation.

The number of children per woman has also decreased among North Africans in France. In 1982, Algerian women in France had an average of 4.3 children, and Moroccan women had an average of 5.2 children. In 1990, these figures had dropped to 3.2 for Algerians and 3.5 for Moroccans. These numbers were lower than the birthrate in the Maghreb: 5.4 in Algeria and 4.5 in Morocco in 1990 (Couvreur 1998).[46]

Long-standing colonial relations between France and the North African countries affect the language that immigrants use with their children. According to one study of immigrants who arrived after age 15, 58 percent of Algerians and 51 percent of Moroccans have a good grasp of the French language, and 38 percent of Algerians and 41 percent of Moroccans can read and write in French (Tribalat 1996). Another study of parents of children in school found that 19 percent of Algerian men, 38 percent of Moroccan and Tunisian men, 43 percent of Algerian women, and 49 percent of Moroccan and Tunisian women speak French with difficulty or not at all (INSEE 1997). The lower levels of language ability by women are because they were less likely to attend school through an age at which French was taught in the Maghreb, but also because of their later arrival in France and their lower levels of employment. Nevertheless, among immigrants with children between 2 and 25 enrolled in school, 37 percent of Algerian women, 47 percent of Algerian men, 18 percent of Moroccan and Tunisian women, and 27 percent of Moroccan and Tunisian men speak to their spouse primarily in French. In addition, 69 percent of Algerian men, 52 percent of Algerian women, 44 percent of Moroccan and Tunisian men, and 34 percent of Moroccan and Tunisian women speak French to their children (INSEE 1997).[47] The more frequent use of French in Algerian families is the result of the longer and more involved history of French colonization in Algeria.

Regarding religious practices there are also differences by sex. When asked about religious practices, 33 percent of Algerian women and 42 percent of Moroccan women responded that they practiced regularly compared with 26 percent of Algerian men and 39 percent of Moroccan men. Approximately one-fourth of all groups said that they practiced sometimes, although women practiced sometimes slightly more than men. Thirty-eight percent of Algerian men and 29 percent of Moroccan men did not practice at all; whereas 29 percent of Algerian women and 22 percent of Moroccan women did not practice. Finally, 15 percent of Algerian men, 10 percent of Moroccan men, 12 percent of Algerian women, and 11 percent of Moroccan women declared that they did not have a religion (Tribalat 1995). Although women of both groups are more religious than men, Moroccans in general are more religious than Algerians, especially Moroccan Berbers. Whereas 41 percent of Moroccan Arab men and 36 percent of Moroccan Arab women have no religion or do not practice, only 33 percent of Moroccan male Berbers and 18 percent of Moroccan female Berbers are not religious. Algerian Berbers, on the other hand, are the least religious (64 percent of men and 45 percent of women have no religion or do not practice at all), followed by Algerian Arabs (48 percent of men and 39 percent of women).

Women are stricter than men about respecting food and alcohol interdictions. Eighty percent of Algerian and Moroccan women do not eat pork, and 76 percent of Algerian women and 77 percent of Moroccan women do not drink alcohol. Among men, 69 percent of Algerians and 75 percent of Moroccans do not eat pork, and 54 percent of Algerians and 64 percent of Moroccans do not drink alcohol. Women are also more likely to fast during Ramadan: 81 percent of Algerian women and 86 percent of Moroccan women, compared with 69 percent of Algerian men and 82 percent of Moroccan men (Tribalat 1995). Muslim women are more likely to pray at home than in mosques, and mosque attendance in general is low: 6 percent for women and 15 percent for men. In addition to differences by sex and nationality in religious observance, immigrants who did not attend school or have a low level of instruction are more religious than their more educated counterparts. Among Algerians, 33 percent of those who are uneducated said they did not have a religion or did not practice compared with 58 percent of those who attended school for at least seven years (Tribalat 1995).

The final area where we see differences between male and female Maghrebins in France concerns naturalization and the desire to return to North Africa. Women are more likely than men to request French citizenship. In 1990, 12.2 percent of Moroccan men, 15.7 percent of Moroccan women, 14.0 percent of Algerian men, 16.2 percent of Algerian women, 27.4 percent of Tunisian men, and 37.6 percent of Tunisian women had obtained French nationality (INSEE 2000b).[48] Those women who arrived after age 15 and who are unmarried are the most likely to become French: 22 percent of Algerian women and 33 percent of Moroccan women, compared with 6 percent of Algerian men and 19 percent of Moroccan men (Tribalat 1995). Women are also less inclined to return to the Maghreb. Whereas 24 percent of Algerian men and 26 percent of Moroccan men wish to return to their countries of origin, only 12 percent of Algerian women and 19 percent of Moroccan women wish to do so (Tribalat 1996).

Participant Characteristics

All of the participants in this study are Muslim, but they differ on age, age at immigration, country of emigration (Algeria, Tunisia, Morocco), ethnicity (Arab or Berber), education (none to doctorate), employment history (never worked to full-time work), marital status (single, married, divorced, widowed), and number of children (0–7). (See Appendix 2 for chart of participant characteristics.) The sample consists of 26 Algerians, 11 Moroccans, and 8 Tunisians between the ages of 25 and 58, who have resided in France between 1 and 37 years. Most were between 17 and 35 years old when they immigrated, but two women arrived when they were in their mid-40s, and two came to France with their parents at ages 13 and 14, respectively. These two participants were included in the sample because they were not schooled in France and spent most of their adolescence sheltered by their families.[49]

Given the time spent in France, and the use of French as the language of instruction in the Maghreb throughout most of the century, the majority of North African immigrants speak French to some extent. The women I interviewed had various degrees of ability communicating in French. Of the 45 respondents, 43 were interviewed in French, and 2 were interviewed in Arabic with the help of a translator. Twenty participants were entirely fluent in French, although some retained a North African accent. Another 11 spoke very well, although they sometimes made mistakes that revealed they were not perfectly fluent. Eight spoke satisfactorily for an interview but made numerous grammatical errors and had a limited vocabulary, and four had a more seriously limited capacity in French. Although they understood the majority of what I was asking, with these four women I sometimes had to rephrase questions, and I often had to make them repeat their answers several times to make sure I understood correctly.

Obviously, language ability is tied to educational level attained. Eighteen participants had at least some college instruction, including 12 who had completed either a master's degree or a Ph.D. Of the other 27 women, 5 had made it through high school (although they had not necessarily passed the baccalaureate), 13 had some schooling but did not reach or finish high school (this category varied from a few months of schooling as a small child to schooling through age 16), and 9 had never attended school at all.[50]

Participants were not only more likely to be better educated than the typical North African population in France, but they also were also more likely to be French citizens. Seventeen women (38 percent) were French citizens, and of the 19 respondents (42 percent) with permanent resident cards, 6 were in the process of applying for citizenship. Of the other participants, one was a citizen of another European country, four had temporary papers, either for one year or renewable every month, one was waiting to receive papers, and one was vague when talking about her status and was very possibly in France illegally.

Respondents were also more likely to be working than the female Maghrebin population in France. Approximately one-third were working full time at the time of the interview, and another third were employed part time. Eleven women were housewives. Of the others, two were unemployed and seeking work, one had stopped working although she was not old enough for retirement, and one was a full-time student in between small-time jobs. Of the women with some type of employment, the majority held low-level jobs, even women with advanced degrees. Of the three women who had doctorates in the sciences, one is unemployed, one works as a ticket seller to a park amusement ride, and the other is a school aide who helps take children on field trips and watches them after school before the parents arrive; she does not teach science. Eleven respondents either cleaned for or looked after the children of private employers. Another four worked in North African associations. A few women held middle-class jobs: one woman was a computer technician, two others ran a small ethnic business, three were teachers, and one was an artist. Malika, the Tunisan woman in the introduction who is a producer at a production company, is by far the most successful woman I interviewed. The higher numbers of employed women and French citizens are probably in part due to well-educated participants in the sample.

In addition, the women I interviewed were slightly more likely to not be religious than other North African women in France. Although they all self-identify as Muslims, approximately one-third do not practice. Several of these women noted that they "believe but don't practice." Another third, however, are very religious, fasting during Ramadan, observing food restrictions, and praying daily. The other third are also religious, respecting Ramadan and not consuming pork or alcohol, but they do not pray daily.[51] The nonreligious group is typical of highly educated Maghrebin immigrants.

Like the overall female Maghrebin population in France, few participants wished to return to North Africa permanently. Only five (11 percent) wished to do so. Twenty (44 percent) are sure that they want to remain in France. Another 13 (29 percent) were undecided, and 5 (11 percent) stated that they would like to live part of the year in France and part of the year in the Maghreb. The other two did not answer this question.

The ethnicity of the women interviewed also reflects the larger population. Twenty-four (53 percent) are Arab, and 13 (29 percent) are Berber. Of the Berbers, 10 are Kabyles. Five women had mixed Arab and Berber origins, often women from Morocco, but sometimes Kabyles as well. The three remaining women had mixed Arab or Kabyle and European or Jewish ancestry. Although ethnicity becomes important in terms of identity negotiation, it does not have a large impact on other areas, such as cultural behaviors. At first I was surprised to find this to be the case with nationality as well. After realizing the enormous importance of educational differences, however, it made sense that illiterate Moroccan, Algerian, and Tunisian women who followed their husbands to France share more of the same behaviors and attitudes with each other than with a fellow countrywoman who came to France to finish her graduate studies.

These educational differences often reflect not only class differences, but also differences in rural or urban origin, age, and the attitudes of women's parents. Several of the women I interviewed were in their 20s and 30s and have lived in France for a shorter period of time than their older counterparts. Younger immigrants are more likely to be well educated because of changes in the Maghreb favoring women's education and French policies that encourage the immigration of more educated groups. Algerian women who fled for political reasons are almost all university educated, and some came to finish their studies in France and then remained after the situation in Algeria deteriorated. Among my sample, 21 women came to join their husbands who already worked in France, 12 were enrolled in French universities, 5 fled Algeria or chose to remain in France for political reasons, 2 came to get away from their families, 2 immigrated as adolescents with their parents, 1 was sent by her parents to help with the children of a relative, 1 moved because she had been offered a job, and 1 sought medical help in France.

Having situated the participants in the wider social context and in terms of their particular characteristics, I now turn to an examination of the questions of this study. As this section illustrates, male and female North Africans differ, and thus I begin the analysis section of this work with a focus on how gender affects the respondents' upbringing and how they have adapted to life in Paris. Respondents compared their experiences to those of male Maghrebins in France and talked at length about their new roles and opportunities as women.

Crossing the Street

Gendered Lives from the Maghreb to France

As other authors note, "[s]tudies about immigration and post-colonial society in France tend to ignore or marginalize the gendered nature of their subject" (Freedman and Tarr 2000:1).[1] Gender affects how people are socialized, how they are treated, and how they view themselves. Pyke and Johnson (2003:34) note that more attention needs to be paid to how racial and ethnic minority women "mediate cross-pressures in the production of femininity as they move between mainstream and ethnic arenas, such as family, work, and school." In this chapter, I examine how assumptions about gender learned in the home country are called into question upon arrival in a new country, and how immigrant women who "do" gender the French way derive unexpected benefits compared with immigrant men (West and Zimmerman 1987). I begin with background on how gender conditions women's lives growing up in the Maghreb. I then explore how being female impacts respondents' experiences of immigration to and life in France.

Female in the Maghreb

RESPONSIBILITIES AND RESTRAINTS

The way girls are raised in North Africa depends on several factors, both within the particular family and without, that result from historical and sociocultural forces. Camille Lacoste-Dujardin (2004a:120) writes that "in Algeria for example, the transmutations stemming from the war of independence, in conjunction with the decline in agriculture, the rate of emigration, and the moving of populations, have led to great changes in family structures that now reveal a rather large variety." At the same time, however, she maintains that "[t]he weight of patriarchal representations and lineage has not been lifted and, in Maghrebin families, people still live, with only a few exceptions, under the power of the honor of the lineage and paternal (patriarchal) authority" (122).

In general, there were two patterns of upbringing for the participants. First, girls who grew up in rural areas with uneducated, traditional parents were often expected to help with household tasks, even at the expense of their schooling. Many of these girls only went to school briefly, and several, especially first-born girls, never went to school at all. Occasionally girls who managed to do well in school were allowed to continue as long as they also consistently met their familial obligations. This was true of Hayat (32-year-old Algerian), who was one of the first girls in her village to attend school, and whose father threatened every year, starting in junior high, that this would be her last year of school:

> *H:*   They did everything to make me stay at home, for me to get married, to not continue my studies. I wasn't helped. Not at all. Even when I went to school, I got home at 6:00, at 6:00, I had to make dinner for my brothers and sisters, because I had a lot of brothers and sisters.
>
> *CK:*   You were the eldest?
>
> *H:*   Yes, unfortunately for me. And a girl. The oldest girl in a Maghrebin family. Honestly, it's no piece of cake.

Hayat's mother argued that because her daughter excelled in school, she should be allowed to continue, so Hayat was able to pass her baccalaureate despite her father's objections. Other mothers were happy to have the eldest daughter at home all day to aid in child care and cooking, and some parents forbade schooling for girls altogether. When asked if she had ever attended school, Fatima (54-year-old Moroccan) answered, "Oh no, never, never, never. Because girls where I come from, they say we have to stay at home and get married, and her husband will work for her. She doesn't need to go to school."

Girls with educated parents, many of whom were raised in large cities, experienced a second pattern. They were expected to go to school, often through college. Even these girls, though, were frequently required to do household chores, including cooking and cleaning, that their brothers were never expected to do. Only in one family were boys also expected to make their beds and do the family's dishes. Women noted that even an educated woman needs to know how to cook and clean in order to be a good wife. As Deha pointed out, "It's clear that when you get married, you have to know how to cook, that's the side, a girl knows how to cook, how to wash. It's clear that a girl who went to medical school, it's very important that she have a diploma so that she can be married, she can be married well, but that she knows how to cook and take care of her man, that's very important." Deha also makes an interesting observation that because girls are trained to be responsible for household tasks at an early age, they carry this sense of work and responsibility through school and into the labor market. Currently, more Algerian girls than boys are passing the baccalaureate and finding jobs, and Deha attributes the successes of girls to their stricter upbringing, which encourages responsibility.

Although differences in upbringing and expectations for girls in the Maghreb differ by region, class, education, and parental beliefs, virtually all the respondents had constraints placed on their movement and their sexuality. In some rural areas, North African women leave their homes only to visit family members, attend to sick relatives and neighbors, and attend weddings. Although some of these women make extra income for the family, they do so by working in their own gardens and fields or, most frequently, by sewing or weaving goods that will be sold. Men do most of the chores that involve going beyond the home, often including the shopping. The story is very different in urban areas where more women work outside the home, but girls find from a young age that the spaces in which they can be seen are limited. Even when parents allow girls to go out for purposes other than school and work, access to public places is greatly restricted. As Mernissi (1996:167) points out, "[s]treets are spaces of sin and temptation because they are both public and sex-mixed." Girls rarely attend movies and are often unwelcome in cafés. The boundaries are maintained by looks of disapproval and sometimes by harassment of women who test the limits. These limitations become internalized. Participants frequently said that smoking, drinking, talking to boys, going to movies, and being out after 6:00 PM are acts that are disapproved of and can cause women to develop bad reputations. Even women who go to cafés, drink, and smoke restrict these behaviors in certain situations. Besma is a 34-year-old from Tunisia, where constraints on urban women are more lax than in most of the Maghreb. Even so, she will not eat pork there and is careful about who sees her drink and where she smokes:

> In my town, I don't go to the restaurants in my town because everybody knows me. I don't like, um, I don't want to be, to have it repeated everywhere and to have them stick a label on me that doesn't match anything really. Because they're going to think of you like a prostitute if you drink. It's ridiculous. But, well, I'll smoke, I'll smoke on the other hand, if I show it, when I'm in a café, in restaurants, I don't have a problem, I smoke. I don't have issues with smoking over there. But, on the other hand, we don't smoke in the street there. Women don't smoke in the streets. No woman does it, so I don't do it. But in public places, restaurants and such, everybody smokes, it's not forbidden, and I don't hide it. But with alcohol, I'm a little more discreet because I don't want problems for nothing.

Many of the restrictions on women are efforts to control their sexuality. A girl who loses her virginity before marriage is viewed as "lost" and can bring shame to her entire family. As Besma made clear, behaviors such as drinking in public or smoking on the street become linked with perceptions of loose sexual morals, and consequently many women avoid these behaviors. The emphasis on virginity remains strong, even for those women with the most "tolerant" parents. Respondents who praised their parents for allowing them to go out in mixed-sex groups still mentioned that the one rule was that they remain virgins. Labiba's parents were very permissive: "I was allowed to go out at night, for example, to sleep out. All along saying, 'Okay, but you have to keep your virginity.' That's the ultimatum." The majority of parents were much more strict. Many would not let their daughters attend even school-sponsored activities after school, and some were opposed to sports and any traveling for girls for fear of losing control over their sexuality. Leila (43-year-old Tunisian) said that growing up in rural Tunisia attending movies, visiting a different town, and participating in sports were all looked upon negatively for girls, "because a girl's virginity constitutes the honor of the family. It's the honor of the family that's riding on it, so if the girl loses her virginity, the family has lost its honor. And still today that mentality exists there. It hasn't changed at all, I think."[2] Nour (34-year-old Algerian) remembers with pain that her grandmother told her to quit horseback riding as a child because otherwise she would lose her virginity.

Like restrictions on movement and visibility in public spaces, women internalized messages about their sexuality and were reticent to go too far. Leila explains,

> When we arrive at the problem of intimate relations between a man and a woman, or having a sexual life before marriage, there I was, um, I got blocked. I repeated what my mother told me, really, I said, "No, a girl who is not married, she's not allowed to sleep with a man" . . . and that's because, well, for us it was the worst thing that could happen to a girl. A girl who's not married and who sleeps with a boy, it's really, it's a prostitute, it's not a girl worth anything. So I never could, I couldn't go to bed with my fiancé before the wedding. I never could, and that's in the education.

Nour, in particular, talked at length about how her sexuality and feelings about her body were affected by growing up in Algeria, even though her mother was Dutch.

> So even in my sexuality, and it's important, I was stuck, you see, by my role as a woman who couldn't have a normal sexuality without guilt. I felt very, very young the way men looked at women in my society. It's a view that's not healthy, you see? And I felt it very, very young. I have a memory really young, six or seven, when a man kissed me by force at the pool, and it traumatized me. And I didn't tell anyone because I already felt guilty, you know what I mean? And it continued that way really. We couldn't have a boyfriend normally. I grew up in an Algerian school, in an Algerian society, even though I was a little different having a Dutch mother and everything, but that weighed on me. The gaze of men weighed on me. The gaze of my teachers, male. I remember that we had a civics and religion teacher who was supposed to teach us good manners and everything, and who openly tried to pick up girls. We were in sixth grade! A friend of mine, in class, like a dirty old man. And that, that can go on in other countries, but I felt it in Algeria where women aren't necessarily free to do what they want. And that

really affected me. . . . [I wanted] to be able to be a woman without others seeing me as a piece of meat. You see? And that was a fight with my male friends in Algeria. And today finally they've accepted me as a friend, and not as a potential wife or a good lay, to speak crudely. And it was really a battle to talk with them and make them understand that there's something more, that, that the woman is not just for sex, but can be a friend. Because in our society, the sexes are separated really early.

Nour goes on to say that she is still not comfortable with her body, but notes that there are Algerian women who feel better about themselves than she does. Indeed, not all women eschewed sexuality before marriage. Respondents talked of girls who found ways to get around the virginity problem. These include having the hymen sewed back together before marriage and engaging in anal sex in order to protect one's "virginity." Deha was open about bucking constraints on her sexuality. At sixteen, she asked a classmate to help her lose her virginity because she wanted to be free of it. At seventeen, she moved out of her parents' house, a move sure to bring shame to an unmarried girl, because even divorced women in Algeria are not supposed to live alone but return home to their parents. She admits she wanted to provoke people and particularly enjoyed having sex on the beach during the month of Ramadan, a taboo, when everyone else was indoors breaking the fast. Yet even Deha was unable to be as free about her sexuality as she would have liked: "My husband and I got married because we had to get married since we lived in a house where we couldn't live as a couple, and so we did it as if it were a duty . . . and there was our son who was going to be born nine months later." Thus wanting to live with her boyfriend and the knowledge of a baby on the way rerouted Deha's sexual freedom back into traditional channels in spite of herself.

RELATIONSHIPS WITH FAMILY MEMBERS

Traditional sexuality is sexuality in marriage, and most North African girls defined themselves around this event. As unmarried children and adolescents, they were under the control of their fathers and often their brothers, who saw themselves as responsible for protecting the family or larger kin group's honor (Charrad 2001).[3] According to Joseph (1996:199), "[t]he notion of family honor facilitates patriarchal power by circumscribing women's sexuality, movement in social arenas, and to some degree, economic opportunities. It enhances the power of fathers, grandfathers, uncles, brothers, and male cousins over women."

The amount of control varies by family, but even in tolerant families, girls often found that their relationships with male family members were conflicted. Fathers usually made the final decisions about school and other activities, and women who were well educated often reached a point where they resisted, challenging their father's decisions and differential treatment of their brothers. Sometimes accumulated grievances were subsumed and expressed in one rebellious symbolic act, such as smoking. In the Maghreb, even boys often refrain from smoking in front of their fathers, a behavior seen as a sign of disrespect. Nour's brothers did smoke in front of their father, and even though Nour did not smoke, she lit up a cigarette in front of her father to test his fair treatment of girls and boys. Malika's painful relationship with her father epitomizes many of the struggles participants voiced. She, too, argued with her father about smoking as a pretext for deeper problems:

> Smoke. Yes. I don't smoke in front of him, and my last big fight with
> him was about cigarettes. Because one day I was there on vacation, and
> he saw a pack of cigarettes . . . in my room, and he said, "I don't want you
> to smoke." . . . So it was a big crisis between us. . . . I smoke one or two
> cigarettes a day, and it's not his business. As long as I don't do it in front
> of him, where I wasn't provoking, or in front of anyone. . . . I don't see why
> he has to get mixed up in it. So we had a big discussion that night, but he
> said that I didn't respect him, and that anyway I did what I wanted, and that
> if his opinion counted so little for me, then it wasn't worth him talking to
> me. And he didn't talk to me during the whole time I was there, and for two
> years I came and he didn't talk to me. . . . But I think that this fight between
> us about cigarettes, cigarettes were a pretext, but they were symptomatic
> of everything. Yes, of everything. Because he is someone who always had
> a really hard time talking . . . he doesn't know how to express his feelings,
> so he's rather violent. He's going to explode or he's not going to say any-
> thing. . . . So he wanted to tell me something. He wanted to tell me that he
> understood or didn't understand, or he felt me slipping away from him. . . .
> I think he wanted to tell me, "I know you're getting away, and I have no way
> to stop you," that's it. "And until the last moment, I'm trying to hold onto
> the last little thing." . . . I asked him to accept enormous things for him, and

he wasn't brought up to accept all that. He wasn't conditioned, um, to see his daughter grow that way. He wasn't prepared for it. . . . Like all men, I think, he wakes up saying, "Oh really? It's like that?" I think it's true for all men everywhere in the world, maybe Arab men more, I don't know, I don't have an opinion on that, but all of a sudden it's too much. I think I'm too much for him, too much. So he's proud of me, but at the same time, sometimes, it poses a lot of problems for him. Had I been a boy, it would have been perfect. He could have been proud without any problem. Now he's proud, but it's difficult for him.

Traditional rules of decency regulating interactions between the sexes and different generations hinder the ability of fathers to communicate openly with their daughters (Lacoste-Dujardin 2000, 2004a). When Malika and Nour rebelled, both their fathers stopped speaking to them. The pattern of conflict avoidance sometimes went both ways. Many women did not or could not challenge their fathers, and some continued to try to meet their family's expectations, or at least pretend to, often even while living in France. Keltouma's (35-year-old Moroccan) story about her father's visit reveals the ambivalence that even independent women in their 30s feel about upsetting their father's notion of how girls should behave. Keltouma was taking night classes after work and consequently did not get home until late at night: "My father visited, and I had to stop my classes because I couldn't tell him that I got home at 9:30, 10:00. He wouldn't have understood. He wouldn't have taken it well." As Joseph (1996:201) clarifies, "Family both supports and suppresses women. This paradox of support and suppression, love and power, generosity and competition compels both attachment to and struggle within families."

Although women were likely to express ambivalence about their father's attempts to control them, they were less understanding of their brother's attempts to do likewise. In some families, brothers were as hard or harder on their sisters than fathers were. They too felt responsible for protecting the family's honor and kept tabs on girls out of the parents' sight. One of Amel's brothers has not talked to her since her wedding to a French Muslim. Hayat noted that her brothers both expected their sisters to serve them and clean up after them, and monitored their behavior outside the house, and that when brothers were not watching out for them, male cousins were. According to Mbruka (33-year-old Algerian), her brother was angry growing up because her parents would not let him take on this role:

My brother didn't have, we had some difficult times, especially during adolescence where a girl doesn't go alone with a friend to the movies, because there are men at the movies. And my brother took it badly with his group of friends, um, boys who said, "Uh oh! We saw your sister at the movies." And he couldn't deal with it at home; it wasn't his business. It wasn't his role. If he wasn't happy about it, that's the way it goes. So the discussion was with my parents, and my brother didn't have any authority over me, unlike the classic way of doing things, it's the father, it's the brother; it's horrible for an Algerian girl or a Maghrebin girl in general.

Mbruka's brother was also the only boy required to participate equally in household tasks. She attributed her freedom as an adolescent and the equal treatment of boys and girls at home to her mother's unwillingness to repeat her own experiences growing up with a very strict father.

Mothers thus made decisions and set standards in some families, but not in all. A few mothers were as strict or stricter than fathers, but many tried to make life somewhat easier for their daughters. Sometimes mothers helped in discreet ways, lending a sympathetic ear or saving money to help pay for a trip to France. Hayat, whose traditional father wanted to end her schooling, was aided by her mother's coaxing of her father and the plane ticket purchased with additional income her mother made sewing. Placing mothers in the role of confidante could cause problems, however, as Malika found when she told her mother that she was living with her French boyfriend, and her mother had to keep the secret from her father. The strain of hiding this from her husband finally led her to have a breakdown. Girls in the Maghreb, particularly the eldest daughters, are often especially close to their mothers, and they may choose to monitor their own behavior so as not to jeopardize their mother's status in the family (Lacoste-Dujardin 2000).

Many participants remembered that their mothers' hands were tied, and that they often suffered under their husbands' familial and sometimes physical control. Isma (36-year-old Algerian) labeled her mother "oppressed," and remembered that after her father's death, her mother threw out all his pictures and the objects he had made for the house. Amel (26-year-old Algerian) related that even after her mother's divorce and election as mayor of a town, she was still controlled by her ex-husband and sons. Despite his own remarriage, Amel's father did not want his ex-wife to marry another man. One of Amel's brothers, who sometimes lived with her father, would threaten every man who got involved with his mother. Because her brother lived at home until the age of 28, Amel says that her mother sacrificed a lot. Warda (58-year-old Algerian) also remembers the double bind in which her father placed her mother. He would allow her to attend weddings and other social events but tell her to be home by a fixed early hour. This meant she had to excuse herself in the middle of a meal in order to make it home on time. Although he never yelled at her for coming home late from work, if she missed one of his prescribed hours for a social event, there was trouble. Consequently, she found herself declining invitations so as not to appear rude when leaving early. Yet at the same time, Warda's mother not only worked outside the home but also controlled the family's money. Warda attributes the amount of power that her mother did have to the fact that she was of a higher social class than her father.

Participants were also quiet about their behavior, or decided to abide by the rules because they wanted to protect their younger sisters. Hayat in particular made great sacrifices in her life in order to open the door for her younger sisters:

> I have three sisters in Algeria, so I tried, I tried to do the maximum so that they wouldn't be badly seen because of me. I had to set a very good example so that they would have the path open to college. . . . I have to be discreet . . . so that my sisters can go to college, so that they can even come to France, you see? So that the parents don't say, "She left. She got us." You see? So I have to do it for everyone, for my sisters. . . . There's a girl who came here at 17; she's been in France for two years. . . . She took off; she left the house. Four months already and she hasn't contacted anyone. Me, that's something I'd never do. I'd never do that, run away, because it would be a catastrophe. It would really mean condemning my sisters.

Although Hayat herself was not able to attend college, one sister has graduated from college, one is currently enrolled, and the youngest is planning to go.

Malika also revealed that being the oldest sister is difficult: "My sister also came to France, and she also kept her life a bit hidden, except that it didn't make her suffer the way it made me suffer. After all, I was the one who was first. When she was born, I was set as the example." Malika's failed romance with her French boyfriend and her confrontations with her father allowed her sister to marry a French man and have children without problems. Malika realizes that her difficulties alleviated those of her sister. Occasionally, as with Hayat, the responsibility to step out of a traditional role and still be a "good girl" also helped women outside the family. The price was not only sacrifice, but also enormous pressure: "I was one of the first girls [in my village] to go to junior high, to go to high school. So actually I opened the way for the girls who are going to school now. I had to give the best of myself really. I had to work more than everybody else to prove I was capable, that I'm not a loose woman." Hayat was desperately trying to avoid marriage, but for many women, marriage was the way out of a difficult family life. Even Hayat remarked that had she stayed in Algeria, she would have preferred getting married to living with her brothers (her father has since died). "You don't have a choice. It's inevitable. It can be an escape. Sometimes girls say I prefer to get married, even if it's not a very good solution. It's not because you get married that you'll be happy, because you're going to rediscover you brothers, your father, you'll always find them again. They'll get you."

MARRIAGE AS A MEANS OF ESCAPE

Marriage, as Hayat notes, is really the only option for most women in the Maghreb, yet many girls look forward to it. It is the rite of passage into adulthood, and although girls know they are still likely to be constrained by their husbands, they relish becoming adult women, establishing their own homes, and gaining the prestige that comes with bearing children.[4] As Najet (46-year-old Moroccan) noted, "It's a pleasure to be married, to be out of one's parents', to build a home, to make a life." When asked about her immigration to France, Najet downplays it. For her, the turning point in her life was getting married: "Marriage, that's it, get out. There or here, it's the same for me. It's the man that changes things a bit, meaning the marriage, that's it. That is in your head, being married, that's all. At 19 you don't understand much anyway." Fouzia echoed the same sentiments:

> *F:*   I was young. I only thought about getting married, later having children, that's all, all that was in my head. I didn't think about coming to France, no, no, no.
>
> *CK:* It wasn't too hard on your parents to see their daughter go so far away?
>
> *F:*   No. Parents, when a girl is married, she has to follow her husband, that's all.

Getting married also means having children, and having children is a form of insurance for many Maghrebin women. It reduces the chances that she can be repudiated or divorced. Once children are grown and married, women take on more importance, and many acquire the most freedom they have ever had (Joseph 1996; Lacoste-Dujardin 1996). Warda (58-year-old Algerian) and Karima (43-year-old Algerian) discussed this important turning point in a woman's life cycle:

> W: With age, women take on a lot of importance. The Maghrebin woman, when she becomes a mother, already she takes on some weight, but when her children are grown and she's about to be a mother-in-law or she becomes one, she becomes the center of the family.

> K: She moves in front then. So really, especially when she has become a grandmother or her children are married, then she has total freedom, right? She's in charge.

As Warda and Karima point out, women can go stay with their adult children if problems arise with their husbands. Mothers-in-law often take advantage of the control they have over their sons' wives. Lacoste-Dujardin (1996) argues that this means of achieving importance explains the lack of solidarity between North African women. Young women are aware of these dynamics, and they recognize that marriage is their means to freedom and more power in the long run, if not in the short run.

For those growing up in difficult homes, marriage can indeed be a blessing. Khadija (44-year-old Moroccan) acknowledges this: "It's me who wanted to come to France, because I had a very unhappy childhood. I was an abused child and everything. That's what pushed me to get married." Bahia (38-year-old Algerian) also preferred taking a chance on a husband to remaining in her father's house: "With my father I was always at home, I worked at home, I don't go out. With my husband it's good . . . with my father a little bit hard. He said to me, 'In my home it's like this, and if you get married, [you'll see] with your husband.'" Bahia got lucky, in her opinion; her husband takes her on car trips and to restaurants and the movies with him. Often participants did take risks with their futures, sometimes marrying men they had never met or men twice their age. Many marriages were arranged with cousins, more distant family members, and men from the same village.[5]

A number of women got married only to live with and work for their par-
ents-in-law when their husbands left the Maghreb to work in France. This
was a common pattern especially until the late 1970s and 1980s, when family reunification laws brought more women and children to France. Some
women lived without their husbands for as many as 25 years, often with in-
laws, but sometimes alone with their children. Husbands sent money and
came to visit for a month or two in the summers. All the women interviewed
said that they preferred living with their husbands, and that it was better to
keep the family intact. Oumniya (50-year-old Algerian) relates her fear that
while she and the children were in Algeria her husband had taken another
wife in France: "Sometimes I wondered why we didn't come [to France].
Sometimes I think he's married to a French woman or a Moroccan, no why
not?. . . . Sometimes there kids said [to my children], 'Your father is married
there; he stays there. He doesn't come to Algeria; he stays in France.' Then
my children are sad in the head. 'Why doesn't he come, my dad? Maybe he's
married now?'"

Young women today rarely marry men they do not know, and few live separated from their husbands. Still, the decision to marry is fraught with difficulty, especially for women who have moved to France. The standard of the
nuclear rather than extended family in France means that women are even
more eager than in the Maghreb to make companionate and egalitarian marriages (Lacoste-Dujardin 2000). Many say they wish to marry a North African man for religious reasons, to make family members happy, or because
they want to be with someone who shares the same cultural background. At
the same time, many young immigrants, as Hayat pointed out, fear finding
the attitudes in Maghrebin husbands that they escaped when they left their
fathers and brothers. Hayat says that at 32 years old, this is probably the reason she has still not married.[6] Other respondents were in similar situations.
Many said their ideal husband would be a Maghrebin man with western attitudes. Unfortunately, they believe this man will be hard to find. Many argued
that North African men in France treat their French girlfriends one way and
Maghrebin women another. They also balked at the double standard that
allows Muslim men to marry Christian and Jewish women, but restricts
Muslim women to marrying only Muslim men. Malika admitted that her
unhappy love life was a result of this dilemma. She has only dated French
men, but feels guilty and unable to commit. Even after finally admitting to
her father that she lived with a French man, and her father's surprising reac-

tion that she was old enough to make her own decisions, Malika still feels uncomfortable dating French men. Amel, who married a white French Muslim, frequently finds herself insulted by Arabs in France even though she respected religious requirements.

A few women stated categorically that they refused to marry Arab men, but only one interviewee had actually married a non-Muslim French man. Cherifa (44-year-old Moroccan) said that even in Morocco she only dated French men, and her parents always predicted she would live in France or marry a French man. She did both. One other respondent had a two-year relationship with a white French man, but he broke up with her after the birth of their child in response to pressure from his parents. Several happy women did, however, meet a North African man who met their expectations, but only two of these men were met in France.[7]

For women who did not marry in the Maghreb, going to France was the other means of escaping their families. Paradoxically, some girls who were not allowed to go to college and live alone in a large North African city were able to convince their parents to let them come to France. Others simply waited until they were in their early 20s and left without their parents' approval. This was Malika's case:

> So I wanted, after my baccalaureate, I wanted to leave. I was 18, and I had sent an application to college, because, of course, studies were the alibi. I wasn't going to say to my father, "I'm going because I can't stand you anymore; I can't stand the country." . . . But, well, my mother convinced me, "You're too young. You want to go there, you don't know anyone. We can't give you money. How are you going to do it? Stay and continue school, get your degree, and we'll see later." Saying to herself, "She'll forget." So I did four years there, at school, and when I got my degree, I said I'm leaving. I'd just turned 22, so I was already an adult, and so that's it. So I left. My father didn't say good-bye when I left because he didn't want me to go.

Nedjma (52-year-old Tunisian) left after trying to live up to her parents' expectations. She married a man her family picked without meeting him, but after four years, she got a divorce: "At that moment I said to my parents, especially to my mother who was very, very conservative and very severe, so I said it to myself even more than to others, I said to myself, 'Now that I'm divorced, before others controlled my life, they took the steering wheel of my life in their hands, now I'm taking it. And if I run into a tree, it is I who will run into a tree, it's not others who will make me run into it. I want to live that on my own.'" She decided she had to change everything in her life, and that meant moving to France.

Female in France

TAKING ON NEW ROLES

Approximately one-third of the respondents, like Nedjma, came to France in search of a radical change; almost half simply followed their husbands. In relation to their lives as women, what has changed for these immigrants, and what is the same? Two of the largest differences involve taking on new roles and having more independence and freedom. These changes varied from woman to woman by family situation and reason for migration, but all respondents noted these effects on their lives to a certain extent. New responsibilities included shopping, running errands, taking the children to school, dealing with French administrative agencies and the medical establishment, and sometimes a paid job for women who had never worked outside the home before. As Hondagneu-Sotelo (1994) highlights, these activities by women help root immigrants into the community and facilitate settlement.[8]

Djamila (39-year-old Algerian) talked about the differences between women's responsibilities in the Maghreb and in France:

> D: Oh she only takes care of the kitchen. Yes, that's it for the Algerian woman. We just take care of the food. That's all. And men take care of all the rest. That's it.
>
> CK: And here in France?
>
> D: Oh here it's us, right? Here we take care of everything. Men work, that's all.
>
> CK: So you have to take care of things because he's at work?
>
> D: Right. That's it. Yes.

Being able to do various tasks for the family involves learning new skills, such as figuring out how to get around by oneself, mastering the metro, improving communication skills in French, and learning how to read. However, much of the challenge comes not simply from learning the new skills, but also from overcoming fears. Hachmia (40-year-old Moroccan) and Faroudja (52-year-old Algerian) discussed all they have learned to do and how intimidating it was at first:

> *H:*   For me it's different. I come here, because I'm from Kabylia; there it's the country. I don't know cities there at home. I live there in the country. But here there are big buildings, um, big offices. . . . There's my husband who teaches me things. He tells me, "Do this, do this, be careful." Actually I remember I went to buy bread. My husband made me: "You have to learn now." The bakery [was] right across the street. . . . I was afraid to buy a loaf of bread. And my husband had talked to the woman at the bakery; he knows her. "Watch out for my wife; I brought her to buy bread," and everything, and the woman was very nice because she knows my husband. I went into the bakery, I put the money down, I said, "Give me bread." She said, "Yes, ma'am," and she gave me the change. I didn't even pick up the change. I took the loaf and I left. And my husband was hidden watching me.
>
> *F:*   I take the metro, I take the bus. I can go to my sister's and to my son's, and I can go out. I know the money here. Before I didn't know, I didn't know anything, 50 cents, especially the cents.
>
> *H:*   Now it's okay. Last Saturday I went to work. I work, I work a few hours on the weekend. I take the metro, and my husband said to me, "Be careful; what direction are you going to take?" I said, "I'm going to take direction Charles de Gaulle-Etoile." He says to me, "Now, yes, you've learned things, haven't you?"
>
> *F:*   Yes, yes. It's not like before. Go to the store now. Because I don't have a shower, I have to go elsewhere to take a shower. I went up, how will I do it? I don't know where it is. I went out at 8:00 in the morning until 1:00, I walked in circles, circles, circles for a long time. Now no. I walk to the park; I know the way.

Certain women took on new chores gradually; others were thrust into them after several years when their husbands suddenly were unable to do it all. This was the case with Rachida (47-year-old Moroccan): "When I came the first time, I was afraid. . . . I didn't talk to anyone. . . . No one, not in Arabic, not in French. I spent six years alone. . . . After six years, my husband went into the hospital. I stayed alone with my children. I didn't find anybody who, I didn't know anything. I couldn't find the stores; I didn't have any money. And afterwards I started to get to know people a little."

Many women realized that they needed to work at least part time to help support their families. Fouzia stated, "Here it's hard. The woman has to work and her husband. . . . Here if the woman doesn't work, she can't make it. Because to pay the rent and everything. . . . There . . . if the man earns well, the woman doesn't work. She works at home, that's all. But here, even if the man earns well, the woman has to work too." Zhora (51-year-old Algerian) concurred, saying that money was one of the main reasons she had enrolled in literacy classes: "Yes, classes. Because we need a little money. We have children, we have papers, we need a little bit to work, something that's paid. That way we help our family a little. We need to because life is very expensive." Despite the economic realities in France, North African immigrants have the lowest rates of female labor force participation, with only 40–48 percent of women active (INSEE 1999).[9] Although cultural norms keep some women at home, others simply cannot find employment as a result of discrimination and the generally high rate of unemployment in France (Gaspard 1998; Freedman 2000).[10]

Various authors (Foner 1986; Grasmuck and Pessar 1991; Espiritu 1997) argue that paid labor is positive for immigrant women because it leads to greater self-sufficiency and destabilizes traditional patriarchal arrangements between the sexes. Fernandez-Kelly and Garcia (1990), on the other hand, point out that for poor women in secondary-labor market jobs, work is rarely liberating. Both of these assertions ring true for the respondents. The incomes of poorly educated women doing housecleaning or child care benefit the family as a unit. These jobs are often exploitative and underpaid. Countless women recounted being paid less than they were told, or being forced to do more work than had been agreed to. In addition, these types of jobs do not help women develop other useful capacities. Rachida was aware of the fact that her husband's job in sales helped him learn to speak French well, whereas her job did not allow her to meet people or practice her language skills: "I did some housecleaning, but it's not the same. Housework, I take the key, and I work alone until I've finished. I lock up and I leave. I don't speak to anyone."

Hagan's (1998) research on Guatemalan women doing domestic jobs in Houston reveals that this work prevents female immigrants from meeting other potential employers, and because the work is often being done illegally, it does little to help them establish themselves in the new country. Live-in positions, in particular, cut women off not only from native contacts, but also from their own communities. Married Maghrebin women in France do not take live-in positions, but some younger single women do work as au pairs. Most of these jobs were unsatisfactory and led women to quit. Illegal work in general, whether in domestic service or in the service industry, created other problems. The women Hagan studied were unable to prove the length of their residence in the United States when they tried to become naturalized because they did not receive paychecks. The situation is the same in France, where illegal residents had to produce proof of living in France for 10 years to receive a residence card, and women working in domestic positions were unable to get affidavits from their employers (Freedman 2000).[11] Not having proof of employment affects more than naturalization: Amina (33-year-old Tunisian) had trouble trying to rent an apartment because she could not prove she had a job. She owed her apartment to her friend, Jawahir's (33-year-old Tunisian), help. "I rented it, and she cosigned. Me, I asked the bank to lend me money because the rent is 4,000 francs, and two months' deposit, and a month paid in advance." Jawahir speaks of her friend's plight: "And she didn't have a cent on her. She doesn't have pay stubs. She has nothing."

At the same time, however, even the worst jobs, and even new, everyday tasks that women took on to help their families, gave respondents a sense of freedom and independence. Many were proud of the new skills they had acquired and were often glad to be contributing to their families' needs in France in other ways. Khadija explained: "I took care of everything, since I know how to read and write a little, so I took care of the school enrollments. I take care of the papers because my husband doesn't have time." Thinking back on her life, which now includes a computer-training course sponsored by her job, she added, "When I joined my husband in France, I was a house-wife, meaning I didn't know much, daily life. But once I found work, there it changed. I discovered lots of things I didn't know before. And especially at the association where I work, I learn a lot, many things that were unknown to me." Mimouna (44-year-old Tunisian) agreed with her: "Every day we get out and everything. We have a lot of things, appointments. Here women, she doesn't stop moving. Always something, even if she doesn't work. That's why I've said I see differences. There it's the husband who does the papers, to pay the telephone or the electricity, he does it. But here, me, now I do it."

FINDING FREEDOM

The notion of *freedom* (in the sense of liberation) was one of the most commonly evoked ideas when women talked about life in France. Participants from all walks of life repeated this sentiment, but freedom was used by different women to mean different things. Young, urban women were pleased by the anonymity of Paris, where they could wear what they wanted and go to any café without being stared at, or fearing that someone would report back to their families. Some participants felt freed simply because their new responsibilities got them out of their homes. Nour talks about the women she knows:

> I think that for the Algerian women I've seen arrive here, there is a big liberation. They feel free. . . . Men don't feel it really. They had that freedom, and the town, the street, all that is theirs in Algiers. It was theirs, so they didn't have a problem on that level, but us yes, women, yes. So women definitely when they arrive here it's clear that all of a sudden they feel liberated. Even if they aren't really because maybe they still live in a traditional milieu, some of them. But, um, but still, because their husbands let them go do the shopping, they'll take on other responsibilities, you see? They'll be present at parent meetings at school. So they'll have other responsibilities. They are, it's clear it's a liberation somehow. If it's not moral [psychological], it will be physical in any case."

These differences were the greatest for women who were not used to leaving their homes very much. Hachmia and Faroudja ended their discussion of all they have learned in France with the same conclusion:

> F: Things are good here in France. We have freedom here, to go out especially, because at home we don't go out, especially women. We don't go out, except to the market. We don't go out. We don't do the shopping, we don't do it. We clean the house, that's all. We take care of the kids, that's all. Prepare the food, help your mother. Here we go out as we like. We walk. Find freedom easier.
>
> H: We're not always at home.

Of course, not all women are able to take advantage of this freedom to the same extent. Many older women still felt that they needed an excuse to go out of doors. Chafiqa (50-year-old Algerian), who began running a day care business in her home once her own children were grown, admitted that one of the reasons she wanted to work was to have a reason to get out: "I can go out with them a little bit, take them to the park. Because all alone I cannot go to the park." She went on to say that women who could not get used to France were those who were separated from their families and thus were not able to go out for social functions: "Because there they have their parents, they have everything. But here, sometimes they are with their husbands, their husbands work, they work, and [the wives], they stay at home until their husbands arrive. If there are neighbors, she can go out with them, but if she doesn't know anybody, for outside, she can't go out."

Freedman (2000:15) highlights the plight of many immigrant women cut off from the extended family structure of the Maghreb: "They have broken with systems of solidarity and affiliation in their countries of origin and have to reconstruct their social position in a foreign society. They may find themselves isolated, especially if they have a limited command of the French language." Bahia spent 11 years at home taking care of her children and felt that her French did not progress because she did not interact with anyone outside the family. She considers herself lucky though to have a husband who takes her places. Not all women are this fortunate. Souad (49-year-old Tunisian) relates the distress of many immigrant women from the Maghreb:

> There are women who would really like to be there. Yes. Because it's true, and I understand these women a little. Um, they spend all day at home. She doesn't have any pastimes. She doesn't go out. I understand them when they say, "I like to be there." Because there they have neighbors, family, that they go to see. But all day the poor thing between four walls; she's waiting for her husband to get home. And all day she takes care of the house, the kids. I understand them. They feel alone. Me, no, personally no. I go out. Even when I was with my husband, he didn't stop me from doing this, or not going out, or you can't wear, put that on, or, I don't have that problem.

Souad's assertion that she controlled her life more than other women begs several questions. Why such variation in women's lives in France? How do women come to different conclusions about how to relate to husbands and how much freedom they should have? Although many participants used the word *freedom*, a conversation between Warda and Karima clarified the fact that respondents had different conceptions of what this meant. Both women felt very lucky about their own situations but somewhat jealous of each other's. Their examples are worth exploring in detail.

Warda is a 58-year-old French citizen from Algeria who has lived in France for 34 years. She comes from a wealthy, socially connected family, and she has a doctorate that she completed as an adult purely out of academic interest, as she does not use it in her part-time work at an association. Her husband, a doctor, helps with the cooking and dishes, does most of the shopping, and even takes phone messages for her, yet he views himself as the absolute head of the family. Warda cannot make decisions about her life without informing him and obtaining his consent:

> I think I'm free in my head, but I'm not free to do anything. I can't do whatever. It's in the things that aren't said. We don't say it, but I know my limits. I know what things I can do without consultation, and what I absolutely can't do without checking with my husband. I can't decide tomorrow to, I don't know, even to go visit my sister. Um, I have to say to my husband, "I'd really like to go visit my sister tomorrow." And yes, that's the way it is.

When her husband told her that a mother should stay home with her children, she quit her job until her children were grown. He also controls the family's finances. As Warda sums it up, "He's very attentive, but in reality, he still needs, it's tradition, that need to feel he is the boss." Her friend Karima's situation, on the other hand, is almost the opposite, although the underlying motivations of her husband may actually be very similar.

Karima is a 43-year-old Algerian who has lived in France for 21 years. Like Warda, she is a French citizen. She graduated from high school but never attended college. She works as a translator, spends her own money, travels without her husband, and even goes out by herself in the evenings to social gatherings. Her husband does not expect to control how she dresses or whom she sees. Yet as Karima puts it, "I have to pay my debt first." She is responsible for everything at home. She makes all the meals, cleans the house, does all the shopping, and even makes her teenage son's bed. If she wants to go out in the evening, she must come home from work and make dinner before she can go. When she went to Algeria without her husband, she had to leave a week's worth of prepared food in the freezer and clean shirts and socks for her husband for every day she would be gone. Reflecting on her situation, she muses,

> Sometimes I say to myself listen, after all, me I work, he let's me work. I, I, I, wear what I want; I cut my hair the way I want. Um, I get phone calls, I do what I want. But, well, I do all that because I have to be really a model woman. On the other hand, family life, I live it, I live it oppressed, because, well, in the morning he has to find his shirts ironed. I better not, really I better not, it's not that, but it's because I don't want problems at home. So I always try to make sure the house is perfect, that it's always clean, as soon as he arrives he finds a pair of shoes left in the hallway, "what's that?" So I avoid it. If you want I've always avoided it, I'm not going to, for the children, I didn't want to, I'm looking for the word, domestic violence. You know, yelling and all, for the kids, I never wanted that. So I always avoided, um, I say to myself, he's like that. So I give in. I give in to his whims, you understand? He's sick; he can get up to get an aspirin. He's watching TV, and I'm resting, doing my crossword puzzles and everything, "Can you go get me an aspirin?" You see? It's something. He could get up. But I don't say anything. Because if I tell him, he's going to say, "Oh, that's it, you—" He's also conservative, my husband. You understand? He is conservative for some things. He is conservative. The woman has to serve him.

Warda and Karima continue to evaluate the different types of restrictions they face and how they feel about it:

> *W:* He does a lot. He leaves me a lot of free room, but only to the extent that I don't have any obligation that's out of his control. That's it. That I don't have any boss other than him. And for everything else, it's true that I find free spaces that he grants me, so he remains the boss, because he gives me free space. In other words, we're not free women in the western sense of the word where the woman leads her life as she wants. . . . We don't do anything that might be refused. It means on my own, I know what I can't do and what my husband won't let me do anyway, or what he'll let me do but be angry about it.
>
> *K:* You have to make concessions. . . . It's true that Maghrebin husbands aren't easy. But that doesn't mean that we're unhappy. Not at all. Not at all.
>
> *W:* No, overall I see myself as happy.
>
> *K:* It's also because we accepted it.

What women will accept differs. In Warda and Karima's cases, both were glad for the types of freedoms they had and did not want to push for more because they knew others who had it worse, and because they did not want to upset family harmony.

GENDERED EVOLUTION

Many participants spoke of the difference between "mentalities" in the Maghreb and in France. Being in France gave them a chance to, as they frequently termed it, "evolve." Some women went as far as divorcing controlling husbands while others lived with almost the same constraints they had in the Maghreb. Respondents, including Khadija, discussed why some women "evolved" and others did not:

> *K:* I'd say there are some people who evolve and others who don't. There are women who stay shut in at home; there are others who are in associations, independent, but it's rare.
>
> *CK:* Do you have any idea why some people are able to evolve and others can't?
>
> *K:* Me, I think all women want to evolve, but it depends on their husbands. Women are afraid of their husbands.
>
> *CK:* So it really depends on him, if he wants —
>
> *K:* If he wants, yes.

Leila reaffirmed Khadija's assertion that most women would like to grow and become more independent:

> The North African woman, or the African woman, or the foreign woman generally, immigrant here, um, lives that situation, meaning the husband tries to, to, to act as if he were still living in Tunisia with his wife. He doesn't want her to go out, he doesn't want, she can't have friends, she mustn't spend the evening out of the house. She should just hold the role of the mother, and that's it. But their wives try to emancipate themselves a bit, and to have a little independence, and freedom. Either it ends in divorce, or it's an infernal life that they lead.

Although divorce was rare, it did occur, and often because of these very dynamics.[12] Of the five women I interviewed who were divorced, four had chosen to leave because they felt oppressed by their husbands. Nedjma divorced in Tunisia and then moved to France, and Zitouna, Souad, and Fatima all divorced in France. Fatima and Souad's stories illustrate women's attempts to take control over their lives in response to increased opportunities in France. Fatima stressed how different she had become since leaving Morocco:

> I came. After my brain had to develop quickly to follow the train, as they say. And so it took off. Even though I don't know how to read French, still my brain reads by itself like a computer. I did good to get out of there [Morocco], because if I'd stayed there, I would have stayed dumb. I understand nothing in life. . . . I'd always be the same; I'd still be looking at the same wall, the same people, so it doesn't advance. So here I say it's good. I did good that I crossed, that I crossed the street to find something else.

Fatima's evolution eventually led her to divorce her abusive husband and raise her four children alone. At 54 years old, she continues to work two jobs to support herself and her younger children while spending her small amount of free time taking classes to learn to read, but she bursts with pride talking about her eldest son, who is pursuing an advanced degree at an American university.

Souad also stood up to her husband when he refused to let her work, even though their children were adolescents. She noted that because men had to be responsible for their families, they learned how to take care of themselves more quickly. This only added to their power in the family, a role they rarely like to see diminished. "It's him [the husband] who's always the strongest. Um, he doesn't want his wife to be independent . . . that's why a lot of men refuse to let their wives work." Souad went on to talk about her own ex-husband's reaction when she told him she wanted to get a job: " 'You don't need to go work. I give you everything. I can shoulder all the responsibility. I don't see why you'd want to go work.' But we see things differently. We want to be independent. Um, when I want to buy something, it's not always, 'give me, give me, I want to buy that, I want to do that.' And that's very important for the woman."[13]

Souad was not ready to attribute all the blame for women who did not evolve to their husbands, because in her case, she preferred to divorce rather than continue to be controlled. She discussed the differences between herself and other immigrant women:

Well, in the beginning I didn't know the language; it was my husband who took care of it. And later, little by little, I started to learn, and especially when I had my children, my husband was working, he doesn't have time to take care of it. I take care of it. And it was not difficult for me. I didn't have problems. Because when you want to do something, you manage, you succeed. I saw a lot of women who came at the same time as me, they had a lot of trouble speaking French, and there are women who don't even know how to take the metro. . . . Because they didn't try, they stayed in their shells, at home, there you go, it's the husband who does it, she, she doesn't even know what's going on outside. Me I, I see that they didn't make any effort. They didn't try to learn the language . . . to learn things, to learn the metro. . . . The moment I know how to read, I can ask how to go to this place. . . . I ask, and I make it. They didn't want to; they didn't look for it. . . . If she wants to go somewhere, to go to the hospital, it's the husband who takes her. She's going to go to cousins with the husband. She doesn't pay attention. She doesn't look. She doesn't say, because you never know what can happen in life. If one day the husband disappears, and that's what happened to a lot of people, the day when the husband left, um, she finds herself in a terrible situation, she can't. And me, that's why I, I tried to learn, to be independent and everything. So tomorrow, if for example I divorce, or my husband dies, or, me I can take care of my papers, my affairs. And some don't have the willpower. It's a question of willpower, I say.

Souad highlights the dangers that women risk confronting if they do not seek any growth or independence. Soraya (25-year-old Moroccan), who works in an association to assist immigrants in a particularly poor suburb of Paris, told the unfortunate story of one such woman. This example is extreme and is telling about the dangers of complete dependency:

S: I'll give you the example of a family that came from Morocco almost 30 years ago; they have children that are born here. The woman, she never, never left her home.

CK: In 30 years?

S: Yes, never left her place. Um, the dad [the woman's husband] had an accident; he lost his sight, and the woman had to take care of things alone. And, on top of it, she doesn't even speak Arabic, she only speaks Berber. So for me already it was an enormous amount of work because I don't speak Berber, I only speak Moroccan. . . . The first time I had to go get her, the mama, from her place to show her where I work first, so she can get me if there is a problem. . . . Everything that concerns her papers, I took care of it, paid her rent. And already there was a colleague of mine who was trying to teach her the tasks of daily life, to do her shopping, show her where the market is. And that I find, I don't know, it's unacceptable for a family that has been here for thirty years. That's, and there are a lot of cases of people like that. People who came from there, now I'm talking about old people, they've been here a long time, and they've kept the same mentality. The woman at home and it's the man who works. So they don't let their wives go out. So his wife had never been to the movies, she never went out from time to time. There are cases where families let the women go to the market, but . . . a lot of families don't let their wives go to the market.

Although this woman had children, they were adult sons who had either been incarcerated or had moved away, and thus they did nothing to help their mother and handicapped father. Soraya went on to explain how two years later she was still taking care of all of the woman's mail and bills. She also accompanied her to the doctor because the woman had never had a checkup. According to Soraya, problems like breast cancer are rampant in this older community because many of the women never get medical care; some women only go to a hospital when their children are born. She also tries, in her opinion usually unsuccessfully, to educate women about contraception and domestic abuse. As she explains: "It's hard for a woman to take charge of herself. And since she's used to, already in her family . . . in the education they've received, it's always the man who decides. So it's hard for a woman to say, 'Okay, that's it, it's finished. It's me that is going to take care of myself now. I'm going to decide for me now. I'm not going to let my father, or my brother, or my husband decide for me.' And that's hard."

Older women, and especially those who were poorly educated, were more likely to face this type of scenario. They also suffered the most from being far from family members, especially if lack of nearby relatives meant they had no excuses to leave their homes in France. When asked if life was harder for male or female immigrants in France, respondents sometimes alluded to these isolated older women.[14] For the most part, however, the conclusion was that in France at the turn of the new century, Maghrebin women were better off than Maghrebin men.

WOMEN WHO PLAY THE GAME GET IT EASIER

Surprisingly, given North African women's multiply marginalized position, respondents viewed themselves as privileged compared with men. Participants believe that immigrant women in France are treated better and are more able to succeed in school and find work than North African men. This is because men face more racism than women; they are viewed immediately as Arabs or foreigners. Women, on the other hand, are seen as women first, and their ethnicity or immigrant status becomes secondary — at least for those women who meet certain requirements, notably the ability to speak some French and often dressing French as well.[15] Although respondents acknowledge that the French are sexist, they realize that this often benefits them. As Nedjma analyzed the situation,

> Since French society is also, how to put it, patriarchal . . . there's still the behavior, let's say everything that is social, exterior, administrative and all that, they are maybe a little more easygoing with the woman than with the man. That's, that's their fault, the macho character of the French that comes out there. It's certain, yes. Yeah, they are, they're going to be much more courteous and gallant with a woman. And it's true that Maghrebin men suffer a lot more at the level. . . . It's an injustice in any case that sometimes happens, um, at that level. To have a comportment, how to put it, um, to live privileged situations because you're a woman.

Camille Lacoste-Dujardin (1992) also found that her respondents, second-generation North African girls, were aware that they had privileges in France by virtue of their sex. She stresses that male North Africans are more likely to engender feelings of fear in the French population. This fear of Arab men in particular, as compared with other immigrant men, is both a lasting vestige of the long and bloody war for Algerian independence and the modern fear of Arab terrorists. Malika explains some of the other reasons why foreign women are viewed as less of a threat than immigrant men and experience less racism:

> People are more indulgent with women in general, so they're less hard. And a woman is a woman, you know? So, well, they bug them less with [racism] than men. Um, maybe men are stereotyped more than woman. Women are stereotyped too, but [men] are more recognizable, that men present more of

a danger to take their places at work, you see, that type of thing. Maghrebin women, it hasn't been long that they've existed in public space.

Keltouma points out that North African woman have more possibilities for work because they are more desirable for "small jobs," like babysitting and in-home care of elderly people. Because there are few small jobs for men, male immigrant students are more likely to take full-time jobs to support themselves and thus stop attending the university. Female students, on the other hand, combine a few small jobs in order to pay the rent and thus manage to make it through school. Jawahir notes that Maghrebin women in general have an easier time finding work than Maghrebin men:

> I find that the woman here, she passes first in France. If you take two CVs, a man and a woman, the same thing, exactly the same thing on the CV, the same level of education, same age, same religion, same customs . . . same origins, all that, they will take the woman because she is less complicated than the man. She's more simple. She's not demanding. She's easy. I don't know. I find, for me, it's not difficult to find a job, to make it all alone here. Everyone helps me because I'm a woman alone. I'm a widow with three children. Wherever I go, they open the door to me, they help me, they take me in. It would be different if it were a widower with three. "You're a man, go work. That's it. You take care of your kids." . . . A widow causes more pity than a widower.

Françoise Gaspard (1998) also argues that North African women are seen as less of an economic threat because they are largely confined to the informal sector of the market or to the domestic sphere altogether. She adds that if anything, when Maghrebin women were not entirely invisible in France, they were welcomed because they would "stabilize" delinquent single, immigrant men who might otherwise endanger French women. Currently, however, with the furor over headscarves and the growing numbers of North African and second-generation women in the labor force, this positive view may be changing (Raissiguier 1999, 2003).

Isma concurs that men experience more racism, but she is careful to note that this is the case only for certain women: "Sometimes women pass a bit better. When there is, for example, an attitude of a man towards a woman, let's say a French man towards a woman, it's always, when it's a woman who's

a little modern, let's say not veiled, not, that stays more or less a gallant interaction, or nice, when it's a woman. It's sure that the interaction with a man is
not the same." Mbruka ties this to a game of seduction between men and
women: "I think that, in certain situations, as a woman, there's always that
notion of woman, thus charm . . . they're more indulgent with a woman,
they're maybe more tolerant. . . . We know how to seduce, because there's
always that notion of seduction being a woman." Woman who veil and who
wear loose, long clothing are automatically refusing to play this seduction
game, at least according to French norms, and this consequently hurts their
chances of being helped by French men. Ultimately, then, they are punished
for not "doing" gender the way that French women do (West and Zimmerman 1987).[16] Likewise, woman who are totally unable to communicate in
French and women who are elderly are also unable to play this male/female
interaction dynamic to their benefit. Yasmine (33-year-old Algerian), who
has some, although limited, French-speaking skills and who wears makeup
and French clothes, has mastered the role of the naive damsel in distress. She
admits that she frequently "plays dumb on purpose to succeed."

Yasmine's example is revelatory. As Jouamana argues, men are at a real disadvantage because they cannot ask for aid: "Men have more dignity, they
can't ask for help. They can be dying of hunger, they can't ask for help. But
a woman, she can." Jawahir's comment about the differences between a
widow and a widower with children illustrates this point; a man, no matter
what the situation, is expected to work and take care of himself and his family. The irony, of course, is that men face more discrimination, particularly
in hiring, than do women. Women have an easier time getting hired, at least
in low-paid service work, and they can also count on more help from others
when they are in trouble.

Respondents were particularly pleased with the French state's readiness to
help them and their children, and even protect them from the men in their
lives. Fatima (54-year-old Moroccan) talked at length about learning how to
work the system to get aid during and after the divorce:

> I'm divorced. I [had] a difficult life with my husband. One time he went
> back to his country, he sees his parents, he left for five months without any
> word, nothing. No news, nothing. I stayed with my children in my apart-
> ment. I live on allocations familiales [government aid to families]. . . . One
> day he came back, and we didn't get along. I stayed with him in the apart-

ment fighting every day. And after a while I'd had it. I filed papers at the court, I did my divorce papers. . . . I asked for my freedom with my children. And, well, for a year I fought, and he refused the divorce. Afterwards I appealed; I appealed and I won my divorce. And I won my children. After I looked for work. I've suffered in my life, with my children, but I get out. They helped me a lot, the French government. He left a lot of debts on me and my back. They kicked me out of the apartment. He left me a 5,000 franc ($800) rent on my back . . . they cut off the telephone; they cut off the electricity. I managed to get everything, everything, and the French government helped me.

Zitouna (48-year-old Algerian) also was thankful that "the French legal system allowed her to free herself by giving her the apartment and putting [her husband] out." Nedjma, who divorced in Tunisia, expressed her gratitude to the French government for helping her retain custody of her son in France. Several participants mentioned that France is a country of rights; they felt that if their rights were trodden upon, the government was there to help them. Nevertheless, they noted that to obtain your rights, you had to be aware of them, and thus more poorly educated, non-French-speaking women are at a distinct disadvantage.

RECOGNIZING AND RESISTING SEXISM

Many respondents articulated the power differences between the sexes and compared the situation in France to that in the Maghreb. While recognizing the advantages of being a woman in France, respondents were careful to highlight that the sexism of French men can also be a detriment. Malika's position as a successful businesswoman gives her a unique perspective on the limits of French men's help. In comparing French men to North African men, she finds that whereas the latter's attitudes can be excused, the former's cannot:

I'd like to say that here the [machismo] is more insidious, but it exists the same. Meaning that the machismo is not flagrant . . . it's hidden, and when you say [something] to them, "Oh, no, you're not going to be the feminist." At least there, well it's like that, and the woman can exist in it anyway. It's not, um, it's not because they're macho that they don't leave a place for the woman. The woman has her place; she is respected. There are a lot

of women with high positions in Tunisia. . . . Here it's difficult. I've gone
through bad times with atrocious colleagues, atrocious. Completely misogy-
nistic. Because, that's it, I'd say there they are macho, here they are misogynist, and I think it's worse, meaner. Because being macho is the result of an
education, it's, really being macho is almost not conscious for them. They're
like that. They were raised like that. They were told that men are better,
more important people than the woman; everything was done to make them
believe that, so it's like that. Being misogynist is having thought about it and
saying to oneself, me, because I'm a man I'm stronger than you — you see
what I mean? I find that, really, I've had more difficulties here at work. I've
come up against obstacles, jealousies, men who were pissed off by my success, doubly too maybe because not only am I a woman, but on top of it, I'm
a Maghrebin woman. Obviously they don't say it. But, um, it's not so common in France to find Maghrebin women in positions of responsibility,
positions of power.

Thus when North African women start becoming a threat in the labor market, the gallantry toward women breaks down. Malika ended her discussion
by wondering what would happen as more Maghrebin girls born in France
enter the labor force, recognizing that increased visibility often leads to
increased discrimination. Raissiguier (1999, 2003) notes that although in the
past the media portrayed second-generation girls as the success story compared with their brothers, who were shown failing out of school and unemployed, this may indeed be changing. In addition to the surge in the numbers
of Maghrebin women in higher education and the labor force, the headscarf
debate has made North African women and their daughters more visible in
the public eye and has presumably increased the likelihood of harassment.
    Women from all walks of life recognized sexism in their lives and were
eager to talk about it. Both old and young, illiterate and well-educated women expressed outrage at the inequalities between men and women, sometimes referring to the Maghreb, sometimes to France, and sometimes to
both. Fatima firmly insists that women have more rights in France:

Women and men are intelligent, why not? It's not only the man who should
go to school. It should be women too. They have their ideas too. . . . Yes, in
Morocco, it's the man who directs the whole family. It's the man who has
the most important role. The woman is for nothing. The woman is there
to shut her mouth and that's it. She eats, she takes care of the kids, she can't

say anything. She's not allowed to talk, nothing. But here we're free. We do what we want. Rights for men and for women. It's true or not? And there no. The woman is off to the side. The man commands. I think it's idiotic.

Other women see the feminine condition as a more universal problem. Houriya (34-year-old Algerian) relates the pain of being female: "I feel like a victim. It's a feeling that hurts. I think that already when you're a woman you're a victim." Leila, among others, pointed out that French women also suffer domestic abuse. Hayat explains why she thinks men are reluctant to give up their power:

> Men are macho there and here. They exploit you at home, they exploit you outside. Men, okay, they haven't changed. They all exploit. They don't want to evolve because they're afraid of that evolution because they always have the impression that you can't complete one another, that if there is a strong one, automatically there's a weak one. If there's a weak one, automatically there is a strong one. They don't say to themselves that you have to stick together to make one. In their heads, if they give up a little bit, that means no, we're going to get ahead of them, and inversely.

Houriya subscribes to this view, arguing that men need to experience sexism before they can really understand and change: "I feel a lot of injustice between men and women, and I'd like for one day them to know that, and that's it's us who would be on top of them. It's maybe mean what I say. I'm not trying to create differences between men and women, that the woman is on top and he is on the bottom, but I dream that one day we'll be equal. And so men can understand our suffering, I'd like them to go through it. So he can know what it's like." She notes this may be needed for western men, although perhaps not to the same degree as with Arab men who have had the experience of racial oppression.

Nedjma believes that when people are treated unfairly, they turn around and do the same to those over whom they have power: "There's going to be the worker who's impoverished, but there's going to be the wife of the worker who's even more disadvantaged than he is because he's going to oppress her. Yes, and it's always like that." Nedjma's recognition of the importance of class as well as gender makes her critical of those who want to fight only one front at a time. This issue is a difficult one for many feminist movements, and consequently, although many respondents had feminist goals, they did not want to accept this label. In fact, all but one of the women who used the word *feminist* insisted that she was not a feminist. First world or western feminism has been taken to task by many authors, including bell hooks, Chérrie Moraga, Gloria Anzadúa, Gayatri Spivak, Chandra Talpade Mohanty, and Nawal el-Saadawi, for neglecting to link sexism with overlapping oppressions based on class, race, and colonialism. Thus, as Johnson-Odim (1991:315) asserts, "[w]hile it is clear that sexual egalitarianism is a major goal on which all feminists can agree, gender discrimination in neither the sole nor perhaps the primary locus of oppression of Third World women."

For this and other reasons, participants took issue with feminism. Nedjma is preoccupied with "the human condition" and says she fights against all types of injustice, not simply sexism. Other respondents echoed another criticism of feminism: that it attempts to separate men from women — an option for middle-class, white western women, but not a possible or even desirable one for many poor women and women of color who depend on their families for support and protection.[17] Deha and Leila both say they do not want to separate men from women or oppress men in attempt to gain justice. Leila articulates this view:

> I'm not a feminist. I'm against all the feminist waves, in Europe or in any other country, especially in America, especially in America, I don't like the feminist movement at all there because it creates a break between two humans. I don't want that break. I want men and women to work together to make all of society evolve and to change certain things that work badly, very, very badly, for everyone, for women and men. I don't want there to be a war between men and women.

Deha, who broke sexual conventions, shares much of the housework and child care with her husband, and argues that all religions are antiwoman, concurs: "I'm not a feminist. . . . Feminist is someone who stands up for the condition of women, and I don't defend the condition of women, not at all, because I defend the condition of my husband, my brother, my son." She goes on to explain that "if we were able to live in, where everything was egalitarian, it's really naive, but if, for example, my son saw his mother respected, he would respect his wife, the girl he goes out with. He'll respect me too. My husband will respect me too. My brother, I'll have a brotherly relationship and not a hierarchical one, you see? And so, somehow, I prefer more to defend boys, so we have normal relationships." She argues that women need men if they are to make progress. Deha, unlike Leila, makes room for non-western feminists, although she remains critical of feminism:

> After all, the best feminists are Arab feminists, not French or western feminists. Women who are on the ground, who work at things, who are totally involved; it's true they're Arab women, Egyptians, Nawal el-Sadaawi . . . but nothing will get done by Nawal el-Saadawi if men don't accompany her. . . . It's men who have to do something for feminists, not women. I'll support a man, he'll say, I support my wife, the next woman, I'll defend my daughter. . . . That's feminism. Feminism, no, it's humanitarian. There you change something.

Participants could not find themselves in French feminist movements for other reasons as well. Besma worked with feminist groups in Tunisia and was initially interested in working with feminists in France:

> I found that I couldn't situate myself in the feminist movement in France. I couldn't situate myself. I didn't have any desire to continue in the feminist movement because at the level of their demands I couldn't really find myself, and I realized that there was a really sexist dialogue in feminist groups in France that didn't correspond to me. . . . I found myself in a group of bitter women, who want to get back at men . . . with relationship difficulties, with men affective relations that failed. And I didn't see myself in their structure. For me, man is not the enemy. So I try more, in terms of women's issues, in union movements, for equal salaries, points they ask for, but not through their structure.

Besma also found ideological differences because she believes in the differences between men and women, and although she wants equal pay for equal work, she does not want equality in everything. She admits she sometimes likes it when men act macho, when they hold the door or pay for a drink. Nedjma also cherished her femininity, which she felt feminists want to abandon: "I don't think I'm a feminist, true and hard, um, I don't negate my femininity at all. . . . Often it's that women sometimes go against themselves." Nedjma related examples of women who either try to be just like men or who go to the other extreme, playing the role of sex object in an effort to manipulate and hurt men.

Although many respondents did not label themselves as feminists, they nevertheless supported goals of women's empowerment. Some participants noted that changes in laws to help women are not enough; mentalities also have to change. Leila notes that domestic abuse can be prosecuted in Tunisia, but that women rarely take advantage of it because people will talk about them and look down on them for turning in their husbands. Although Leila and Deha argued that men and women have to work together to change the situation, others admitted women's responsibility for supporting the status quo. Souad and Zitouna, both uneducated women, stood up to oppressive husbands and divorced. Souad thus argued that other women just needed willpower to make their lives better. Other women focused on the future. Houriya is insistent about not leaving changes up to men: "Only women can change things. If we wait for the men, it's, men can't do anything for us, it's true. And well, we're a society of men, right? . . . . It can change inside the family, already. As for the level of the family, we can change things. We can even change things at the societal level. But it's really up to women, especially to change things." As Warda recognized: "Maghrebin women, it's transmitted, yes, they're responsible, I was going to say, themselves for the situation that is done to women. Because the mama transmits to her daughter that it's shameful if she doesn't clean well, if she doesn't take care of her house, et cetera. She'll never think of saying to her son, 'Hey, after all, why don't you clean?' or 'Why do you leave that dirty?' That's it. It never enters their minds. Even when we're evolved." Karima, who described herself as oppressed because she had to do all the work at home, then admitted that she still makes her adolescent son's bed and that her daughter helps her with the housework.

Conclusion

Paradoxically, the intersecting, marginalized identities that are often seen as problematic for minority women line up in a way that can sometimes benefit North African women in France. In general, respondents concurred that female Maghrebin immigrants in France were better off than men because they were viewed as women first and as Arabs or immigrants second.[18] Thus they were not experiencing "double jeopardy," discrimination based on race *and* gender, but rather were deriving benefits from being seen first as women and only secondarily as Arabs/Muslims/immigrants. This was particularly true of women who played the game, "doing" gender according to French norms, and thus got more aid from French people.

Despite a lifetime of struggle, Fatima was pleased with what she found on the other side of the street, but how did other women feel about adapting to life in France? The next chapter addresses cultural differences and patterns of acculturation. As immigrants, the respondents faced numerous choices about how to run their lives. Given the choices available in France, how do women decide how to dress, what to eat, how to practice their religion? How do they feel about these decisions? What do they prefer in France, and what are they sorry to have left behind?

THREE

Everywhere There Is Good and Bad

Cultural Choices

Immigration to a new society with different beliefs, values, and behaviors forces immigrants to question their own taken-for-granted cultural traditions. Because culture is the conduit for experiencing and expressing meaning through language, rituals of daily life, stories, ceremonies, and beliefs, one's sense of community and place in the world can be profoundly affected by migration. When people immigrate, "there is an ongoing process of negotiation taking place in their lives between the cultures and traditions of their communities of origin and their new social positions in France" (Freedman and Tarr 2000:5). This chapter examines the participants' behaviors such as cooking, dress, and religious practices, and explores their beliefs about what is better in France and what they preferred in North Africa.

Culture consists of the "publicly available symbolic forms through which people experience and express meaning," and these expressions of meaning depend on shared understandings common to a group (Swidler 1986:273). In her groundbreaking essay, Swidler (1986) articulated culture as a "toolkit" of "strategies of action" that people use to fulfill their goals. This definition implies a range of choices, a range that will necessarily be expanded during the course of immigration when new models of action become available. Lamont (1992:135) takes issue with the concept of "culture as toolkit," noting that the toolkit is not limitless but rather is "largely shaped by culturally available accounts of what defines a worthy person and what behaviors are reasonable." Rather than being entirely voluntary, cultural choices are constrained by structural (national, sociohistorical, economic, political) factors. She particularly urges us to pay attention to issues of class and racial differences within national cultural repertoires.

The case of immigration provides a unique window for looking at how cultural repertoires change or persist given the context of a new pattern of relationships between social actors. Immigrants from North Africa to France encounter differences in the educational system, the media, the view of the nation, and even the calendar, just to name a few. Immigrants provide an example of "unsettled lives," "[w]hen people are learning new ways of organizing individual and collective action [and] practicing unfamiliar habits until they become familiar." Settled cultures, on the other hand, encapsulate their members who "naturally 'know' how to act and may not exhibit much commitment to cultural behaviors that are nevertheless constrained by a limited set of habits and resources" (Swidler 1986:278). As Swidler (1986:284) points out, studying unsettled cultural periods provides unique research opportunities:

> Settled cultures constrain action over time because of the high costs of cultural retooling to adopt new patterns of action. In unsettled periods, in contrast, cultural meanings are more highly articulated and explicit, because they model patterns of action that do not "come naturally." Belief and ritual practice directly shape action for the community that adheres to a given ideology. Such ideologies are, however, in competition with other sets of cultural assumptions.

Therefore we can use immigration as a case for studying which cultural behaviors and values "take root and thrive, and which whither and die," and who resists and who acculturates (Swidler 1986:280). This chapter thus examines which everyday behaviors continue to be influenced by immigrants' culture of origin, which they choose to take from the new culture, what conditions these choices, and how they feel about them.

Dislikes and Preferences

CULTURAL PREFERENCES?

Anthropologist Ruth Benedict (1961:46), famous for her national character studies, wrote that "culture, like an individual, is consistent." Those, like Swidler, who see culture as malleable, critique her approach for being too deterministic. Moreover, the hope of studying untouched, "primitive" societies in order to uncover what about human nature is universal and what is culturally constructed has long since faded in an era of increasing globalization and permeable national boundaries. As a result of the long history of colonization, the Maghreb continues to be heavily influenced by French culture. French words, cultural productions, and modes of dress have been incorporated to various extents in all three countries, depending on generation, social class, and rural or urban residence. The extent to which interviewees were exposed to French media and the French language varied by region and education. Higher education in the Maghreb follows a largely French model, and being educated in the French language and exposed to great French thinkers obviously brought these respondents more in line with French cultural repertoires than their lesser-educated compatriots. This supports Lamont's assertions about the variation of culture within a nation along class levels.

Nevertheless, even the women who came to France to pursue advanced degrees found themselves shocked and displeased by certain French modes of behavior. The frequency with which participants mentioned these behaviors and attitudes provides evidence of underlying cultural patterns and the difficulties in adapting to a new set of values and norms. Their answers point to a middle ground between Benedict's fixed concept of culture and the potentially limitless individual choices of an ever-expanding toolkit. In addition, the women interviewed engage in boundary work, drawing distinctions between themselves and others and the times and places in which certain behaviors are acceptable. Respondents identified both a North African and a French "mentality," and they talked at length about what they preferred and disliked in each country.

DISLIKES IN FRANCE

Lamont (1992) has studied the values and attitudes that upper-middle-class men in France and the United States use to draw symbolic boundaries between themselves and others. More recently, Lamont (2000) has expanded her research to look at working-class men in both countries. She interviewed white and black men in the United States, and white and North African men in France, but her section on Maghrebin men deals primarily with their reactions to racism. France is a tightly bounded society, with less tolerance for cultural deviance and fewer possibilities for upward social mobility than loosely bounded societies like the United States (Lamont 1989). The United States has less stable symbolic boundaries as a result of its regionalism, large size, weak high cultural traditions, and ethnic diversity (Lamont 1989). Whereas people can succeed in the United States without a knowledge of high culture or an intellectual background, economic success without these other symbolic markers is looked down upon in France (Lamont 1989, 1992).

Bourdieu's (1977) concept of "symbolic violence" — pervasive, hidden norms that control access to power through an accepted view of reality that benefits some and disadvantages others — helps us understand why immigrants are prevented from becoming members of the dominant class. The inability to fully join in the dominant cultural landscape may encourage immigrants to reinforce the boundaries that separate them from French people. Lamont (2000) found that Maghrebin men often employ particularistic cultural and moral boundaries (for example, caring North Africans versus individualistic French people) when making comparisons. To get at the boundaries North African women use to distinguish themselves from the French, I asked what they disliked and what they liked in France. Like the men in Lamont's study, respondents also judged French people according to moral criteria.

The most frequent sort of complaint made by 16 different respondents about the French was that they were cold, distant, unable to communicate, and individualistic.[1] Several indicated that this was the biggest shock upon arrival in France. Besma remembers writing to her mother in Tunisia during the winter: "It's maybe minus 30 here, but the people are minus 40." Summing up the differences between the two countries, Isma said, "The difference is clear. The difference is already in the attitude and the approach of people, it's clear, very clear. People are much less forthcoming, less warm, less than in Algeria. . . . People [in Algeria] get on the same public transportation and smile, or at least yell at one another, or say things, speak loudly. That's it. It's true that people talk with gestures. Here people remain frozen. It's true that that surprises me." Houriya speaks about her first year in France with a sadness that she has not gotten over:

H: It was very difficult for me to adapt the first year. Oh yes, I had a hard time adapting.

CK: To what?

H: To what, well the society, um, this society of individualists that really shocked me, it's, it's mostly that really. Yes, that's all. That's what shocked me the most, especially this society of individualists that differs some, you know, from our society where really people feel more solidarity, I'd say, warmth. . . . I was really disappointed, but really disappointed. French people are cold, I'll say it, they're cold. They don't even look you in the eye. When you look at a French person, he lowers his eyes. . . . And French people are really wary, and so it's very difficult to make, I've noticed, to create a friendship with a French person. If he wants to be friends with you, it has to go through friends, or people he knows, or family . . . they don't take the risk of meeting someone in the street or the metro.

Soraya concurred: "I was disappointed by the relations between people, that's all. I don't have much contact with people. That's what disappointed me here. . . . There [in Morocco] we love contact; we love to go see people. And here I find that everybody stays at home. Me, I know all of my neighbors over there, but here I've lived in the same building for three years and I only know the neighbor across the hall."

What participants often identified as personality was linked to cultural boundaries. Some of the most common personality traits respondents mentioned when asked to describe themselves were sociable, open, welcoming, and enjoys being around people. They often made the connection between the way of life in their countries of origin and their personalities. Some noted that they had a Mediterranean outlook and thus shared more in common with Italians and Spaniards than with the French. Others labeled the preference for being in groups and sharing "African." Cherifa talks about how she likes to spend her time:

We always have short weekends, because we love to have people over. We always, always, always have people come over, but that's, I guess it's a bit of my African origins coming out. I love having people at the house, so weekends I'm always calling left and right. . . . I have a boyfriend who is French, pure French line, from an aristocratic French family, who says to me, "When are we going to be alone?" I say, "If you're not happy, leave," nicely. And so it's true, he comes around. When he met me a few years ago, he knew about my origins.

Oumniya enjoys even bigger gatherings, particularly weddings: "I like to party. I like to dance, talk, smile." Given the importance of being with others, the French reserve and tendency to stay home alone were particularly hard for participants to get used to.

Isma explained that she feels lonely even in the middle of a crowd in France: "When I get on the metro at 7:30. . . . I look at the people around me and I realize that the people are terribly sad; it's awful. . . . Either they read the papers, I don't know if they're really reading or if it's just to not have to look at others, look others in the eyes especially, otherwise they're really like robots. . . . You really feel, you feel the solitude."[2] Several women mentioned the inability of strangers to communicate with one another, and many respondents felt that French people only cared about themselves and were egotistical, always putting their concerns and needs above those of others. A few recounted stories of themselves or their friends getting hurt in public without receiving any assistance from the people around them. The pain of being ignored was worse than the physical injuries. Lina (32-year-old Algerian) described running after a bus, twisting her ankle, and falling to the ground, where she briefly lost consciousness: "There was a couple next to me; they didn't do a thing for me. In Algeria that doesn't exist. And that, that hurt. I went home, I canceled work, I went home, no, I went to work. In the metro I cried and cried and cried. I wasn't expecting that."[3]

Leila also focused on moral boundaries. She cringed when describing how French people cared more about a lost dog in the street than about the homeless person. Like other respondents, however, she was the most shocked when this sort of indifference was also extended to family members. Coming from the Maghreb where family is everything, participants were horrified that family members in France rarely saw each other, and that even worse, parents abandoned adult children, and children refused to take care of aging parents — a finding echoed among the men Lamont (2000) interviewed. A few respondents mentioned hearing of nursing homes for the first time in France and their inability to comprehend people who could leave their parents there and rarely even visit. Participants whose biggest complaint about living in France was that they only saw their families once or twice a year had trouble understanding French people who live in the same country, or even same town, and choose to visit their parents only occasionally. Leila recounts:

Family relations for us are very strong. . . . We can't allow ourselves to go without seeing the family for three, four months; we can't, we can't. We have to find the time to see each other, to get together, to eat together. For example, me and my cousin, um, I can't go a month without seeing her; we have to see each other at least once every two weeks. Either she comes to my place, or I go to her place, um, see her daughters, I see my uncle, and those things are very important for our equilibrium. What goes on in France is something different, because I have friends, I have a French friend who sometimes goes six months without seeing his mom. And it doesn't bother him, not at all. And me, still now, after years in France, I can't accept that. I can't make myself accept that.

Respondents talked about their families as a source of support and aid, and 31 women said that being far from family members was one of the hardest problems to cope with in France.[4] Cherifa noted that child care would never be an issue for her in Tunisia because a family member would always be available to help her, and Besma realized that coming to France made her truly independent because no one was there to stick up for her anymore. These feelings of isolation were then exacerbated by the difficulties in interacting with French people they perceived as cold and distant. As Besma puts it: "This explains why the experience of France has been something that, in the beginning for me, I felt, I didn't feel at ease at all, and I felt tremendously rejected."

Linked to the individualism and coldness were other characteristics of French culture that participants pinpointed as hard to get used to. These included the stress of everyday life and French people's view of the role of money. Respondents liked to say that in France, everyone runs in circles. Mbruka spoke about life in Paris: "It's very stressful, very tiring. What's funny is the expression we used in Algeria, we had a hemorrhage of time we had so much time, and a lack of time in France." Lina and Rym (32-year-old Algerian) also compared Algerians to the French:

L: [In Algeria] people are cool, relaxed . . . it's not the morning you find them running to work, all stressed out and everything. You take your car, you go to school or work cool. All calmly. It's not important and everything. It's not the same.

> *R:* Slow in the morning, not too fast in the evening. That's it. And you
> know the first time I came [to France], a friend showed me the metro
> and everything, he told me how to do it. I said, "But tell me, why
> are they all running?" He said, "Rym, in fifteen days you'll run too,
> I promise you," and it's true. And that's also proof of integration,
> you see, we threw ourselves in right way. You have to run, work,
> make money, pay the rent, everything. But it was hard.

Women noted that although there were problems in North Africa too, the
stress was not the constant stress of France that made one sick and unable to
appreciate the good things in life. As Souad pointed out, "There, even if you
have little problems, you don't feel it because you are with your family, at
home." Attitudes also made problems seem less serious in the Maghreb
because people took things "coolly."

People also needed to work for pay in North Africa, of course, but the
relation to money was different.[5] Respondents expressed their dismay that in
France, when people eat out together, they split the bill down to the last
penny. Leila told a story about a neighbor she barely knew coming to ask her
one evening if she had any aspirin because her husband had a bad headache.
Leila gave her a package of aspirin and then forgot all about it.

> Two days later her husband knocks on the door; he brings back the package
> of medicine. I said, "Listen, we don't do that where I come from. . . . We
> don't work like that. I can't accept it." He said, "No, no, no, it's yours."
> I told him, "I'm sorry, I can't accept it. . . ." Something like that still sur-
> prises me. For them, they think it's totally normal. They say, she bought it,
> we'll give it back to her. But us, a neighbor comes to your door, he asks for
> anything, if you have it, you give it to him. We don't expect him to give it
> back afterwards.

Hayat also discussed the emphasis French people place on money and the
way they order their lives:

> Sadly, they're very materialist people. You have a lot of money, people know
> you, solicit you. If you don't have much money, they don't know you. Sadly.
> And that shocks me in France. . . . People are too materialist. We don't
> have that in Algeria. No. In Algeria we go to everybody's, eat at everybody's,
> drink at everybody's. You don't have to call a week in advance to say, "Hey,

I'm coming by this date, this day, this time." There everyone is welcome at any time, any day. It's true. There isn't that in France. I miss it a lot.

Telja (44-year-old Algerian) and others noted that in the Maghreb you can get by with very little because other people will help you and stores will let you buy on credit: "But not here in France. Here, if you don't have a wallet you can't live." After critiquing the French, Hayat admitted that living in France forces you to become materialist: "You have to think about earning a lot of money, earning a lot of money why? To be able to go to the movies, to be able to cultivate oneself, to be able to go work out." Mimouna said there are too many choices in France, and that maybe Tunisian women who stay home are better off not seeing all the things they cannot buy. A few women explicitly said that the problem in France is capitalism.

The final complaint respondents voiced frequently about life in France was the weather. This, in addition to the cold people, made them homesick. The long winters and the rain were depressing and difficult to adapt to. When asked what was the hardest thing about being an immigrant, Deha responded: "It's the climate. That's all. It's atrocious. I assure you. It's painful." Some respondents said they had adapted, but like Chafiqa, they still spoke nostalgically about the light and the warmth: "There when you wake up in the morning you have the sun. . . . You get used to it. You get used to it." Others, like Souad, remained unchanged: "Still now I hate the winter. I really don't like the winter. . . . Here in France . . . one day it rains, one day it's nice. But there, it's always beautiful, and I feel like a different person when I'm there." Nedjma used the weather as a metaphor for her adaptation to France:

> I've lived 20 years here in Paris, always saying to myself that I missed the sea and the sun. When I went back there, I stayed a year, and I came back, and I found that the Paris sky was really beautiful. Today I looked at the sky, it was raining, and I said, my God, it's great what we discover here, to be able to appreciate. . . . I'm maybe not yet at the autumn of my life, but in my head to be able to say one day I'd say at the autumn of my life that I appreciate the winter. It's amazing because before I never liked the winter.

When speaking about the weather, participants noted that the south of France would be better than Paris. Many also stated that they thought life would be less hectic and stressful outside of the capital. Yet, as we will see in the next section, some of the things they liked best in France had to do with being in Paris.

As Swidler (1986) points out, in the midst of "unsettled" lives in France, immigrants are exposed to new cultural options and develop new perspectives on life in their countries of origin. Although respondents dislike certain aspects of the French mentality, they are also critical of North Africans. Whereas they describe the French as obsessed with work, running all the time, and perpetually stressed out, they say that Maghrebins lack a strong work ethic and discipline and are sometimes too easygoing. Cherifa laughs about her favorite discovery in France:

> There's one thing that I was pleased to find in France and regretted never doing in Morocco. It's going to seem idiotic to you what I'm going to say, two things even, and it's true when I talk about it, it's funny. It's the line in stores. You know? When you wait in line to buy bread, I find that fantastic. . . . And another thing, when you drive, um, people don't honk, and the lines are all straight; in Morocco it's total chaos. You see, it makes you laugh, but it's impressive because you go into a shop in Morocco, um, people, Moroccans, whether it's in a store, the post office, the bank, whatever the place where you need to form a line, they're all pressed up against the window, against the counter. They don't know how to form a line.

Others found the differences less funny. Both Malika and Nour felt that the laid-back attitude in North Africa made it hard to accomplish anything at work. This, in part, led to a feeling that the Maghreb is in stasis, or at least not evolving as quickly as France. Various women characterized their countries of origin as "traditional" and "static." These descriptions echo those of French colonizers, and it is worth noting that Malika and Nour are both well educated, have worked in middle-class jobs in Europe, and have European relatives (Nour's Dutch mother and Malika's Italian maternal grandmother). Several young women especially were critical of a system where North African women believed the only option in life to be marriage. These respondents had chosen to come to France to continue their educations and for the other opportunities France provided, and therefore they may be more representative of a certain type of relatively privileged Maghrebin woman.

Both young and older women, those who had chosen to come deliberately and those who followed husbands, found that France did provide a wealth of opportunities. Although younger educated women focus on their university studies and careers, older women take advantage of paid work and literacy classes. Immigrants who had arrived illegally or with student visas that do not authorize employment, and illiterate women with few skills were particularly thankful for the numerous small jobs that were available such as picking up children from school, grocery shopping for elderly people, and cleaning. Keltouma expressed her gratitude for these opportunities:

> It's true that small jobs have not entered Moroccan culture yet. And I find that it's great that a student can do something parallel to be able to do whatever, to study, or whatever. I'm proud of all the small jobs I've done that allowed me to obtain a thesis that I never could have done in Morocco. I'm sure that there are a lot of people who can't go on in graduate school in Morocco because they don't have ways to make money on the side.

Even though these jobs were often poorly remunerated and sometimes exploitative, as we saw in Chapter 2, women were often glad to have them as they helped make ends meet, and for some women, such jobs simply gave them a chance to get out of the house.

Several women stated that although France was very expensive to live in, they could do better than in their countries of origin. This was, after all, the reason many, like Fouzia, had come to France:

> CK: In general, vis-à-vis money and work, can you do better in France than in Morocco to earn a living?
>
> F: To earn a living, yes.
>
> CK: It's better?
>
> F: That's why we stay. Yes. It depends, because there are also people there who earn well, who have good positions. If you have a position like that, on average you live okay, but unfortunately there aren't, so we prefer to stay here.

Mimouna also said that in Tunisia it was difficult to find good jobs: "If they stay there, even if they go to school, there isn't much; they can't find good jobs. . . . More chances here." Algerians especially talked about the inflation that has spun out of control and prevents young people from marrying, or that forces married couples to live with their parents. Lina compared what she could buy in France on a small salary to what she would have in Algeria: "I think it's a country that gives a chance to everyone . . . you can aspire to a minimum. You can aspire to have your little apartment, to furnish it as you like, in your tastes, buy a small television, a small radio, buy a used car, go on vacation from time to time, take a charter to Italy, Spain, et cetera, things you can't do in Algeria." Returning to Algeria for vacations, they were also shocked to find that sometimes the water did not come out of the faucet or the electricity would go off, conveniences they had become accustomed to in France. Another advantage immigrant women see in France compared with the Maghreb is the social support system that provides government aid to poor families. Although respondents were sorry to be unable to count on friends and family members in France, they were pleased with the state's aid when jobs fell through or spouses got sick.

In addition to opportunities for work in France, North African women are also grateful for access to education. Many female immigrants, particularly those who came in the 1970s and early 1980s, had little or no education in the Maghreb, and the rates of illiteracy are high. Literacy classes are provided in France for free. Women participate in order to improve their French-speaking skills and to learn how to read and write. Sometimes these classes lead to internships that can turn into employment; often they simply help women feel more confident and gain skills such as reading metro maps and filling out forms. Almost all of the women who had never been to school or who were forced to leave school at a young age voiced their regret about their lack of studies. Asked at the end of the interview if there was anything they would like to add, several spontaneously said that all they wanted is to learn to read. When talking about their children, they mentioned that they pushed them to work hard in school and to benefit from the educational system. Hachmia regularly checks to see if her eight-year-old son has done his homework: "And I look close at his exercise book every day, 'Pay attention. You must go, you must go [to school], because it's a chance we're given.'" Mimouna compared the facility of making it through school in France compared with Tunisia: "If they study there, it's too difficult. They don't have a lot of, oh, I don't know, libraries, things, transportation, you understand. It's easier here to complete studies than there. There a lot give up because of all that. Because there isn't much transportation, ways to pay for school and everything . . . here they help the students, they give scholarships." Keltouma left Morocco expressly for this reason:

> I did my master's in Morocco . . . but in the library in my city I found prac-
> tically nothing. . . . So I can tell you that I did my thesis with one book that
> a friend sent . . . from Casablanca, the economic capital of Morocco, and
> a few photocopies that my professor made for me when he was visiting
> Paris. . . . And when I find that, the luck French people have to have all
> these large libraries, all these main sources, I, honestly, I say to myself,
> "How can one not come study in Paris?"

Respondents also appreciate being able to take advantage of big city life in France. Soraya enjoyed the nightlife: "I didn't go out dancing there because there aren't any clubs, that's for sure. Going to the movies too, because there movies are for men, so here I take advantage of it." Several participants mentioned the cultural opportunities and the many means available for self-improvement. Leila noted: "It's a country that offers, on the artistic and intellectual level, a lot of opportunities. Paris. Especially Paris." Houriya raved, "Paris is the cultural capital. We can go to the theater, we can go to concerts." Amel also thought about the differences: "It's true that the cultural side is much more interesting here than there. Museums there only cost two dinars, that's two francs [30 cents], which is nothing, but well, there's nothing in them either. It's true that I, since I've been here, I've opened up to the world, I mean to culture and everything. . . . I think I've learned a lot here." Besma concurred, saying that it would be difficult to go back because of all she would miss: "The cultural richness, I would miss it. Paris for me, it's inexhaustible. Tunis in comparison is the little capital of the suburbs really; it's not enough." She also felt that in Paris she had been able to learn more about the Arab world, including music and literature, that she had not been aware of while in Tunisia. Hayat added, "Here we can educate ourselves. Even if sometimes you have [financial] difficulties . . . you can take books out of the library. It's really great. You can get informed."

Other women appreciated the diversity of the population in Paris. Hayat reflected on living in Paris: "It's allowed me to see the other, it's positive really, to meet other peoples. It's true in Algeria, between Algerians, we don't know others, whereas here there's everything. There are blacks, Chinese, there's everything you want. It's true. It helps you become more tolerant." Rym agreed: "It's taught me to see other people who live differently than in my country, learn other mentalities, other, it's allowed me to open up to the world, to see how people live elsewhere." Leila marveled, "Paris is one of those rare cities where there are different cultures, and cultures where you can, you can have a vision of Turkish culture, or Hindu, or Pakistani, without having to go to Pakistan or India to, you can go see the Pakistani and Turkish communities, and I don't know what, to have an idea of the traditions and cultures of those countries." Thus immigrant women appreciated Paris for the culture it provided, both high culture and access to cultures of the world.

The other aspect of North African mentality that respondents disliked is the machismo and strict supervision of women. As we saw in Chapter 2, participants felt liberated in France, where they could be out in public without feeling like someone is keeping tabs on them and where unmarried women can live alone. Freedom was the aspect of French life that most of the interviewees preferred when asked to compare France with their countries of origin. Houriya summed up the sentiments of many:

> Sometimes I walk at midnight, at 1:00 in the morning. I say, "Shit, I'm free. In Algeria I can't do this." . . . It's an exploit, and I feel an immense joy. . . . I say in spite of everything, in spite of all the difficulties, I'm free. That's what counts for me. I do what I want. No one is going to tell me, "Where are you going? When will you be back? What time are you going out?" Over there, you can't have that; it's out of the question. If it's not the family, it's the environment. . . . And, well, the girls that we know there, they get married just after school, so I think that they are girls who have never known what it is to be independent or responsible.

Georg Simmel (1950:337) writes that cities lead to indifference and antipathy, but this can lead to a hidden benefit: "[M]odern life has developed, in the midst of metropolitan crowdedness, a technique for making and keeping private matters secret." Respondents took advantage of this. Nedjma noted that Paris confers a sense of anonymity that allows a person to act as he or she chooses:

> While in the beginning, I complained about the anonymity in Paris, when I arrived in Tunisia I appreciated the anonymity. . . . I say when you can, when you can exploit the anonymity, it can be a very good thing. Because you can make friends in Paris . . . share things with them; you don't have to share

with, when you want to be anonymous, you go out. You can have a romantic life, all that, and when you go out, it's possible to also be anonymous.

Of course, some women are in a better position to take advantage of the opportunities they like in France than others. Some women continued to be under the strict control of their husbands. Even for those who are allowed to go, movies cost money, and free books in libraries do not help illiterate women. Nevertheless, all were cognizant of the differences between the Maghreb and France and were able to criticize both. The ability to view the good and bad in both countries is the first step in actively choosing how to live one's life, what to incorporate from each place. Asked about differences between the Maghreb and France and what she preferred in each, Khadija answered, "Everywhere there is good and bad. . . . What I'd like to take from there is the customs and keep here is the freedom, the evolution." Some women went further than others in one direction, but all were negotiating between cultural choices — in other words, engaging in selective acculturation.

Selective Acculturation

THE BEST OF BOTH

Immigrant women have been consistently represented in one of two ways: as either "barriers to assimilation" because of their insistence on maintaining cultural traditions, or as the opposite: "vehicles of integration into dominant society" (see Deutsch 1987:719–20; Kibria 1994:248). According to Freedman (2000:15), immigrant women in France have not escaped these binary portrayals:

> Women of immigrant origin are thus represented as both the bearers of "tradition" and agents of "modernity," responsible both for perpetuating the boundaries of ethnic groups within France and for ensuring that these boundaries are made permeable to French culture. These dominant representations are often both stereotyped and contradictory, and little has been done to moderate them by analysts of immigration, or, indeed, by French feminist researchers.

Integration is the French term for the incorporation of immigrants into the host nation and usually implies assimilation. However, recent researchers

(Portes and Zhou 1993; Rumbaut 1994; Portes and Rumbaut 1996) have pointed out that the old models of assimilation, becoming truly indistinguishable from members of the host society and taking on a new identity, are problematic for racially visible immigrants. Because of racial and/or economic discrimination and enclaves of coethnics, immigrants may recommit to an ethnic identity even as they take on the behaviors of the host nation, leading to segmented assimilation (Portes and Rumbaut 1996). In addition, cultural maintenance and cultural change may go hand in hand, so that immigrants accept certain values and behaviors from the host society while actively working to preserve others from their countries of origin, a process referred to as selective acculturation (Portes and Rumbaut 1996). Although some acculturation is involuntary because immigrants must learn the ways of the host country to a certain extent in order to survive economically, selective acculturation implies an active process of picking and choosing among cultural beliefs and behaviors.

The Maghrebin women interviewed were all engaging in selective acculturation, with some leaning toward greater maintenance of North African customs and others toward greater incorporation of French ways in their lives. The cases of Najet and Cherifa, both Moroccan immigrants, provide interesting examples of two different patterns of acculturation. Najet is a 46-year-old woman who arrived in France with her husband at age 19. Her husband is a member of her extended family who married her in Morocco during a vacation from his job in France. She has three children, all young adults who continue to live at home in a northern suburb of Paris, and she has never worked other than some occasional babysitting in her house. She prepares three meals a day and does all the housework. She keeps very busy with traditional tasks and hobbies, sewing, embroidery, cooking, and making Moroccan pastries, and has made many decorations for her home such as pillow covers and tablecloths. The majority of other household decorations come from North Africa, including a large gold tea set and the quote from the Quran on a plaque in her entrance way. She also enjoys having friends over, listening to North African radio stations, and watching programs from the Maghreb on satellite television in addition to French soap operas. "Everything we do is Moroccan. Even our glasses, our plates, our meals, our desserts; everything we do is Moroccan. Even the TV, we watch things from home, a lot."

Najet is a devout Muslim, praying five times a day and respecting all the holidays. She buys only *hallal* (religiously acceptable) meat and never eats pork or drinks alcohol. She cooks only Moroccan food with a few French additions, mainly salads. She wears a djellaba and headscarf at home but wears modest western clothing when she goes out. Although her last year of schooling at age 16 was partially in French, she did not speak French when she arrived. She has learned to speak well enough to get by thanks to her children and French television. At home, she and her husband speak Arabic and Berber between themselves; the children, who speak French among themselves, are fluent in both Berber and Arabic, although they cannot write. Najet says that her life has changed little in coming to France, other than being far from her family and missing the sun. She does appreciate the freedom in France and the ease of leading one's life without being constantly watched and critiqued by family and neighbors. She returns to Morocco for one or two months every year, sometimes with the whole family and sometimes alone. Despite having lived in France for 27 years as a permanent resident, she has never asked for citizenship.

Cherifa is a 44-year-old woman who married a French man at age 30 and moved with him to France. They had one child before her husband died unexpectedly, and she is currently living with her 11-year-old son and her French boyfriend in an almost entirely white suburb of Paris. She works as an administrative assistant in a company in the city. Cherifa always dated French men, and therefore her parents were not surprised by her marriage and decision to live in France. Even in Morocco, despite her parents' complaints, she went out with boyfriends, drank alcohol, and smoked in the street. She has always worn French clothing except to an occasional Moroccan reception. She was never very religious, celebrates Christmas with her son, and does not keep any Muslim holidays. Her son, who does not understand Arabic, is one of only two children in the sample to have a French name.[6] Cherifa herself speaks French with her parents. She also prefers to have them come visit instead of going to Morocco. She rarely goes for more than two weeks at a time, and after her arrival in France, she spent five years without returning to North Africa at all. When asked about what she has kept from Morocco, she mentioned her sense of sociability and cooking Moroccan dishes for guests. She admits, however, that she can also serve friends pasta and salad and rarely makes Moroccan food for her family. She has been a citizen since her marriage.

When asked about issues of integration, Cherifa is adamant about immigrants making an effort to fit in:

Me, I'd be a bit radical . . . because if I want to wear a *gondelah* and a djellaba, then I should stay in my country. I feel that when you are somewhere, you try to blend in. There's an old Moroccan proverb that says "do as your neighbor or leave." That means that I shouldn't come to France to affirm my convictions, be they cultural or religious and all. If I want to wear *babouches* and put on the veil . . . well, I stay, I should stay in my country, or I blend in. Otherwise, if I'm in France, well I'm sorry, I dress like the French. If I eat with them, live with them, if I go to their schools, I don't see why I'd make myself be noticed.

Yet she does believe in preserving certain aspects of the culture, as long as they are the aspects she believes are positive and do not disturb others.

Me, I say often that I've kept only the best of my culture. That's, that's my motto, keep the best, the most positive in the culture. I kept good dishes, the good little things, the politeness, the welcome, the smile, the availability, um, the sensitivity, et cetera, et cetera. . . . You have to know, it takes a long time; not everyone gets it. Um, it's preventing children from yelling in the street, under the pretext that they think they're still in Morocco, in the "jungle," um, avoiding that kids' talk with their hands and everything. When it's the negative side of cultures, try to, I don't know, brief them, talk to the parents, or I don't know. But try to, so that really Africans have the opportunity to preserve their culture, which is their most absolute right, but to not spread out that culture, the negative side of the culture in a context that doesn't fit. When people yell and sing in the street, or play the tam-tams, it's great in Africa, but it's out of place on the banks of the Seine. You see? Cook shish kebabs in my garden, either here or in Morocco, but make shish kebabs next to the metro, I don't like that at all. You see? It's trying to transpose things in a context where they don't bother anyone. It's simply, dress Moroccan, fine, but not to take the metro or when I go to a meeting. You see? That I wear a djellaba at my place, at least in a context where it won't bother anybody. That I yell *youyous* [traditional North African cry] because my daughter is getting married, no. I think I have to rent a house in the country where no one can hear me. Same for the sacrifice of the sheep; I find it an aberration. It's a phenomenal aberration . . . when in a building they kill a sheep in the bathroom or in the bathtub and everything, I find it out of place. . . . I find it lamentable. So yes, all that, I don't have anything against all the people who kill sheep, but elsewhere, in Mecca, but not in public housing in Paris.

Thus even the most "assimilated" participant in the sample, whose discourse is remarkably similar to that of right-wing anti-immigration politicians, believes that immigrants have a right to preserve facets of their cultures. Cherifa puts limits on this cultural maintenance, however, and stresses the importance of selectivity. She clearly disagrees with Najet, who believes that immigrants "can do the maximum" in terms of living as they did in North Africa. For Najet, the only constraints on culture are structural, such as not being able to keep all the rituals of a holiday when one must work all day: "If it's not possible, it's not possible." What is possible, on the other hand, should be practiced. This does not mean rejecting everything French, though. Najet learned French, wears western clothing in public, and has grown to appreciate not only French salads, but also French soap operas. Cherifa and Najet, while representing opposite ends of the spectrum, are both engaging in selective acculturation.

A few respondents, like Rym, made arguments for integration in the sense of assimilation, at least outward assimilation:

> Me, I think that, talking about a principle, from the moment where you live here . . . from the moment when you're here in a foreign country, you integrate. For example, you know me, I was offered a hand of Fatima [a North African protective medallion], and well, I don't wear it outside. It's not because I'm ashamed to be Algerian, no, you see, I don't wear it, I don't want it to be written here, to label myself, to provoke, you see?

A few others felt that immigrants should not want to give up anything cultural. Souad argued this point:

> Me, I don't see why they should change. I don't see the point. But, well, everyone's free to do what they want, but I don't see the point. Why do they want to change? Because our culture is too rich, um, I don't see the point, who wants to change it? As they say, everyone their culture, and there are different cultures, we have different religions.

Many more women, like Yusra (31-year-old Moroccan), nuanced their arguments in some manner, looking for a limit: "[They can] preserve their culture up to the point where they don't disturb the laws of the Republic, which is a respect. They can do what they want, you see, preserve their culture as they like, but not disturbing the laws of the Republic."

The majority of the participants fall in between the extremes of near assimilation and total cultural maintenance. Several made specific arguments about selective acculturation. Amel expressed her views on the subject: "There are good traditions that you should keep and others that you can eliminate. I think you have to, you can sort them, and then, um, you can integrate like that, keeping the positive." Tinhinan (34-year-old Algerian) agreed: "I'm attached to many traditions although I'm against a lot of things, Algerian traditions that oppress." Respondents argued that Maghrebins in France could do without traditions like taking four wives or putting brides on display the day before the wedding, but they usually wanted to keep the sociability and generosity, certain dishes, and to varying extents the language and holidays. Leila discusses her life:

> There are things, there are things in our culture . . . that I don't want to reject or ignore and that I'm proud of. And there are also things that I've learned living in France that are maybe different from ours, part of western culture, and that I find great, that I've adopted in my life. Which means that, well, I take the two sides. I don't reject one or the other. I try to have a certain equilibrium. . . . I've tried to keep the enriching sides of both cultures. I've stayed typically Tunisian in my relations with people, and um, maybe French when I go there.

For Leila, taking some of each culture helps her feel balanced and enriched. Other respondents picked up on this idea but also noted the dangers of going too far in one direction. Keltouma argues for flexibility in order to prevent marginalization in the new society and a complete loss of the traditions of the old:

> I believe it's very important to still keep one's culture, to keep up the contact with one's country of birth, to explain that well, the traditions and everything to one's children, without going to the point of shutting oneself in on that, which unfortunately happens often. Because then you find yourself marginalized, and you find yourself really a stranger in the country you live in. So, um, I think that you have to open up to the culture that takes us in, know its culture, know one's traditions, respect differences, because it's with difference that we enrich ourselves, and that doesn't mean neglect your own. So I think that you have to be pretty flexible to welcome the differences, new things, while still keeping the old of course, and the traditions of our origins.

Labiba (35-year-old Algerian) concurred with Keltouma, speaking of customs that should be kept but at the same time fearing the effects of ghettoization:

> Well, I think the learning is to take. Um, from a cultural point of view, you shouldn't lose your language. There are religious customs, I think that in a secular country like France in principle the problem should not pose itself. You are what you are; I am what I am. Each person, I don't have to do like you do to integrate, because it's pretending really, because it's not coming spontaneously from the person. And I think there are nice little European traditions. That's it, I think that I have things to give you like you have things to give me. And it depends on the people. And it's true that making ghettos isn't good. Nor is seeing French people rejected by Maghrebins or seeing Maghrebins rejected by French people.

In addition, Labiba notes that how much acculturation occurs depends on the person. For her, this is not simply a matter of individual choices, but also a matter of generation.

> The generation that's been here since maybe 10 years ago, or 15 years, they mix both [cultures] without any complexes. But the older generation, that came in '62, it stopped in '62, knowing that it came to an enemy, and that if they took anything at all from that enemy, it would mean at the loss of their culture; it would mean being erased. But this generation is spontaneously open, at the same time knowing that it keeps, that it doesn't get erased. Because they're at ease in their culture. They're already open before coming here.

Yusra links this difference between generations not only to the political climate in Algeria and France in the 1960s versus the 1980s, but also to the reasons that brought the different generations to France:

> A woman of 50, 60 . . . she's never going to integrate in the French cultural world. For her, that's not it. I think there are two sorts of immigration, an economic integration, and an immigration searching, that aspires to something else, to another way of living, and that's what permits assimilation. The first, the economic integration, the people don't feel obligated to leave

their culture. Well I don't feel obligated to leave my culture, but I'm fine the way I live, you see, in France.

Although several respondents noted that the Maghreb is changing and is not now as it was during their childhoods, only one situated immigration within other changes brought on by technological developments and an increasingly globalized world. Besma rejected the idea that there can truly be such a thing as a national culture:

There's no doing it the French way, or doing it the Italian way, there's no doing it a way. Me, I don't believe so. That doesn't exist for me; it's a concept that doesn't make any sense. There are things that will get forgotten, and things that will remain. The fundamental will stay, and the details will get mixed up. Some will take from others, and in general it's the details, but there's an evolution that happens naturally, be it here or there. I don't believe that immigration specifically is concerned by that question, because it's a question of time finally. We're facing other methods of communication, we're facing other modes of transmission, and we're facing so many things that make it so in spite of ourselves we have to readjust our comportment, readjust our points of view. Everybody is moving. But culturally you can have roots that come from somewhere else, an origin that is elsewhere, but that's at the same time an additional richness. It's not to banish, to toss away, to throw out, but rather it should be revalorized. . . . I find it frustrating that we always talk about a power relationship between two cultures, and that power relationship should not be. It's not legitimate. There's no, there's no under-culture and over-culture. There are two cultures that are brought to live in interaction and to take from one another.

Given the two cultures brought to live in interaction, what specific behaviors are North African immigrant women taking and what are they keeping?[7] Observing Najet and Cherifa's examples, we see that the range is vast. Are there any patterns?

BEHAVIORS LOST AND GAINED

Food

Behaviors like cooking and getting dressed are simple, everyday actions, and yet they have symbolic meaning. They tell us a great deal about people's negotiation of cultural boundaries. What are Maghrebin women serving to their families in France? Some women, like Djamila, make all the same foods they ate in their countries of origin: "We make the food there here. It's the same. We didn't change the cooking." Yet even women who only cooked North African food admitted that there were a few slight differences. Occasionally they added a French side dish here or there, and frequently they skipped some of the steps of traditional cooking. Some bought frozen food or canned rather than fresh vegetables. Many women said they did not make homemade bread but rather purchased it. Others, including Mimouna, went further: "Me, sometimes, when I don't have the time, I don't like to cook. The children, I say, 'Well, I'm doing like the French.' I put things in water and all that, and after they say to me, 'What's this? We eat this at the cafeteria every day . . . we're sick of eating this every day at the cafeteria, at least in the evenings we eat well at home.' . . . So I say, 'Oh la la, it's my fault,' because they're very spoiled now, even the husband too, the same." Hiba's (43-year-old Algerian) children also prefer North African food: "My children always say, 'Mom, the weekend you're here. You have to make the food from home.' They love it, they love couscous, they love it all. I do everything by hand, good." Other women who wanted to cook Maghrebin food, like Hachmia (40-year-old Moroccan) and Assia (36-year-old Algerian), feel pressure from their children not to:

H: [We eat] French a lot because the children like fries and steak, pasta. They eat a lot of things like that, things for children . . . pizza, stuff like that.

A: Me I prepare good the meals at home. Either I make *tangines* or I make couscous. The children say to me, "Mom, we don't eat that." They prefer McDonald's. You have to force them to eat a little bit of couscous.

A few participants themselves preferred the taste of French food or liked to experiment with cuisines from around the world. Yasmine talks about the changes in her culinary taste: "Me, I like French cuisine. I mix, me. I mix. I don't distinguish much because me, I buy a lot of cookbooks. When I came here in '83, I loved crepes. . . . It's in '83 that I started buying French books and Spanish books, I mix. Before I had never eaten Chinese. . . . The first time I ate Chinese I didn't like it . . . and now I like it." Fouzia also likes to vary what she eats: "We like to change, to not eat the same thing every day. Yeah, sometimes I cook Moroccan cuisine, sometimes I cook French cuisine." Although most women generally believed that North African food is healthier, many women cooked Maghrebin dishes only occasionally, usually citing a lack of time for the preparation required. Amel reflects, "The days I have time, I do a little bit of Algerian cooking, but when I work, we're rushed, no, I, a little of everything. It varies." Joumana (36-year-old Moroccan) agrees: "When I have time I cook a little, Moroccan main dishes, or French, and sadly we don't have enough time here in France because of administrative papers especially and work. We eat what there is and that's it. We eat quickly and badly, badly especially. . . . It's too bad, but we don't have time." There was one general exception to this rule for women who said they usually made French meals. Many respondents stated that they cooked Maghrebin food on the weekend, not simply because this was when they had the most free time, but also because this was the time to spend with family and friends.

Eight different respondents stressed that when they invited guests over, be they Maghrebin or French, they would serve exclusively North African food. Mbruka says her husband threatens to invite people over just to get the chance to eat couscous: "I rarely cook Algerian, usually the weekend when I have time, but very rarely. Especially when I have friends who come, to have them discover the cuisine. When I have people over, I never cook other than Algerian, because it's always nice to have friends discover the food from my country." Nour explained that whenever her mother-in-law visits from Algeria, she brings certain food products, "and then it's time to have a great dinner. We invite someone over, you see, and we make Algerian dishes, definitely *chorba*." Extended family members are also treated like guests, as Hachmia notes: "When I have family over, on the weekend, we make ourselves happy, we make food from home. On the weekend we make *tangines*, sometimes couscous, it depends, or balls of ground meat, when there is family." Having extended family for a meal makes it a festive atmosphere and thus requires preparation of appropriate dishes, as Faroudja highlights: "Well, yes, the weekend from time to time we go to visit family, or they come to our place. We talk among ourselves. We make like a party because we are happy when the family is together. We eat. We make couscous. We eat together."

The importance of meals with extended family or friends is a part of

Maghrebin culture. Deha shakes her head at the nerve of French people who invite her over for a simple salad and piece of meat when she spends hours preparing complicated dishes for them: "You didn't go to any trouble; it's good, but it's not how you invite me." Babès (2000) writes on what she calls the "sacredness" of the traditional North African dish, couscous. Couscous is both a gift, often distributed to the poor, and a sacrifice, because of the ritually slaughtered meat it is often served with. Couscous is composed of semolina and varying accompaniments, different combinations of vegetables and/or meat, depending on the occasion. It takes all day to prepare when made in the traditional manner in which the individual grains of semolina are rolled in between women's palms. "Despite being the dish of the poor, couscous has always been the festive dish par excellence" and predated the arrival of Islam in the Maghreb (Babès 2000:14; translation mine). Couscous is made for family meals, holidays, weddings, and other important occasions.

For immigrant women in France, couscous continues to fulfill these functions, remaining far from what Babès calls the "desacrilized" couscous served in Mediterranean restaurants. Warda explains: "Couscous is not the fundamental dish, it's the dish of parties, the dish of commemorations, big occasions." She reveals that although her immediate family typically eats French food, "the cuisine for occasions, for religious holidays, or commemorations, or other things, it's specifically traditional Algerian cuisine, like it's made that day by the family." Oumniya talked at length about the importance of different dishes and desserts, the ingredients, and the order of consumption, at a wedding she had recently attended between an Algerian man and a Tunisian woman in France. Women would often help friends and relatives prepare enormous quantities of food several days before such an event, much as they did in the Maghreb.

Dress

Weddings and other social events were also the occasion to wear traditional clothing. Only two women veiled in the street in France, and none wore a djellaba or other traditional dress out, other than to special occasions.[8] Eight participants mentioned that they wore traditional dresses to weddings. Karima also stated that she continues to put henna (plant dye) on her and her children's hands for holidays. Faroudja and Hiba discussed their clothing habits:

F: When we're at home, we dress like there, Kabyle dresses for the inside, at home. At home Kabyle dresses, but when we go out, we don't put on dresses from home, we dress like in France. To go out you have to respect people here, because we're here. We wear clothes from home here for parties, Kabyle dresses. I'm a seamstress. I make here for women, there are women who like the costume, long dresses for women. Yes, I make dresses, beautiful dresses, for marriages, when we're at a party, a marriage, Kabyle dresses. Yes. The Kabyle belt, the gold bracelets. . . . We're happy when we have parties like home, it's magnificent. Parties we go out, we wear the dresses from home.

H: The weekend. The weekend I do it, all together the guests. Um, if I don't go out to go shopping, I do it at home.

F: I put on the headscarf when I cook so that my hair doesn't fall in the food.

CK: And in the street, do you wear the headscarf?

F: No, no, me, no. I do it at home.

H: At home we do it, but not elsewhere. When I cook. When I pray, always, yes, my head.

Chafiqa dresses the same way: "I wear French clothes, but when I go to a party, I put on my Algerian dress."

French clothing, however, does not mean the same thing for all the women. Older, religious women, many of whom wore the veil in the Maghreb, wear "long" clothes, skirts that reach the ankles and long-sleeved shirts. Hachmia explained: "Wear long things there. It hasn't changed. I don't wear short things. . . . We wear skirts, that's changed. Wearing the scarf on the head, here no." Zhora revealed the point of dressing this way: "I like clothes that are a little bit classic. Something that covers the skin." Clothes that cover the skin can still be French clothes, and thus permit women to "respect" people in the host country. Salima (38-year-old Algerian) and Bahia (38-year-old Algerian) disapprove of the way French women dress:

S: Me, here I find the women here, French women, they're, how to say it, they're too, too naked, that's it.

B: In France, I see a picture, in the post office, before in France, clothes like us . . . before France like Algeria. The headscarf, the headscarf and the skirt, maxi. . . . Young people now, it's not like old ladies and men. It's different. . . . Us, no, still the same, still like before. We wear the headscarf like before, the maxi skirt like before. . . . Women look at me not good. I don't know why. If it rains, she too, she wears a headscarf.[9]

Both Fouzia and Bahia, who continue to veil in public, also wear long clothes rather than traditional North African clothing. A couple women noted that although they wore head coverings in their countries of origin, their husbands did not like them to wear them in France. Mimouna talks about some men compared with her husband: "Here I don't put [the headscarf] on, I don't put it on, but, even my husband, there are husbands who don't like their wives, they are very religious, and they like their wives to wear the headscarf even here, but there are others who are modern . . . he likes his wife modern. . . . My husband doesn't like for me to put on the headscarf and everything." Nassima (50-year-old Algerian) wore the headscarf in Algeria until coming to France at the age of 43. Now, at the age of 50, even when she returns, she wears the headscarf only over her shoulders:

N: Because I'm older now. Yes. My husband's not jealous, he lets the face [show].

CK: Before you covered up more?

N: Yes, I covered the beauty, for my husband, so he's not jealous.

CK: And your husband, he's not jealous here?

N: No, because everyone walks like that.

Thus the change in veiling is not simply a function of living in France, but is also related to aging and consequently reduced fears about sexuality and the family's honor.

For younger, less religious women, French clothing means anything French people wear, including miniskirts and low-cut blouses. Although several adopted these clothes without any trouble, and a few even wore them in North Africa before coming, some still had hang-ups. Wearing pants, especially in the Maghreb, was often a way to dress in western clothes without having to fight with parents or worry about other people's reactions to skirt length. Seven different respondents mentioned that they wore pants frequently in their countries of origin, and some kept this up in France. Malika is a case in point:

> When I was there I had enormous problems with my father because of my way of dressing, because he always thought it was too short, too transparent, too this, too that, that I wore makeup, that I shaved. . . . So, as a means of revolting, I said, okay, if it's like that, I'll never wear another skirt, I'll always wear pants, and effectively that's what I did. When I was there I always wore pants. When I arrived here, it's not because I'm far from him and there, the country, that I do it differently. . . . I'm always in pants, and it took me years before I could wear a dress, a short dress. I do it in the summer, but, um, it hasn't been long that I've let myself do it. The prohibitions, I have them in my head, although I could do whatever I wanted because no one looks here.

Nour behaved similarly:

> In Algiers I always dressed without any ostentation. I tried to look as much as possible like nothing, or like a man, you see? Meaning nothing that would make me stand out from the masses. I called it the war uniform, meaning pants, or sometimes even a skirt, but usually pants, cool, sweatshirt. The most basic possible. And here, it's true that I like to wear miniskirts in the summer; I'm more someone who wears pants in general. . . . I have a few skirts that I wore when I came here before, and I wear them occasionally, but otherwise, basically I haven't changed my way of dressing, other than sometimes when I go out at night or during the day I wear a miniskirt that I wouldn't wear in Algiers, that's for sure.

Religion

As Muslims in a secular society, Maghrebin immigrants have the choice of resisting, "establishing strong boundaries with the broader culture, resisting cultural encroachments as much as possible, and setting the group up as a radical alternative," or accommodating, "adapting certain features of the religion to make it more consonant with secular ways of life" (Davidman 1991:32). The women I interviewed practiced accommodation.[10] Although some traditions were modified and some lost altogether, other new ones were gained. The majority of women continued to celebrate Muslim holidays, but some had also added Christmas. According to Souad, celebrating Christmas is the only thing that makes her feel French: "I celebrate Christmas with my children, since I've been here more than 30 years. My kids are born here, we celebrate Christmas. . . . I do it because I like it. I like holidays, and I do it for my kids. Other than that, I do everything like there, but I always try to, I don't change my customs. I do Ramadan, I, we celebrate our holidays." Zhora also celebrated holidays from home and from France: "Yes, we celebrate holidays here. We mix the holidays everywhere. We celebrate all the holidays, the Arab holidays, the holidays of Christmas, all the holidays are okay." Rachida actually celebrated with French people: "I do Christmas with the French people here. Everybody has a big celebration with everyone. Eat alone during the holidays, it's not good." Recounting her pain at having nowhere to go for Christmas, Yasmine said: "Even New Year's, I spent it at home. . . . I like someone to invite me here. I didn't find anyone to invite me, either for New Year's or for Christmas . . . nobody invited me. But I wanted to know their holiday, know it. And it was, it marked it for me, I said, oh la la, I came to stay here and I didn't celebrate. I don't like that. There are some who say, 'No, you shouldn't celebrate.' I said, 'No, me I like to learn the holidays of all the races.'" These four women are all religious Muslims and do not neglect their own holidays; they simply see no problem adding in Christmas.[11] Islam continues to play a very important role in their lives, and yet many say that although they want to celebrate their holidays and engage in other Muslim behaviors, such as prayer, these things are often hard to do as they would like in France.

Although one-third of the women interviewed do not actively practice Islam, they all self-identify as Muslims. Several of these women noted that they "believe but don't practice." Others explained that they were Muslim simply because they were born Muslim. As Yusra put it, "I was born Muslim without ever having practiced." A few even noted that since being a Muslim was taken for granted in the Maghreb, they could do whatever they pleased as long as they did not make it too obvious by eating in front of others during Ramadan or by drinking alcohol in public. Malika found this to be the case: "Every Tunisian is supposed to be Muslim, and he's never asked, 'Are you Muslim or are you something else?' It's like that. You are born in Tunisia, you are obviously Muslim, so somehow, since nobody asks you, they leave you alone. So you have the right to be nothing if you want to be nothing. It's so obvious for them that you can't be something else, that they don't ask you the question." Another third of the respondents are very religious, fasting during the month of Ramadan, observing food restrictions, and praying daily. The other third are also religious, respecting Ramadan, and not consuming pork or alcohol, but do not pray daily.[12] Those participants who are religious talked at length about the challenges of practicing Islam in France.

HOLIDAYS   Coming from a Muslim society that follows the Muslim calendar to a Catholic country that follows the Catholic calendar poses problems. One of the most frequent complaints women mentioned was the difficulties involved in celebrating Muslim holidays in France. The main religious festival is Ramadan, which commemorates the month during which Mohammed received the revelation of the Quran. During the entire month of Ramadan, practicing Muslims abstain from all drink and food between sunup and sundown as an act of repentance for sins. Each night, the fast is broken with a large meal among family members and friends. The experience of fasting is a uniting experience for the members of the community all showing their obedience to God in the same manner at the same time, and in Muslim countries, the workdays during the month are often cut short. Because Islam follows a lunar calendar, the holidays fall at different times of the year; consequently, people fast for fewer hours when Ramadan falls during the winter than they do when it falls during the summer. For the celebration of Eid-el-Kebir, which commemorates Abraham's sacrifice and lasts three days, Muslims ritually slaughter sheep and then feast with others. Sharing food with neighbors is an important part of this holiday. Both of these holidays are hard to respect in France the same way they are carried out in the Maghreb. Fatima explains that work interferes with the holidays:

> Ramadan . . . is very tiring here because we work. Because there, in
> Morocco, when it's Ramadan, we only work half a day. We have to work,
> but we work a half day, but not the whole day. Here you have to work your
> whole day without [eating]. As the French say, they don't give a shit. You
> have to do your day, and that's it, they don't want to know anything. You
> do your religion, you don't, you do your work, and that's it, no discussion.
> So I can't leave my job. I have to take care of my children and not find
> myself in the street, so I prefer to work. It's too tiring, too tiring.[13]

Souad discussed the differences between holidays that fall during the week, and those that fall on the weekend:

> For the holidays . . . especially when it falls during the week, the kids work, my cousin too, it's not the same. It's not the same thing as over there. There when it's a holiday, no one works. The family is all there, but here it's not. But when it falls on the weekend, we spend it together. And even if it falls during the week, well before my girls lived with me, we celebrated in the evening when they got home. But now that they have their lives, either they stop by in the evening, or they come the weekend after . . . or I go see them. I make pastries, for example, for Ramadan, we make pastries. If they can't come, I go see them, I take them some.

Having to work is not the only factor that makes celebration difficult. When asked about celebrating the holidays, Telja raised other problems she faces:

> It's too difficult because we can't make noise as we'd like, we don't have room, space like we'd like to celebrate. If we do a wedding, we have to search a year in advance. And that's what is missing, and it's a shame. Holidays are joy. That gets ruined. Sometimes going I don't know how many kilometers to do a wedding. We have to work when [a holiday] falls during the week. It's a shame that there aren't days like that for us, because the Muslim holidays are sacred, like Eid, the end of Ramadan, like Eid, the festival of sheep, it's really sacred. But when it falls during the week, we work.

One of the stereotypes commonly raised about Muslims in France is that of a family killing a sheep in a bathroom for Eid. Few respondents slaughtered sheep themselves, and those who did usually went to a farm to do it. The majority bought meat from a butcher. When asked whether she buys her meat or slaughters a sheep for Eid, Hiba responded:

> There's a farm, but it's far, people with a car. We go buy there, and people slaughter there; they bring it back. But people without the means, who don't have a car, well. . . . In '83 we bought a sheep, we slaughtered it in the courtyard. We had a party. The concierge came to eat with us, neighbors, and everything. And after, we can't do that, because there are many,

many Arabs, because if I slaughter my sheep, and you, you slaughter your sheep in the courtyard, it's not good. And after that we go each year to the farm, he buys there, my husband. He pays someone to slaughter it. We put it in the car, we put it in the freezer. Otherwise we go buy meat, that's all.

For other respondents, like Mimouna, the hardest part of the holidays is being far from their families:

It's for holidays that I don't feel good, I miss my family, especially for holidays, religion, because there everyone gets together with my brothers and sisters, my father, everybody, and I'm alone. Sometimes I don't feel like it's a holiday. . . . Sometimes when the children have a test that they can't miss, they have to go to school even on holidays; they can't leave school if they have important things to do. And me, I stay at home and cry. Yes, because I, for me, it's not a holiday.

Despite all these constraints, a few women noted that it has become easier to celebrate Muslim holidays in France in the past decade because French people are becoming increasingly aware of Muslim traditions. Warda and Karima talked about the changes they had witnessed over time:

> *W:* I'd say this year everyone knew it was Ramadan. And since we
>   worked it so people knew we were fasting, they finally understood,
>   but before it didn't enter their minds. They could invite you over
>   for champagne, they don't understand, not only do I not drink,
>   but it's Ramadan. Um, because my neighbors were totally ignorant
>   of Ramadan. But now I see that even they, who are bourgeois and
>   conservative, et cetera, French, they've understood that something
>   else existed, that it's respectable, but we had to impose ourselves.
>
> *K:* And now even the deputy, during Ramadan, he wrote my husband.
>   [The political party in power], they wrote for the holiday of Eid.
>   Even the deputy writes to wish you a happy Eid.

PRAYER   Other women, however, felt that practicing their religion correctly remains difficult, and that French people are generally still ignorant about Islam. In addition to holidays, participants spoke about prayer. Religious Muslims pray five times a day, but as respondents pointed out, work, and life in France in general, make the hours of prayer hard to keep. Joumana notes that the "rhythm of life" in France makes prayer difficult, and that the French do not respect the Muslim day of prayer: "Catholics, Catholics don't care. They know our religion, they don't know. Have to work on Friday. Normally, Friday is the day of prayer. It's sacred. And to make couscous to give to people to eat. It's the day of couscous, give to people. . . . And prayer too, the day of prayer, Friday." Despite having seen progress in this domain in France, Warda still notes that it is hard to pray regularly: "It's very difficult to adapt; nothing is set up for it. Um, the environment doesn't lend itself to it. In other words, you have to organize yourself and since I want to do a lot of things, well, God forgive me, it's the thing I neglect, saying to myself I'll make it up by something else."

Although Khadija explains that "for people who work, yes, yes, they can do their prayers by saving up all the prayers for the evening," those who did work full time, like Fatima, often found this challenging.

No, I don't pray. I don't have time. It's hard. I'm not lying because I say well, I do it or I don't do it, but I don't do it. I'm telling the truth. I don't do it because it's hard . . . prayer you have to stay at home to pray each morning, but you can save them, you do it at night. Me, when I get home at 8:00, it's not at that moment; I have to shower, cook. So I'm totally exhausted, my feet hurt, my head too, so I eat and I sleep, for the next morning and everything. God forgive me. And when I'm retired, if God lets me live until retirement, I'll do it.

Amel agreed:

Prayer, I did it in the beginning, but with my hours and everything it's hard. I remember in the beginning when I came, I already did it in Algeria, when I came, I tried to do it, but sometimes when I got home at 10:00 at night, I had to make it all up. And honestly, I wasn't concentrated on those things. When I was praying, it was, "When am I going to finish and be able to go to bed?" So I said to myself, it's hypocrisy; it would be better to stop. So I stopped. And it's true, I say to myself that God sees what I'm doing, so I don't have to think about praying, well, maybe I'll do it someday, but the day when I think I can assume it, meaning do it well.

Joumana also said she would not start praying until she could do everything in her life according to her beliefs. For her, the problem is not just time, but the conditions of life in France:

> I like my religion, I'm proud. And it's a shame we don't practice very well, because of the time . . . because I'm losing it a little, but not all of it, thankfully. But I like my religion; it's a beautiful custom, Islam. . . . I practice, but not really everything, but my heart practices the most. I do Ramadan, though. Yes, but how to put it — religion, it's really, it counts in Islam for us to not talk about people, talk badly about people. That, too, you have to avoid. And to help people. That's Islam. . . . So I love my custom, and I follow, but, um, not like, prayer for example. Normally I should do it. You can't lie when you do it, but sometimes I have to lie. But when you pray, you can't. You really have to follow it all the way or it's not worth it. But now, when I'm young, I have to lie to survive. . . . Normally you have to be very, very clean, psychically and on the inside; it's the body more on the inside. You can't lie, insult the neighbors, talk badly about people.

She says that one day, when her life is more stable, she will start praying: "Afterwards I will go to Mecca, sweep up all the sin as they say."

Even in North Africa, people sometimes do not begin to pray five times a day until they are in their 40s or even older. Chafiqa, for instance, explained that she will start praying when she no longer has children around to interrupt her. Other women, like Assia and Salima, also noted that when they are older they will begin to pray, but that life is too difficult for them to do so right now. Souad is an example of someone who started praying after living in France for several years: "Yes, I drank for a while. Occasionally. Now, no. It's been years. I do my prayers. It's not allowed in our religion. I started drinking when I went out with friends in the evening and everything; I drank with them. Here. And afterwards I stopped. I decided to pray. . . . If I work, like my last job, I worked at people's, in the house, I did it there. But when I work for companies, in the evening when I get home I do the prayer." Najet believes that when there is a will, there is a way: "If you have faith, you can do anything. Pray on time, Ramadan, we do it all." When pushed, however, she too admitted that her husband's schedule revolves as much around work as it does around prayer and the holidays.

Those participants who do pray, whether five times a day or just occasionally, find that it brings them peace and a sense of well-being. They talked about what Islam means to them and what it gives them. Souad explained why she started to pray:

> I do my prayer so that my conscience, I'll be tranquil vis-à-vis God. Later we'll be punished if, it's like a debt, it's a debt to God. If we don't do Rama-dan, we don't pray, um, it's a debt, and I'm happy to do it, to be at peace. It's like someone, you owe him money, and you don't pay him, your conscience isn't tranquil. This, it's more even, because later you pay more, much more. And it's good to read the Quran at home. It brings a lot, it's good. It saves us from a lot of bad things, lots of things, yes. As they say, when there's someone in the house who prays, it's always safe. It's not that there are no bad things; bad things can happen to anyone, but it's protected from the devil, as they say.

Hachmia noted that prayer is not the only way to please God: "Praying to God, it's like someone who owes you, a credit, it has to be given back. That means praying is a credit to give back, but also doing good, like giving a gift, not hurting people; it's like praying, it replaces it. . . . Loving one's neighbor, that means it's a real Muslim who's going to help others. Yes, be there for oth-ers if they need him. If he needs it someday and he finds no one, it doesn't matter, but he has to always go toward others." Zhora concurred: "Religion is justice . . . choosing to do something good for us, our neighbors. . . . Prayer gives a little peace, health, yes, because it's good things for morality."

In addition to pleasing God, women also felt personally aided when they prayed. Yasmine reflected: "When I do it, I feel good. If I do it, my day is always good for me. Sometimes I don't do it, the day is not good for me." Keltouma spoke about prayer and about the role of religion in her life more generally:

> I think that religion is an element that helps me . . . that helped me sur-mount difficult moments in my life. For me, it's a moment of peace when I do my prayer, honestly I feel very, very good. I relax as if I were doing an exercise that I like. . . . I think it's good to have something you're attached to, a chore we do. It's like an assignment at school, and when we've done it well, we're peaceful, and we feel good; it's the same with religion. And it's true that . . . in any sacred book I think, we have lots of stories and things, words that make us think, and it's pleasant reading, very enriching, and that does good. It's sure that taking time to pray, forgetting everything,

absolutely everything, it's like a sport, you forget everything and you concentrate on something, and it's true that you're not the same afterwards.

Although Warda fluctuates on praying five times daily, she insists:

I don't go to bed without asking God forgiveness for everything I could have done that's not very moral, and where I concentrate a little on essential things. But it's, I mean, it's an individual prayer, profound, that doesn't need any exterior manifestation. I don't put down a rug, no one sees me do it. But I always give myself 15 minutes to think about what I've done. Is it good? I'm a Muslim, have I conformed to what I believe? It's very important to me. It's a crutch I can't do without.

A MATTER OF THE HEART Warda's focus on an individualized relationship in Islam echoes the feelings of many other respondents. Several women do use a prayer rug and wear a headscarf to pray, but they point out that this is done in the home and is therefore not a public expression of religion. For many older religious women, Islam is between oneself and God. It should be practiced in private and should not interfere with life in French space: on the street, and especially at work or in schools. Chafiqa explains, "It's Maghrebin, you do it for you; you don't do it for others. Me, I do Ramadan, I don't ask others to do it with me, or show others that I do it. If they ask me, okay, I'll say I do it, but if they don't ask me, it's not their business what I do at home. . . . Intimacy is kept at home. You want to do your prayer, you do it at home." Telja sums up this view: "My religion, I keep it inside of me. I don't show anyone, because it belongs to me and God, nobody else."

Many participants disapproved of wearing the headscarf in France, arguing that the veil is not really required in Islam, that other facets of the religion matter more, that a woman can dress modestly without covering her hair, or that one must not show off or try to stand out.[14] Despite being raised in a society where many women veiled and often having veiled themselves while in the Maghreb, none of these respondents believe that to be a good Muslim woman one must veil. They focus on other aspects of their religion, asserting that Islam is "not doing bad things," "helping people," being tolerant," and "respecting the religion of others."[15] These answers point to the "ethical voice" of Islam, which includes an insistence on the equality of all humanity and highlights the multiple possible interpretations of Islam (Ahmed 1992:229). Souad, who prays five times a day, shuns alcohol and pork, and celebrates all the holidays, draws the line at the headscarf:

I am Muslim, and I am against this, against people who dress like this, who wear veils; I can't stand it. Because when you want to follow the religion, as we say, religion is in the heart. It's not wearing the veil and then behind it doing things that are against the religion. I am Muslim, I practice, I do Ramadan, I do my prayers, and it stops there. It's not worth it that I wear a headscarf, or that I have to go to work like that or to school. That I don't accept.

This response is especially revealing about a whole group of Muslim women in France.[16] Many immigrant women, many of whom grew up with the veil in their countries of origin, abandoned it in France to work, to be hired, to fit in. In coming to France, they have become members of a minority group, and many were cut off from most of their family members. Religion, a communal affair in North Africa, became a private affair in France, as five participants phrased it, an affair "of the heart." Writing about Islam, Babès (2000:32) discusses the importance of intention and "heart":

Let us keep in mind that Islam is a religion of belief that postulates the *primacy of the heart*. The social constraints of morality, of the community norm are not superior to eschatology. Religion of the Law, Islam remains a religion of equilibrium, of moderation, but also of the *niyya*, the purity of intention. So let us remain attentive to the evolution that is taking shape within the community. The question of religious practice is inseparable from faith and extends beyond orthodoxy. Canonic rites say nothing (or very little) on the question of deep belief, nor on practice in a broader sense (individual ethics). The relationship between spirituality and the norm is at the heart of the evolution of the relationship between, on one side the normative logic of the community, and on the other the demands of universal faith and spirituality in the middle of secularization. [Translation and italics mine.]

Yet this leads to a crucial question. When respondents use the word *heart*, is it out of a conception of deep individual belief, or is it simply a reaction to trying to practice Islam in a context that shuns it, an instance of making religion internal and private because of external pressures? The heart Babès discusses is about intention, what one feel on the inside. An example of this is Amel's decision to stop praying because she was thinking about other things and therefore her actions were hypocritical. This may be different from the insistence on the heart that comes when one realizes she is not allowed to show on the outside what she feels inside.

What does this tell us about Muslims in France? These immigrant women have redefined what it means to be a good Muslim woman, by focusing on intentions, the purity of one's heart, and private acts, instead of conforming to the norms they grew up with in the Maghreb. For example, in discussing her life in Morocco, Najet says that "a real Muslim woman does not meet a man without her brother or husband, or someone from the family. A stranger, she won't sit next to him, talk, discuss, won't say anything." Yet in France, going shopping, riding the bus, and other daily chores necessitate a breakdown of this segregation between the sexes, and Najet feels no less Muslim for it. The respondents have made compromises between their cultural customs and the requirements of French society (such as wearing French clothes in order to "respect" French people), but they are compromises they feel comfortable with. Many of these women came in an era when immigrants just wanted work and hoped to be overlooked by the French.[17] Although they did not expect to fully belong to French society, they saw little reason to purposely mark themselves as foreign and other.[18] For them, it is important to fit in wherever you are. Instead of mixing some of each and creating new patterns of behavior no matter where one lives, these women feel that with people in North Africa one should follow North African norms, and with people in France, one should follow French norms, at least up to a certain extent. Oumniya adapts her behavior to the country she finds herself in: "Me, here in France, French habits. There I have Algerian habits. Here we live the French way; there we live the Algerian way." Najet agreed:

> N: Different countries. There it's different, and here it's different. The other culture is different, and here it's different. You shouldn't mix it all up. We distinguish between things, we know, we don't force . . . we let it go, meaning their habits, their culture. You shouldn't say, "No! Don't do this and then that." Okay. You see?
>
> CK: So you should do a little when you're there like there?
>
> N: Yes. Do like there. If we're here, we do like here. That's it.

This blending in and doing like the French is only important in public spaces in the host country. The home, or even a hall rented for a wedding, is a private location, free from the need to conform, and thus becomes a site of cultural expression. The transition from one mode of behavior to another can be a spatial boundary, crossing one's threshold, or a temporal boundary, certain days of the week or times of the day.[19] In Fatima's case, it was both:

> *F:* Saturday and Sunday I dress like at home. I put on my long dress, and I tie my headscarf around my head, and I clean the house, and the next day I'm dressed European.
>
> *CK:* So it's really for the weekend?
>
> *F:* For the weekend. Yeah, I take my shower, and I put on my long dress, and then tie on my head the headscarf, and that's it, work at home, Saturday and Sunday like that. I don't go out; I stay in. When I finish my work, I watch television. And then, or somebody comes over, a friend and we talk, we drink tea, and that's it. And the next day, I fold my dress, and I put on my skirt or my pants, and that's it, get going. It's finished. It's over.

When asked later whether immigrants should try to assimilate or to hold onto their traditions, she replied,

> *F:* They should do like I do. I don't let my culture get away, and I follow the French culture. I do both. In each role I find myself, I swing into it, and I come out good. I don't leave this or that. And it's very good. I don't have any difficulty; I don't, none.
>
> *CK:* And you manage according to the situation?
>
> *F:* Yes. If I have a French party, well I go there, I'm always dressed like this [she is wearing a skirt with a sweater over a blouse]. And if I have, for example, a wedding from home, and I'm invited, well, I'll do the same culture as them; I'll be the same thing. And that, why not? It works very, very well. Last year, there were two weddings, and, well, I went with my oldest daughter, dressed like at home, the orchestra, the party, and everything. I was dressed like there. And the next day, the next day I went to work in European, as if the party in the evening hadn't happened. That's how you should do it. You

> shouldn't drop, for example you, you are American, when you go back to America, you do like there, but here you live like a European. It's the same thing. Like you are seen in the street, they don't say it's an American, they're going to say it's a French person.

As we have seen, many other women, like Joumana, behaved the same way, changing clothes for the weekend or for festivals: "The djellaba, kaftan, *gondoura*, that's Moroccan clothing, it's very pretty, very comfortable, but at home or a ceremony. For work everyday, going in a djellaba to work, it's not [good]." Others, like Hiba, change the food they eat: "The weekend we cook almost only food from home. During the week, we make the food from here." Aside from sometimes wearing Maghrebin clothing and cooking North African food, some participants also tried to feel more at home in their houses by decorating with objects from the Maghreb. Najet was not the only respondent to furnish her home with North African decorations; Karima spoke about her home:

> At my place, the decoration in my home, I'm opening a parenthesis, this year, I have a cousin that came to visit last year, and this year I went to visit him, there were paintings of the Eiffel Tower everywhere, of the Arc de Triomphe, and when he came to my place last year, he couldn't believe it, because in my home, all the paintings that I have are Algeria. Everything. Everything, everything, everything. So for me, in my son's room, it's paintings of the Quran. In my daughter's room, there's the Quran and a few photos of Zidane [a famous French soccer player whose parents immigrated from Algeria], soccer and everything, but otherwise all the decoration in my home, it's Algerian.

By practicing selective acculturation and actively alternating between Maghrebin and French cultural behaviors, participants said they could feel comfortable in both their countries of origin and in France. Souad noted, "I'm happy to be here. I love my country, I only spend my vacations there; I feel really good there, but I'm good, I'm good here." Chafiqa concurred, noting that she does what she wants in Algeria, and is freer than other women there: "I'm not against what they do there or here. I'm good there, when I go there, and when I'm here I'm good. I am as I am. I practice as I want here. There I'm at home. . . . I do the same. No one tells me what time it is. My husband agrees. I want to wear pants, I wear pants there. I want to go out, I go out. When I want to go see someone, I want to go, I go. I'm not shut in like the women there." Thus, some of these older women take some of what they have become accustomed to in France back to the Maghreb. The interchange of culture flows in both directions.

Conclusion

North African immigrant women in France demonstrate a range of cultural behaviors, spanning the gamut from involved maintenance of traditional customs to high levels of acculturation. Despite this variety, all the women engaged in selective acculturation, albeit to varying extents. Whether they choose to take the best of both worlds and refashion a consistent mode of behavior accordingly, or whether they follow the alternation model proposed by LaFromboise et al. (1993) by trying to conform to French norms in public while preserving Maghrebin customs at home, they all are actively making choices, picking some behaviors and not others from their expanded cultural toolkits. The ease with which this is done, and the awareness of both cultural systems, point to the adaptability of people in situations of migration. Previous research highlights women immigrants' incorporation of certain beliefs and behaviors without a wholesale adoption of the culture of the host country (Naidoo 1986; Kibria 1993, 1994). My findings, in connection with these other studies, point to the generalizability of these processes.

> Crossing the border, they change, they westernize. It's a bit the image I've often had taking the plane from Algiers, of women who are in *hidjab* in Algiers, and who take it off in the airplane before arriving in Paris, who put on makeup . . . and who crossing the border are different women. You would barely recognize them. And in the opposite direction, it's the opposite that happens. It's an image that I've always wanted to keep . . . because it's significant, you see, because with the makeup, or the veil they take off, there are also comportments that go with it. When you put on a dress and take off the veil, um, you change your attitude, so you change, you change your way of being. . . . And the ideas are more open. They can handle a girl who smokes in the waiting room here in Paris for a flight to Algiers — I smoke comfortably in this direction, but in the waiting room for

Paris in Algiers, I don't smoke comfortably. You see what I mean? And it's curious. But it's also an adaptation. It's an adaptation, and it's our duality, us Algerians. Because we have that duality in us, even those whose parents are Algerian, they have modernity and custom, that are often opposed in them. That they manage to reconcile sometimes, but that still are often opposed in them.

Nour provides an excellent image of the flexibility in navigating between cultural patterns, but her example raises questions: How problematic is this duality? What does migrating back and forth between countries and cultures do to one's sense of self? Do respondents really feel as if they are a part of both cultures, or do they continue to identify primarily with one or the other? How do they view themselves given their cultural positioning, and how do they react to French people's perceptions of them? The next chapter explores the identity negotiation of immigrant women.

FOUR

Wherever I Go, I Have My House

Identity Negotiation

Moving to a new country not only affects cultural behaviors but also calls into question one's identity. "Within their families, as well as within society as a whole, women of immigrant origin are in a dynamic process, creating new social spaces and negotiating new identities" (Freedman and Tarr 2000:5). As members of a low-status, visible ethnic minority, identity is particularly likely to be problematic for North African immigrant women. As Freedman and Tarr (2000:6) point out,

> The question of representation is particularly problematic in the context of a nation whose universalist Republican principles make it reluctant to recognize difference (a problem which affects women of immigrant origin both as women and as ethnic or racial "Others"). The dominant culture continues to obscure the problematic bicultural or hybrid identities of women of immigrant origin who are French residents, and, in many cases, French nationals, but who also feel allegiance to their culture of origin.

Freedman and Tarr correctly highlight the importance of examining the connections between gender and race and the unique position of minority women. This chapter examines how women from North Africa living in France construct and manage their identities.

In the first section of this chapter, I explore whether the participants ever truly see themselves as equally belonging to both countries, or do they align themselves as one or the other? When, if ever, do they identify as French? In the second section of the chapter, I examine the consequences for immigrant women of the conflict between their self-perceptions and the perceptions of them by others. I find that visible ethnic minority members' identities are not as constrained as once believed, and, in particular, I highlight the fascinating case of immigrant women who deny that they are immigrants. I conclude with a discussion of the special situation of Algerians who have been affected by the country's recent civil war. They provide an interesting example of how both self and meta-perceptions are affected by context.

Self-Perceptions: French or North African?

PATTERNS OF IDENTIFICATION

According to social identity theory, identification as a member of a group occurs when people self-categorize as such and also feel an investment in or attachment to that group (Tajfel 1981; Turner 1985). In this section, then, I examine to which group(s) North African women who live in France feel they belong. Mary C. Waters (1990:16) notes that "ethic identity is a social process that is in flux for some proportion of the population." In her study of third- and fourth-generation white ethnics in the United States, Waters (1990:36) realized that people change responses about their ancestry when questioned at different times in their lives, "a finding that challenges one of our commonly held beliefs about ethnicity — that it is a physical or permanent aspect of oneself." Unlike later generation white ethnics, Maghrebin immigrants are both more and less likely to experience shifts in identity over time. The process of leaving one's home and creating a new life in a different country can have profound effects on one's identity. At the same time, first-generation immigrants know where they come from and were well steeped in a particular cultural background growing up.

When asked whether they feel more Algerian/Moroccan/Tunisian or more French, 18 women chose their country of origin, 7 respondents answered "French," and 20 answered "both." In picking an identification, participants mentioned maintaining or losing Maghrebin cultural traditions, having or not having French nationality, and amount of time spent in France or North Africa.[1] Thus, although some participants' answers supported Roberts's (1995) claims that a temporal perspective, including duration of time in the host nation and life events such as naturalization, affects identification, others used different markers. Interestingly, some women used the same criteria to arrive at different conclusions about their identities. For example, the meaning of citizenship differed by respondents. For some, citizenship mattered as a means of self-definition, and therefore whether or not they had become French was important. Others, however, argued that a piece of paper does not determine how they view themselves, thus discounting this symbol of identity. In addition, some thought that they had changed because they had lived in France for many years, whereas others believed that they were permanently marked by having spent their childhoods in North Africa.

MAGHREBIN (ALGERIAN, MOROCCAN, OR TUNISIAN)

Many women who view themselves as Algerian, Moroccan, or Tunisian do so because they maintain North African customs.[2] Thus, for respondents like Najet, cultural behaviors affect how they define themselves: "Still Moroccan. Everything we do is Moroccan." Chafiqa leaves room for including some French practices, but she maintains that because she has kept her culture, she will always be Algerian: "I've adapted to their culture, but I still practice mine. You can't adapt like that right away. I speak French, I do French things and all, but I still have my culture . . . you have to keep your culture. We can't change." Labiba and Hayat noted that even if they wanted to be French, Algerian behaviors would continue to crop up and give them away:

L: We're far from being French.

H: We're cool maybe, but not to the point of—

L: We can't be French finally because we aren't.

H: Even the nationality, we don't have it.

> *L:* Yes. We're immigrants. In parentheses. We can't be completely
> French. . . . We can't completely deny ourselves and say we're
> French, we've forgotten to be Algerian. First of all, even if we
> wanted to, we can't. Talking, even between us, for example, I'll
> end up saying two or three words in Arabic without you realizing
> it, or in Berber.

Other participants, including those who were very acculturated, continued
to identify primarily as Maghrebin according to more fixed criteria: being
born and raised in North Africa. Soraya explains: "Well, I'm still Moroccan.
That's for sure. Because, after all, I grew up there. I was born in Morocco, and
I grew up in Morocco. I'm still Moroccan. Maybe I'll get French citizenship,
but it won't change it, I'm still Moroccan. . . . Twenty years there, five here,
for me, I'm not really in my own country." Keltouma agrees:

> I think I came pretty old, really old. . . . I was 24, 25 when I arrived in
> France, so I believe that the essential part of human life I spent it in
> Morocco. That's where my childhood education was spent, and I think
> that's what affects us the most, and what determines our mode of being.
> And I think it's really hard to change now. It's true that I really like France.
> I have French friends that I love. I get along with everyone. I feel a little
> bit French, but I feel more Moroccan.

For these respondents, and numerous others, identity is not only a matter
of culture and customs but of attachment. As Hiba puts it, "I'm still Algerian. . . . When I sleep, I'm there, not here. . . . My heart, it is still there." Lina
reflects on her life: "It's sure that there's a cord there, inside. Inside we're
Algerian. . . . Maybe in 20 years we'll talk for France, but it's still fresh. We
lived everything in Algiers. All our memories are in Algiers. We did our studies, our pranks, especially the time during college. I think it's a very, very
beautiful time, the end of high school, when we pass our baccalaureate, and
the years at college are very important to us. And all that we lived in Algiers."

Despite identifying as Maghrebin, many participants admitted that in certain situations they do feel French, supporting Waters's (1990) finding that
identification changes not only over time but also in different contexts. Lina
describes this fluctuation in identity: "We feel it more, we react more, when
someone touches Algeria than when someone touches France, that's for sure.

But, at the same time, um, me, I've been abroad where people have insulted the French, because they hear us speaking French and everything, I also defend France." Mimouna said she felt Tunisian, but when asked if there were any situations in which she felt French, she replied, "Yes, like when I vote, for example. I've voted before. And when I, for example, when I talk with, I have a few friends now, French, when I talk with them." For Souad, participating in Christmas is the only time she feels truly French: "Tunisian, always, that doesn't change. I still feel Tunisian. I've never felt French, no, except, well, Christmas. I celebrate Christmas with my children because I've been here for more than 30 years. . . . Other than that, no, I don't do anything, I don't feel French."

FRENCH

A few participants did feel French, or, like Joumana, at least increasingly French, because they were losing their traditions:

> *J:* More Moroccan in the language. And in everyday life since I've been here a long time, that, I've started to lose our customs a little bit, not too much. And it's a shame.
>
> *CK:* You feel more and more French?
>
> *J:* Yes, almost, but more, 85 percent.

Jawahir concurred: "Me, in the end, I feel more French. I've lost a lot of my Tunisian customs. A lot of things that I lost, that I don't do anymore, that I did in Tunisia. I did them when I arrived in France, but I'm losing them little by little. I didn't realize I was losing them, my customs, my religion too."
Some women felt French not because of a loss of customs but because they had received French nationality. Rachida is an example: "Now, no, I've changed like a French woman. Not Moroccan. It's changed a lot. . . . French identity card, me too, I change with the kids." Amina's adoption of a French identity, however, has more to do with her problems in Tunisia (a family unaware of her illegitimate daughter) than her own behaviors or legal status: "I feel French. Anyway, with my daughter, Tunisia is complicated."
Like respondents who realized that they had begun to feel personally insulted by comments about the French and defensive of them, others, like

Nedjma, came to an epiphany about their changes in identity as a result of a specific event:

> Me, I lived the World Cup when France [won]. It was marvelous. That, I, I had the best time. I'll tell you something, I said, "I am French." Because seeing people of all races shout, be together, feel the same emotions, it's fantastic. Finding everyone in Paris. . . . Tunisians, blacks, Africans, Pakistanis, Hindus, French people, Americans, I don't know what else, Asians, and everything. Everyone was in the street. Paris was theirs, France was theirs. We all greeted one another. It was the blond French saying hello to the black French. They were together. They belonged. They were French, in short.

Mbruka, on the other hand, believed she belonged almost from the start. She never pondered whether she felt more French or Algerian because she always felt confident in and comfortable with her choice to make her home in France: "I don't think I have an identity problem. I'm French with Algerian origins. . . . I'm happy here, I'm happy with this culture. I think I lead my life the way I would have liked to lead it, more in France than in Algeria." This was even more the case for Cherifa, who purposely left Morocco because she believed she had never fit in there: "More French. More French because already when I was in Morocco, I 'bothered' a little, in quotes. I was a bit marginal in relation to life, the community and everything. I acted really more like a French woman. . . . So for them, Morocco, I had to leave for France. Had I stayed in Morocco, I would have finished my life in prison."

BOTH

By a slight majority, more respondents said they identified with both countries instead of identifying primarily as Maghrebin. For women like Yusra, this was the result of going from being a member of the majority to being a member of the minority and a resulting stand taken on identity:

> I'm closer to French culture than Moroccan. . . . It's been 11 years that I've lived in France, and even before my life in France, I had affinities, if you like, with the French culture, because we mix. I've been bilingual since six or seven years old, so that marks you. You can't get rid of it, but, well, that said, I absolutely don't deny my Moroccanness. . . . When I was in Morocco,

I didn't feel like a Maghrebin. I didn't feel at all African, for example . . . this African conscience, I, it's when, it's when I crossed the border really that I acquired it.

Yusra's recognition of her Moroccan identity after her arrival in France supports recent research highlighting a recommitment to ethnic identities by racial minority immigrants, frequently termed segmented identificational assimilation (Portes and Zhou 1993; Rumbaut 1994). Warda (58-year-old Algerian) also talks about making an identity stand while at the same time being bicultural; she situates hers in its specific historical context[3]:

It depends on our age because we're born French. Already me, when I came for the first time, obviously I was still French because I came before the independence of Algeria. It never came into my head that I was abroad. . . . So we always felt French. But I'd say that even before independence, we also always felt Algerian. So they are two identities that complement one another, that aren't automatically opposed. Me, even when I was French, I said I was Algerian, at the time. I always said, "I'm Algerian." . . . I never said I was French when I was little. For me the French were the colonizers, and we were Algerian, even if we had French nationality. We started to understand that after the beginning of the war of Algeria. But, and afterwards we were still conscious that culturally France was part of us. It was inseparable. For our generation it was inseparable.

Karima adds, "We juggled the two cultures. We couldn't escape it." Besma recognizes that this continues to be the case today for urban North Africans educated in the French language:

I think we're both somehow. We're both somehow because we're steeped in both cultures. . . . I always lived there believing myself to be completely Tunisian, but what's inculcated through education, even through school, bilingual school from seven, eight years old, so we're brought to open up to Francophone literature, to read works, to read newspapers, to have access to French cinema and all, but it brings us, it causes us to question a lot of things. We don't perceive it, we don't notice it, but it's part of the baggage you take with you. But it's in really conflictual situations . . . you realize that you have different ways of seeing that aren't completely Tunisian . . . we've completely integrated them. We've completely, um, adopted them; they've taken hold in us.

Although some of the younger women labeled themselves Algerian, Moroccan, or Tunisian as a deliberate identity statement, several older, often very traditional women, did not claim to be Maghrebin but rather both. Some, like Fatima, felt partially French because of the amount of time they had spent in France: "I still keep Moroccan culture, but I live the French way. Because it's not today that I come to France. It's been, I came to France in the year '65. There was General de Gaulle; he was president of the Republic. May '65 I came to France." Fouzia, a religious woman who wears the headscarf, also identified with both countries: "The truth, um, both. When I'm in Morocco, I feel Moroccan. When I'm here, I feel, the truth is it's been a long time that I've been in France. I like France too." Several more women said they felt both North African and French because they were comfortable in both places. Hachmia states, "I always feel at ease in both. When I go on vacation, I'm Moroccan. I'm at ease. I know that I'm on vacation. That I'm there, that I was born there, and when I arrive here, it's true that it's a country that's welcomed us. I've been here 20 years, so I'm at ease, that I have my children, that I have my life." Bahia and Salima felt partially French because of nationality and simply because they live in France:

> B: I did the French card [nationality] with my husband. I did the application, that's it. I'm waiting, I don't know when. Half and half. A little here, a little there. More here than I would have been. Since the summer, me, almost seven years that I haven't gone. Seven years, yes. Already there is no one there. My mother is dead, and my father. All the family here, yes, that's why.
>
> CK: And you, do you feel more French or more Algerian?
>
> S: Yes, half and half. French and Algerian.
>
> B: Because she lives here.
>
> S: Yes, we live here.

Although many women identified with both, a few stated that they never really fit into either. Nour says she always felt a little bit like an "extraterrestrial" in both places: "I feel very close to Algerians, and at the same time I'm different . . . the same thing with the French." A few women said that growing up in the Maghreb they were labeled French derogatively by peers because of their attitudes. Unlike Cherifa, who felt relief living in France and adopted a French identity, the others realized how North African they really were after moving to France. Amel (26-year-old Algerian) recounts her high school years:

> I was confronted with a lot of, my teachers made comments because my mother was a town mayor. They said to me, not directly, but there are religious education classes in Algeria, we were in class, the teacher . . . in the middle of class [said], "Those that don't pray, stand up," so I didn't stand up, so I did the prayer and everything, and he said to me, "*Gaouria,*" *gaouria* is "the French one," because we lived like Occidentals, my mother, my father, so he called me "*Gaouria,* you say the prayers?" He said, "You know you can do it in French if you want?" He outright mocked me, and me, in the beginning it bothered me, because everyone looked at me funny, but after I didn't care. . . . I see myself as Algerian. I don't feel French. I feel like an Algerian living in France.

Deha explains how both in Algeria and now in France she continues to be the odd woman out:

> When I was in Algeria, they took me for a French woman, and when I got here, people took me for an Arab, an Algerian. So I don't know . . . do I feel more Algerian? I feel Algerian, for sure, when I approach people. I have a contact with people that is much more Algerian. But I feel French because I feel western. I feel free of all the taboos, the taboos from home. But that, you see, is exactly the same as in Algeria. In Algeria or in France, it's the same. In Algeria, people said to me, "Ah, but you're not the same. You're a *gaouria.*" And here people say to me, "Oh, it's normal, you're from over there."

Yet even some women who were originally at home in the Maghreb now find that regardless of how they feel about themselves, they are singled out as different when they return on vacation.

Meta-Perceptions

CONFLICTING PERCEPTIONS

Although people can choose how they wish to identify themselves, they cannot always control others' attempts to classify them. A second-generation white ethnic will rarely be labeled as different unless he or she chooses to purposely play up some aspect of ethnicity, whereas immigrants are often easily recognizable as such because of their names and accents. This is particularly true of racial minorities for whom ethnicity is an ascribed characteristic. As Waters (1990:18–19) notes, "Black Americans, for example, are highly socially constrained to identify as blacks, without other options available to them . . . [I]f one were part African and part German, one's self-identification as German would be highly suspect and probably not accepted if one 'looked' black according to prevailing social norms." There are costs, both material and psychological, to classification as a member of a low-status group. In this section, I explore how women immigrants react when meta-perceptions conflict with self-perceptions. As we shall see in the first part on how emigrants are perceived when they return to the Maghreb, even being evaluated as a member of a higher-status group can cause stress if it does not correspond to one's self-image.

IN NORTH AFRICA

Although earlier generations of emigrants, particularly from Algeria, faced a certain level of general disapproval at home for abandoning their country and their families for a life in France, this condemnation has waned over time (Sayad 2004).[4] Yet respondents today still complain about how they are viewed by people in North Africa. Some found that they no longer fit in or were labeled as French. Jawahir explains what people think of her when she returns: "They see me, because I live in Paris, that I'm superior to them. Because I don't have the same mentality anymore. I dress differently. And I don't have a lot of time for everyone. . . . They think we're superior to them because we live in Paris, because we earn French francs, because we dress well, not like them. For them, we are someone." Mimouna tries to fit in as much as possible when she visits Tunisia, including her style of dress, because otherwise, "they'll say, 'because you were in Paris.'" Zhora (51-year-old Algerian) hides the fact that she asked for French citizenship from friends in Algeria and worries that they will find out.[5] Yasmine has encountered similar perceptions, yet she resists others' definition of her: "There are some who say, 'You have a French character.' . . . Inside I feel Arab, me, inside I feel Arab. There are others who say no." Called an immigrant by neighbors in Algeria, Chafiqa also argues,

When I go there, they call me "the immigrant." So I say, "I'm not an immigrant, I'm like you!" I say it. I take advantage of both sides. I'm fine. I have my house here, I have my house there. I'm not unhappy. I say, "You, you are immigrants, you are immigrants in only one country." Me, I'm not an immigrant! Me, I'm a winner on both sides, me, I say, because I come here, it's my country, I go there, it's the same. Wherever I go, I have my house.

Five women talked specifically about the image North Africans have of emigrants. A couple, like Jawahir, mentioned that growing up, they too believed that everyone who went to France became rich:

Question of money, I find it's not at all how I imagined it. There people say, yes, money in France, all that, you live like a princess. You see? For example, my father-in-law, he said, "You'll go to my husband's store, you are there, you'll buzz like that, they'll bring you everything. You'll have workers, all that." Well, no. I have to work. . . . So I found you have to work to have money in France. It's not always easy in France. It's not how I imagined it at 16. Not at all the same.

Keltouma also realized how erroneous the image of immigrants to France is: "Sometimes the image that they gave us was false. So for us, I say for us because I think that it was everyone's opinion, most people, an immigrant was to have a nice car, very pretty clothes, money, he spends money, um, that was it. It's true they didn't realize the difficulty, the misery of Maghrebins here." Because immigrants are expected to bring presents and help others when they return for a visit, this image is often perpetuated, as Cherifa explains in detail:

After a week, I'm saturated . . . we take on everyone's problems . . . money problems. It's not that we don't want to, but we can't help everyone. And after, it's because we live in France, the cousin wants a housing certificate to come, et cetera, et cetera, et cetera. . . . We feel badly because we can't help everyone, neither financially, nor, we can't house everybody. We're not the Salvation Army. We can't pay everyone's plane tickets, um, because often it's that. Often when I bring my mother and father, I pay their tickets from A to Z, round trip and while here, and it ends up being cheaper than me going for a week. . . . It's always the same problem . . . because they have a girl who works in France, it's like this in all African countries, the fact that they have a relative who works in Germany or Holland, they think he earns millions, and that all they have to do is ask. They don't know that he kills himself at work from 8:00 in the morning until 8:00 in the evening to have enough to live decently. They think that all he has to do is bend over. . . . What's generated this reasoning error is that natives who work abroad . . . going to the country of origin for vacation take advantage of everything. Why? Because all year we saved. It's vacation; we give, we're generous, we buy big, um, when we go to the supermarket, it's enormous carts. So the native who lives in the country sees all that. He says, "It's all year like that. He doesn't suffer." They don't understand that it's false, a false idea of vacation.

Of course, close family members or those who come to visit soon learn the difference between the image and reality, as Yusra points out: "My mother, my father too, I tell them, 'If I live in an eight by eight meters apartment . . .' I tell them, they know it's very difficult. They know it's not easy." Yet others do not understand, and Yusra feels the need to set them straight: "We can't hold up that image of an immigrant that comes back with a car, you know? We can't. Me, I say we don't have the right to hold up that image. Immigrants, I think, well, it's a very difficult situation; it's a choice one has to assume. It's tough, so, um, others need to know that it's tough, and that if you come, you mustn't think that; you have to leave your illusions behind to come."[6]

Deha also noted that she encountered hostility from Algerians who had remained in Algeria, but for slightly different reasons. Instead of allowing herself to be hurt by their comments, she turns it around to reflect on them: "With good friends, when they start saying shit to me, I send them spinning. . . . It's clear that they don't understand why we've left. So it is also 'jealousy,' I put that in quotes, in parentheses. Jealousy because on the contrary it's people who only ask to evolve, to be freed elsewhere. So when I say jealousy, it's, 'Why are you leaving me when you, you [get to] go.' It's clear there's some of that too."

IN FRANCE

When North Africans in the Maghreb make negative comments about emigrants, some women view this as a consequence of the status they have gained by living in France. By attributing the hostility to jealousy, they can dismiss negative evaluations, thus using external attributions as a coping mechanism. In addition, trips to the Maghreb usually do not last more than a month, so the tensions engendered are short-lived. In France, however, disjunctures between immigrants' self-perceptions and the perceptions that French people have of them are a more constant source of stress. Maghrebin women in France are very aware of the fact that they are of lower status because they are immigrants, Arabs/Berbers, and Muslims. According to social identity theory, people need to feel positively about their individual and social identities (Tajfel 1981; Snow and Anderson 1987; Swann et al. 1987). Being a member of a low-status group poses problems for the maintenance of a positive identity. Whether Maghrebin immigrants are recognizable as such by French people, however, depends to a great extent on their physical appearance, especially skin color and hair type. Some women, therefore, are more able to hide their "stigma" than others (Goffman 1963). As predicted by social identity theory, those who can pass as members of more desirable ethnic groups often do (Hogg and Abrams 1988).

Although many respondents said that they looked Maghrebin and were identified by others as such, several stated that they could easily be confused with other Mediterranean groups or Latin Americans. Women mentioned being taken for Italian, Spanish, Portuguese, Mexican, Brazilian, South American, Polynesian, and Jewish. Rym is a case in point, and she realizes that this works to her advantage compared with those who are more obviously North African: "You see me, for example, people see me outside, it's not clear I'm Algerian. People take me for a Jew, or they take me for Portuguese, you see? I pass. I'm not typed. Yes, I am typed, me, I'm typed; it's clear that I'm not French. It's obvious. But, I don't know, [others] have more problems than us." All the participants recognized that those who could pass as white enjoyed advantages, as could a few of the respondents, like Telja, "Me, I'm lucky, all my children are light. They all pass for Europeans."

Women who have darker skin, on the other hand, like Fatima, not only cannot pass, but also are frequently mistaken for immigrants from other low-status groups. Fatima, for example, is often thought to be an immigrant from the Caribbean: "Sometimes they even think I'm from Guadeloupe or Martinique. And they, sometimes they make mistakes, because they are the same color as me, but I say, 'No, I'm not West Indian, nor am I Guadeloupian; I'm Moroccan.'" Yusra was thought to be Caribbean or sub-Saharan African, but Fouzia, who is also dark enough to be taken as black, does not encounter this perception because her North African headscarf automatically identifies her as a Muslim from the Maghreb.

Participants complained that people often do not take the time to get to know them as individuals but rather associate them with a group image, as foreigners and/or as Arabs. Many stated that because of their physical appearance, language difficulties, dress, or simply their Maghrebin names, escaping these perceptions is difficult. Tinhinan explains: "They see us as strangers. That's for sure. Even if we have French nationality, they still see us as strangers. Just saying we're of origin, or having a name, an Algerian name, for them we're foreigners, that's clear." Mimouna agrees: "Yes, I know they view me as a foreigner, not French. It's normal because even the language, I don't speak well, and the clothes, they show anyway. I don't wear many things from over there, but it shows anyway." Soraya noted that outside of cosmopolitan Paris, reactions are even more blatant. She was visiting a sister-in-law's family with her French-born husband of Moroccan origin and his mother. After arriving in town late at night, they rose in the morning and decided to go buy bread for breakfast: "I went out, me and my husband, his mother was with us, we saw, they were French, 'Oh la la! Arabs!' So I was surprised by that reaction. I mean it's okay, it passes in Paris, but it doesn't pass everywhere. In France we're still Arabs. But, well, it's true that it's a little village. They're not used to seeing, they're among themselves. . . . We always remain Arabs."

Negative evaluations lead immigrants, like members of other low-status groups, to engage in "identity work": "activities individuals engage in to create, present, and sustain personal identities that are congruent with and supportive of the self-concept." One strategy is "the verbal assertion of personal identity" — in other words, "identity talk" (Snow and Anderson 1987:1348). Mbruka, who views herself as French, argues back when others insist that she cannot be French: "Even when I take a trip, I have a French passport, et cetera. I remember a trip I took to Cyprus where the person asked me where I was from, and I said, 'From France; I'm French.' 'No, you're not French.' 'Yes, yes, I am French.' He said to me, 'No, you don't look French.' I said, 'Yes, I don't look French because I'm of Algerian descent.' And he said, 'Ah yes, I understand now.'" Isma, however, believes she can never become French because of her name and appearance: "I don't feel French because I don't have a French name. I can't change my name because I don't have the look, not completely. . . . People of foreign origin sometimes, especially peo-

ple from the Maghreb or the south even, I'd say, are so cataloged, that sometimes, well, we're all the same." Najet concurs and points out that the French
rarely distinguish between various nationalities or ethnicities. When asked
how French people view her, she replied, "No, not like a French woman.
They see right away if you're a foreigner or not. It shows. It shows right
away. . . . A French person, it's a Moroccan, um, an Arab, Arab. They don't
distinguish between Algeria, Tunisia, Morocco. Arab, Arab."

Whether they view Maghrebin immigrants as North African or simply as
Arab, the images French people associate with these terms are frequently
negative (Khellil 1991; Geisser 2003). Burke's (1991) identity-control model
focuses on the distress that people suffer when their identity processes are
interrupted by appraisals, comments, or behavior by others that do not
match their own conception of their identity and that they have trouble
changing. Several women felt this stress and talked about their efforts to
influence others' perceptions of them. When asked what the most difficult
thing is about being an immigrant in France, Besma responds,

> It's the gaze of others, which is devaluing, and assimilating you to something
> other than what you are, that sees in you right away a whole package
> of things that don't have anything to do with you. An Islam that is a sign
> of fundamentalism, um, as soon as you're an Arab they assimilate you to
> someone who's violent, because of the war in Algeria. There are a lot of
> other things that are bandied about it the mentality of your average Joe . . .
> when they look at you, they always judge you, and it's unbearable.

Nour explains that newer, more positive images of North Africans are slowly
beginning to appear: "In the movies . . . the Maghrebin was always the little
[drug] dealer, or the crook, or the little prostitute, or, and we're starting to
see Maghrebins who are successful in society. All of a sudden their image has
started to also become, you see, to appear through the media. It's new, but it's
extremely important."

Distancing oneself from negative associations is an important means of
identity work, yet supporting Burke's (1991) assertions about stress, Nour
realizes that the need to stand up to these negative images is very taxing for
individuals: "You ask questions about yourself. It's very complicated in relation to your personality, because you have to zap your strength, correspond
to an image. You have to give an image of yourself even if you're not neces-

sarily what you give. You reflect it, you see?" Sayad (2004:286) provides the context for the phenomenon that Nour is describing:

> A sort of hypercorrection is required of the immigrant, especially one of a lowly social condition. Being socially or even morally suspect, he [*sic*] must above all reassure everyone as to his morality. There has never before been so much talk of "republican values" in France. That is because it is a way of denouncing what the social and political morality of French society regards as the deviant behavior of Muslim immigrants: wearing veils to school, statutory discrimination against women, the political use of religion, which is referred to as fundamentalism, and so on. Being conscious of the suspicion that weighs upon him . . . it is up to the immigrant to allay it constantly, to foresee it and ward it off by repeatedly demonstrating his good faith and his good will. He finds himself caught up in social struggles despite himself, because they are of necessity struggles over identity.

Deha engages in exactly this type of "hypercorrection" about Muslim women. She relates how both she and her husband try to dispel the idea that all North African women are oppressed family servants, the type of woman called pejoratively a "Fatma":

> People are quickly surprised . . . for example, when my husband introduces his wife, they're surprised that it's an emancipated woman. . . . He, vis-à-vis other people, he needs to show that. And me too, I need to show that my husband is very emancipated. I need to break down the image they have of us. . . . I can't stand a woman like people describe the Fatma. . . . So I have to provoke to show that I have nothing to do with all that. I'm not a Fatma.

Isma is careful to note that various French people react differently to her, and that much of how others see her is related to their socioeconomic level:

> It depends on the milieu I'm in. It's clear that if I'm in my work environment [teaching school], people are more, I'd say a little more cultivated, so a little more knowledgeable about other countries. So they know, they understand when I say I'm from Algeria, that I'm Maghrebin. They situate it, they see where it is, they can see. On the other hand, a milieu where they've never been out of France or Europe, for them I'm Arab, it's clear. So I'm an Arab with all that has that is bad. It's an Arab seen as someone, first of all, someone of a different skin color, frizzy hair, um, who doesn't know how to talk,

doesn't know how to present himself, bad manners, and all the rest. All the negatives. Whereas, well, there's not just negatives, but well it's sure that for a lot of people I'm seen like that. It's sure that the people I worked with in the store, the women in the store, they saw me as the Arab.

Besma also points out that people have different reasons for trying to find out a person's origins: "Effectively the question of what origin you are . . . it depends on the milieu. It can be a question of pure curiosity, or a question where there's a need to differentiate. It depends on who asks it." Some respondents thus engage in another form of identity work: "selective association with other individuals and groups" who will be more supportive of the self-concept (Snow and Anderson 1987:1348). They strive to interact with acquaintances and colleagues who are better educated, interested in the outside world, and less likely to hold stereotypes.

The responses French people have to immigrants also depend to a great extent on both the class level of the particular immigrant and on her perceived attempts to fit into French society, as the following quotations illustrate. Bahia admits that she receives negative reactions because she wears a veil in public:

B: Sometimes I find people, for the headscarf, it's not good for me. I tell the truth.

CK: People don't like it?

B: Yes, they don't like. They go "hmfff," like that. Oh yes. That's why sometimes I don't talk. I'm ashamed, I don't talk.

CK: They look at you?

B: In the metro, sometimes I find a woman, "Ohhh!" Oh yes, it's like that. Sometimes men, more women . . . all the women, "Ohhh!" They look at me not good like that. I don't know why.

Nedjma, on the other hand, as a well-educated artist who speaks French fluently, can wear a traditional North African accessory to a party in Paris and receive nothing but compliments: "If you're, I don't know, dressed in your traditional manner, a little folkloric, but, above a certain level, et cetera, they'll accept it. But if you wear, I don't know, a Bedouin dress, me, if I want to do something original, I wear a Bedouin scarf, they'll think it's beautiful. If it's a real Bedouin in the street who is wearing it, no."[7]

French people in wealthy arrondissements and suburbs of Paris may feel differently about the occasional North African they meet than people in more ethnically mixed, poorer suburbs. Cherifa argues that how she is perceived depends on the neighborhood she is in, insisting that because her suburb has few Arabs, she has no problems: "Like a French person. I live in a neighborhood where I don't see any difference, where people that I talk to also respond automatically, we stop to talk sometimes. And I even have the impression that the fact that I'm a little, that I'm Moroccan, means there's also that search for exoticism and everything." For Cherifa and Nedjma, a touch of Maghrebin flair is appreciated by people of a certain level of social standing, as long as it is a minimal accessory, a mere touch of the exotic, and not an integral part of life. These examples illustrate how managing one's personal appearance to fit others' expectations is another form of identity work (Snow and Anderson 1987).

A few women noted that close friends and acquaintances view them as individuals, and some French people are shocked at how "western" they are. Labiba recalls, "People said to me, 'Oh, it's not possible that you, you come from Algeria; we had the impression that you've always lived here.'" To elicit these comments, however, respondents have to engage in extended interaction, as Jawahir explains: "In general, not personally, they see us as people from over there. Because I've talked with a lot of people. But me personally, personally, they see me as a French woman. All the French people who are, I'm surrounded by almost only French people, my bosses, my French friends, and everything, they see me as French. For them, they say to me, 'But you're like a French person, it's not possible! You're not Tunisian.' Other than my accent." Houriya has had the same experience:

> It depends. There are French people I work with, they consider me differently. They consider me as someone who is westernized. I have French friends too who consider me, who say to me, "You're really western; different from the others." Now for those who don't know me, um, well, of course if I say I'm Algerian, they consider me as Algerian. I mean if they don't know me, know my insides, my ideas, um, for them I'm Algerian, and when they get to know me, they have an idea about me. And if I go to the prefecture, I stay Algerian. It's clear.

Of course, an attribution of westernization occurs only for those who speak well, dress French, and frequently, as Keltouma point out, those who are well educated: "Well, listen, it depends. It depends. If I don't talk like a Moroccan, of course, because I'm typically Moroccan, as you can see, I don't have blue eyes or blonde hair, so Moroccan, but it's true that when I talk to them, it's different, it's already different by the language . . . by the education. I think I'm a little, it changes, I think they consider me like a French person of foreign origin."

Resistance and Redefinition

PROTECTING THE SELF

Clearly, self-presentation is important, but participants were divided on how much they could control others' reactions by the choices they made. A particularly telling example is the frequent belief that minority members can control perceptions of themselves, even to the point of preventing racism. Certain respondents, like Souad, believed that they were able to protect themselves from racism by always appearing clean and well dressed in public, having well-behaved children, and so on:

> I know there's a lot of racism. There's a lot of racism. They make us feel that, seeing the TV . . . but each person knows how to comport himself. Because me personally, or my family, or my children, we've never done anything to be reproached. "Because it's an Arab who did that," no. When you respect yourself, everyone respects you. Where I've lived I've always been neat, always honest, always. I know they won't talk about, I mean behind my back, "she's like this or that," or "her children aren't good," no. I haven't felt that. Always, um, always the opposite. I only hear compliments.

Rym generalizes: "If you're well-behaved, they're well-behaved with you. It stops there. The French are racist with people who aren't well-behaved." Labiba agrees: "As long as you don't do anything stupid, [people] don't notice you." Of course, being "well behaved" is not always enough to prevent negative evaluations. Despite Labiba's comment, she had been harassed repeatedly by local police officers at her store in a northern suburb with a large immigrant population.

When faced with racist comments, those who were able to stand up for themselves could take out some of the sting. Fatima relates an incident that occurred when she worked in food service at a Paris university cafeteria:

A French woman called me, she said to me, "Go home. You came to eat French people's bread. Go home. You foreigners aren't wanted here." Well, I said, "Me, there are French people who exist at home in my country, so I have a reason too." I said, "Me too, I work here. You want or you don't want, it's the same thing." I said "Go, go tell the president of the Republic to repatriate me home." We're truly, often here, often they've said to me, "Go home. You don't belong here. You come to steal the bread, rip away our bread, to eat our bread, and they'll put the French people out." It's caught me twice, but I don't pay attention because they're old. Me, I say, "I respect because you're as old as my mother, but if you were the same age as me, we'll box." I said, "Because you're the age of my mother, I don't box you." So me too, I speak meanly, um, the words that come into my head. And that's all. I feel relieved, and that's all.

Whether women who argued back believed they had convinced the offender or not, just being able to assert herself went a long way toward protecting her sense of self. This begs the question of whether the stress in Burke's (1991) identity-control model can be mitigated simply by *trying* to set misperceptions straight, even if the ultimate goal of correcting misperceptions is not achieved.

Women who were unable to defend themselves, either because they were in a situation with a large power differential (for example, with a police officer or an elected official) or most frequently because they lacked French-language skills, carried the pain of these interactions with them for much longer. Mimouna recalls a comment she received 20 years earlier before she had learned to speak French:

One time I went downstairs with my daughter . . . before I came and stayed like a tourist, and my daughter was young, not now, it happened before. Like a tourist, and my daughter was very small, her and her brother, children. They were running in the courtyard, and two women said, "Come talk to me." In French, they said, for example, "Don't let the children play in the courtyard; it's forbidden." Me, I didn't know because there we play in the grass . . . it's not the same here. Here, like this building, you can't play. I couldn't, I understood, but I couldn't explain or answer. She said to me, "Oh la la! The donkeys!" That really, really shocked me. . . . She said that, it's been a long time, it's been 20 years already. She said to me, "Oh la la!" It hurts. I remember it all the time. Because I can't answer. She said "the donkeys." But if she spoke like me, Arabic, like I speak, if I answered in Arabic, she can't answer me in Arabic; I can say the same thing to her, but in Arabic. It hurts inside. I cried. I said how, maybe it's someone, a racist, but she thinks I don't understand because when I didn't answer, she thinks I don't understand. Me, I understood. I understand, but I didn't speak. Because I'd been to school. . . . I understand the words, but I couldn't respond. But she said to her neighbor, "Oh, the donkey!" I cried. I couldn't answer.

Rachida had also been deeply affected by racist comments to which she was unable to respond. One incident in particular involved her daughter, Latifa, who helps her explain:

R: Sometimes we find really mean, people who are very hard, but I can't respond. Yes, it's true. Each time I'm sick about that. I fell sick; I got a fever. It's true. Each time someone, it's like that in stores especially.

L: Racist young people who always have their word to say. It's true that when you can't answer, it's hard on the person.

R: Yes, when I have errands to run or I go to the mayor's, it depends on the people you get. There are good people, explain well, and people who are really hard. I drop it, I can't respond, and I fell sick each time. . . . [One time a deputy] said, "Good thing [your daughter] is here. She can walk the streets." Really hard words. He says, "Keep your girl for the streets."

L: "I'm a regional deputy, I'm not a county deputy. I don't take care of helping people."

R: I can't do it, I left. Why did he say that word, it's not normal. I didn't look for a fight. . . . Me, I fell sick when he said that. It's true; I had a fever. . . . I kept it in my heart, and I cried.

Whereas Fatima, who fought back verbally, said that she did not let the incidents bother her, both Mimouna and Rachida were still so deeply troubled by situations in which they felt they had no control that they physically shook and cried when recounting the past events.

Women sought to change not only racist reactions, but also other attributions they felt were misperceptions. Several respondents had issues with the division of North Africans into Arabs and Berbers. Still others worked to distance themselves from the immigrant label altogether.

Ten women objected to distinctions between Arabs and Berbers. Many felt that the colonial history of the Maghreb needed to be set straight, and some explicitly criticized the French specifically for creating unnecessary divisions between various groups of people in the same country. Silverstein (2004) argues that the Arab-Berber split in North Africa is neither an inherent and unchanging social fact nor a complete creation by French colonists (see Chapter 1). Berber-speaking groups have historically existed as identifiable groups, and yet they have always mixed with other groups to varying extents depending on the time period, location, and circumstances. As Silverstein (2004) points out, however, the repression of Berber culture and language in Algeria and its renaissance in both Kabylia and in France has been played out along lines that perpetuate colonial divisions and that contribute to the lasting tension around these labels.

Historically, the indigenous residents of the Maghreb were various groups of Berbers who spoke different dialects. Labiba explains, "The Berbers were the first population that lived in North Africa, in Tunisia, Morocco, Libya, the Canary Islands, western Sahara, Mauritania, they were the first population. Then, within Berbers, you find ethnic groups." Deha enumerates a few of these groups: "There are different Berbers. Kabylia is the north [of Algeria], and a little west, and to the east there are others who don't have anything to do with Kabyles; it's the Chaouis, east-south [Algeria]. And then there are Touaregs who are Berber. After there are other different Berbers."

After Arab invaders conquered the region in the seventh century, the Berber tribes converted to Islam. Subsequent invasions by the Turks and then the French, with smaller groups of Spanish and Italian colonists, have also affected the racial composition of North Africa. People who come from rural Berber areas in Algeria and Morocco often continue to identify primarily with their villages. People unaware of origins outside of the metropolitan areas, and most Tunisians generally consider themselves to be Arab.

As many respondents, like Amel, pointed out, however, centuries of intermarriage make it hard for anyone to be sure of their origins: "I'm definitely Arab, but, um, I know that in our family there are a lot of Berbers. And I think all of Algeria is like that because, I believe that, well the Arabs, when they invaded Algeria, they came without wives, so I think they married Berbers and everything. So I think we're all, um, a little bit Berber." Isma is aware of her Berber origins but also realizes she is mixed:

I'm from the west; my parents are from the west, but Berbers from the west. I say Berber because the Berber is typed. My grandmother, my great-grandmother, my grandfather was someone typed, meaning he had a Berber type. Someone who lived, the Berber is someone who lived a little in tribes. A bit from the mountain. But, well, very touched by Arab because of the Arab colonization, and that gives the mix there, and it gives what we are, I think, it gives what we are. So, um, I don't think I belong to an origin, an origin, how should I put it, very clean. It's mixed. I'm sure it's mixed. In the west of Algeria there were also Spaniards, so there were lots of mixes. I know that somewhere there's a mix between Berbers, Arabs, colonizers, the French colonization, and I think I belong to all that.

Whereas remote Berber villagers resisted invaders and continued to live among themselves, Deha argues that origins are especially hard to pinpoint for Arabs:

The seaside was invaded all the time by everybody. The Spanish, the Turks, the French, always invaded by somebody. So all of the north hid in the mountains, and the Kabyles, that's how they lived where they were able to see the invaders coming. . . . Kabylia is like something that's closed, the language and other things. People from Oran speak Spanish; they're more open. Algiers is very, very cosmopolitan, and it's Berbers more than any-thing else. But because geographically we were so invaded, finally it doesn't mean anything. Arab doesn't mean anything to us. But from Tclemcen means something, because you come from, it's still family, you have to give names and everything otherwise. Algerian-Turkish families, that means something, but not everyone. Arab doesn't mean anything.

The majority of Algerian Berbers in France are Kabyles, and according to Nedjma, "It's funny, we say Kabyle, Berber, equals Berber, but we never talk about Chaouis or other Berbers in Algeria." Sensitivity about Arab/Berber distinctions in large part arises from French policies of treating Kabyles and Arabs differently during the colonization of Algeria. The French preferred the Kabyles because they viewed them as less attached to Islam and as better workers (Silverstein 2002b). They appreciated the Kabyle language and Kabyle culture more than that of Algerian Arabs. The French focused their conversion attempts in Kabylia, as Deha notes: "The French, when they entered certain villages, there were brothers, monks who came to the moun-tains, and they Christianized a lot of villages." The monks provided not only religious instruction, but also schools for children and other services. In the first part of the century, when Algerians could only become French citizens by giving up Muslim law, very few chose to, and the majority of these were Kabyle schoolteachers (Mansell 1961). When the French needed workers or soldiers from overseas, as in both world wars, they encouraged migration of Kabyle men. Kabyles continued to go to France because of these good relations, increasing demographic pressure as French colonists took over more and more land, and because, as Deha explains, of social networks: "There are more Kabyles in France because immigration, as you know, is done by families, between Sicilians, all that. It's the family. So Kabylia, there was nothing to eat, you went to work in France, [sent] money to the family."

A few respondents, including Rym, highlighted that the French preference for Kabyles was part of a strategy to better control Algeria: "Divide and conquer. When they colonized Algeria, it was the Kabyles are Kabyles, the Arabs are Arabs, when really we're all Algerians." Nedjma agrees:

> I've seen, taking a taxi and all that, he asks, "What country are you from?" If I said Tunisia, he says, "Me, I'm Kabyle." He doesn't say I'm Algerian. Why? Because here, they tried to say, to transmit, and to say, all the time repeating it, that an Algerian, to be Algerian is to be, not good, bad, aggressive — it's the negative image. Whereas the Kabyle is the educated one, the cultivated one, the refined one, et cetera. He's not going to say he's Algerian. . . . Divide and conquer . . . when you set Kabyles against the others, it's already partially won.

Deha worried about the persistence of this image, asking me if I thought a Kabyle was more modern than an Arab. More than 40 years after the Algerian war, when Berbers and Arabs fought each other in an effort to shape the newly independent country, the animosity between Kabyles and Arabs continues. Berbers have worked to prevent the term *Arab* from being used instead of the word *Algerian*, and Kabyles in particular have fought for the use of Tamazight in schools. Issues of Arabization have continued to spark riots and further Berber nationalism in Algeria, a movement heightened in the 1990s in response to Islamists' attempts to take over the government. When talking about the differences between Arabs and Berbers, Yusra says, "It's an ideology that I'd say is manipulated."

This is not to say that Kabyles and Arabs made no distinctions among themselves before the arrival of the French. A prohibition on marriage outside of Kabylia, and traditionally even outside of a particular village clan, has persisted for centuries. Tinhinan, who is Kabyle, talks about her feeling on intermarriage: "I was a little against it. I'd say it's the education; it was always forbidden to us. Even among us, they forbid us to marry, for example, I'd say personally for me, it was forbidden to marry an Arab. Since they always separated us into Arab/Kabyle in Algeria, it's not allowed to marry an Arab. Before, it was out of the question to marry an Arab." Likewise, Nassima, who is Arab, admits she gets upset when in France she is mistaken for a Kabyle.

Others, however, are against this regionalism. Those who argued against this divisiveness were usually not Kabyles, though. Lina is a case in point:

> Origins, me, you know, I don't like this thing, it's not that I don't like it, but, well, we have a problem with regionalism in Algeria with the Kabyles. Me, you see, I don't speak Kabyle, I'm not Kabyle, but I call myself Berber, because everyone, whether they like it or not, all of the Maghreb is Berber. The whole community, the whole population is Berber. But I don't call myself Kabyle because I don't speak Kabyle, my parents aren't from Kabylia, et cetera. I don't speak Kabyle other than a few words. But you see it's a problem of regionalism. . . . I don't like when they say to me, "Where are you from?" "I'm Kabyle." Say you're Algerian first. It's not a nationality. It's not a country, Kabylia; it's a region of Algeria, like you'd say Brittany, or the south of France, or Normandy. Don't tell me, before even giving where you're from, "Kabyle." No, stop. And that's a big problem for us; it's a shame. . . . I understand people who want Kabyle to be in school, that demand that, but there are so many other problems that that comes second; it's secondary, I mean. There are more difficult, more important things to work out in Algeria right now than the Kabyle problem. Maybe I say that because I'm not Kabyle.

Oumniya also argues that everyone is Algerian first and believes in unity: "Because we're all Algerian except for the language. All Algerian except the language. There they speak Kabyle; where I'm from, they speak Arabic. It's not the same language, but we're all Algerians. A difference of language."

Nevertheless, distinctions continue in France. Amel related how she contacted a Berber cultural association to sign up for Tamazight classes after work. Her first telephone conversation, when they assumed she was Kabyle, went well. When she went to the association for more information, she was asked if she was Kabyle, and when she said no, she was asked, "Your parents aren't Kabyle?" She was then told that she could not take the class because students had to know a little bit already, even though on the phone she had been told that the class was for beginners. Yasmine finds discrimination in hiring by Kabyles against Arabs in France:

> They think I'm Kabyle because I lie. The truth is a Kabyle is a little special here. They don't like to hire Arab girls. They like to work among them-selves, Kabyles work among themselves. And when I'm looking for work, they always ask, I lie. They say, "You're Kabyle?" My friend said, "[Say] you're Kabyle." I said, "No, I don't speak Kabyle, and everything, I'm afraid." Yes, a lot of people ask, "Are you Kabyle?" I said yes. I'm afraid here people are racist. I find the racism here, not there. It's here people say, "You're Kabyle? You're Arab?". . . . So now for them I'm Kabyle. I said Kabyle on purpose to find work. . . . I say, "Talk to me in French because I don't understand. My mother wasn't Kabyle."

In addition to being sensitive about the Berber/Arab label, many women also refused to categorize themselves as immigrants.

REJECTING THE IMMIGRANT LABEL

In her groundbreaking work on women of color and feminism, Mohanty (1991:35) "challenges the idea that simply being a woman, or being poor or black or Latino, is sufficient ground to assume a politicized oppositional identity." Here we see an example of women who are actively resisting the imposition of an identity by others around them, an identity that at first glance seems to leave no room for negotiation. In a volume on recent devel-opments in identity theory, McCall (2003) urges us to study disidentification in self-presentation as a form of reactive identity work. He asserts that deny-ing an identity resists others' altercasting, and in refusing received identities, people create a "Not-Me" that is equally important to the "Me" for consti-tuting identity. Nine participants specifically stated that they did not feel like an immigrant.[8] By distancing themselves from the identity of immigrant, participants were refusing to be a part of a low-status group. According to social identity theory, this is a common strategy when boundaries are permeable (Hogg and Abrams 1988). Yet how did women who had moved to France and intended to stay manage to not view themselves as immigrants?

Hachmia never felt like an immigrant because she has always felt comfortable in France:

> Some live differently, because they have a hard time, some have a hard time getting their claws out, as they say. There are some where it's true that it's difficult. There are some where it goes well. It depends. If you feel at ease, it goes well. If people feel they're bothered, they feel something that always makes a difference. Me, that wasn't my case. I'm fine. It went well. I never felt like an immigrant. I feel, I'm here, I'm like others. There are no differences.

The majority of other women who rejected the immigrant label for themselves did so because they felt that they came for a different purpose than others, and often that they were of higher socioeconomic class than those they viewed as immigrants. Like Yusra, they drew a line between those who immigrated for economic reasons and those who immigrated "in search of something, who aspired to something else, a different way of life." Malika differentiates herself from the former: "Me, I don't feel like, um, I'm not an immigrant. I don't feel like an immigrant worker. I don't know how to put it. I'm not an immigrant. I do after all have the papers of the country. I don't, I haven't had to feel or suffer racism." Thus not simply having French nationality, but also how others perceive her, affects Malika's ability to reject the immigrant label. Isma is also careful to point out who she is not: "It's clear that I'm not comparable to the wife of an immigrant who arrived in France because she lived in the country, her husband worked in a factory here, he went back, married her, brought her here. It's sure that she comes out of another context completely."

Like the other women (with the exception of Hachmia) who did not want to be seen as immigrants, Isma is well educated: "I don't speak the language at all like an immigrant because an immigrant has a very, very strong accent in French. They learned a new language. . . . It plays an important role for sure. But I, well, I want to note the difference because it's true that we're not perceived the same way." Warda also distinguishes herself from immigrants on the basis of class: "I'm not an immigrant person who came here to find work. The situation that I left there, the patrimony that I left there, is much better than my social situation here. On top of it, there we were high class, we were from a traditionally well-known family, respected, all that. So it was an advantage on the social level that I practically never found here." Like Isma and Warda, Keltouma also emphasizes how her reason for coming to France differentiates her from immigrants:

> I don't know if the others one day felt like an immigrant, but I've never felt like an immigrant, and if, I don't know, if someone asked me if I was an immigrant, I believe, without thinking, I'd say no. When I was a student, I said, "I'm not an immigrant; I'm here to study; I study." And it's crazy, I'm still not able to consider that I'm an immigrant. First because maybe I feel a bit more French, um, I don't know, I feel either Moroccan or French, but not like an immigrant.

Nedjma feels the same way: "I don't know, I wasn't forced to immigrate, to come look for work here or something like that. It's a choice I made. I came to do my studies; afterwards I stayed. It's a choice I made, without saying to myself, without asking myself questions. I'm here; I'm fine. But, um, I don't feel like an immigrant."

Time spent in France was not a factor for rejecting the immigrant label: Isma was the most recent arrival in the sample, having been in France only one year, and Warda, with 34 years in France, had been in the country the third longest. Although having French nationality and feeling like they belonged in France helped, the main determinants of not feeling like immigrants were reason for migration and socioeconomic status. These women felt that they controlled their lives and their choice of where to live more than immigrants did. This, combined with their educational level and their ability to speak French correctly, separates them from immigrants. Their experiences demonstrate how the self can affect, or at least stand up to, society. Ultimately, however, this apparent resistance may only serve to legitimize dominant stereotypes of immigrants. Because the women who reject the immigrant label have internalized a negative conception of what it means to be an immigrant, they are seeking to distance themselves from that label rather than working to rehabilitate it by changing its meaning to something more positive.[9]

Two respondents, Lina and Rym, took the definition of immigrant even further. For them, the real immigrants were not just people who had come as poor laborers, but also their children, called Beurs. Lina and Rym categorized as immigrants members of the second generation whom they described as poorly adjusted, even though they had been born and raised in France and had never migrated anywhere.[10] Their insistence on distancing themselves from these groups and redefining the term *immigrant* is a telling example of self-disidentification and is worth quoting at length:

R: We don't consider ourselves immigrants.

L: I don't consider myself an immigrant. Not at all. Not at all. In fact we have that problem, someone says to you, "Are you an immigrant?" I say, "No, I'm not an immigrant." I'm not an immigrant because I don't have the same mentality as them. When someone says to me, "What are you?" I say, "I'm Algerian," or even I say I have both nationalities, I'm Algerian and French, but I don't have the same mentality as them.

CK: So who are immigrants? When you say, "I don't have the same mentality as them," who is them?

L: It's people that are born and have lived here, and who have an identity problem. Me, I know where I'm from. I'm fine in both societies. I've integrated very well here, you see? Other than missing my family, the climate, et cetera, a few things like that, the stress, the anxiety, people who run, the coldness, et cetera. But otherwise I've integrated well. Whereas they, they have a problem. . . . But us, no, you see? We don't insult the French because on some level we are French. We recognize that France gave us our chance. . . . Somewhere we're grateful. Me, I'm grateful to France. I admit it. But them, no: "Yes, [the French] are bastards. There's no work. They take us out of the academic track by high school, and everything. They stick us in ghettos."

R: Their parents are poor workers, at Renault, they haven't gone to school . . . they had 10 kids to get 2,000 in public assistance; they don't care about their kids. It's not, you can't compare us to them. It's not the same mentality. And us, never, never will people say about us or our kids that we're immigrants. We don't feel like it, you see? Our kids won't be immigrants, they'll be French, you see?

L: French people, when they see you sometimes, "Where are you from?" "I'm Algerian." "Oh, you're different." Different from whom? Immigrants in ghettos, the suburbs and everything. . . . Somewhere, you see, when we're called immigrants, it's not an insult, but for us it's pejorative. Right away someone says to me, "You, you're a Beur." I say, "No, I'm not a Beur, because a Beur is —"

R: We correct them, you see, we rectify.

L: Because we don't have the same mentality. We haven't lived the same things, in regards to France, our way of seeing things, or in regards to Algeria, or in regards to religion, or in regards to customs, it has nothing to do with us.

R: And what pushed us to come here, it's not the same reasons . . . people who came 20 years ago, they came to work, earn money, build a house over there, fill a car, no. We came for a better life . . . we have blossomed.

L: Our first thing was our studies. Our studies, and after two, three years, go back to Algeria. In the meantime, the events [the current civil war in Algeria] happened. And that's when we decided to never go back.

ATTITUDES TOWARD THE SECOND GENERATION

Like Lina and Rym, a few other respondents expressed very negative reactions to children of North African origin born in France. In large part, this was because they felt that Beurs were giving Maghrebins a bad reputation. Vehement feelings about this group signal a need to draw a line between "them" and "us" for younger immigrant women who can easily be confused with children of Maghrebins born in France. Amel spoke at length about her opinion of members of the second generation:

I know that there are Beurs that are born here that are fine, very good, but, well, it's true that what we see is mostly the young people from the suburbs who can barely make it. I don't agree when they say, "Yeah, [the French] don't like us. We can't work." I'm sorry, I think that in France, I say to myself if I were born here, you have all the opportunities. I mean to study, you have the libraries, you have the choice, I mean you have a lot of things that can interest you here, you have museums, you can open up to a lot of things . . . when you hear them talk, I'm sorry, there is work, but what they don't want is to get up at 7:00 AM to work, to earn money. . . . I'm sorry, when you want to, you can make it here . . . they've decided to stay in their neighborhoods, their suburbs, stealing, [drug] trafficking. . . . That's how

I see things. I think a lot of people see it that way. . . . They should thank France or God to be born in this land.

Amel argued that members of the second generation who complained about life in France should be sent to Algeria for a little while to see how good they really had it:

> I'm waiting for one thing, I'm waiting for the government to say, I'm a little mean, but that Beurs who screw up, we kick them out, we send them back to their countries of origin. No, it's true, because I find that the fact that they're French, they take advantage some. They say to themselves, "We're Algerian." I think they tarnish the image of Algerians. But when you talk to them, they have nothing Algerian about them, honestly. . . . You'd say they don't know anything about Algeria. You speak Arabic to them, they barely understand two words. You talk to them about Algeria, Algeria is vacation where they change one franc for fourteen, and they spend luxurious vacations in hotels, and the others, Algerians who live there, "They're savages; they don't understand anything," or "They dress badly; they don't speak French." . . . So I'm waiting for the government to pass a law so Beurs who are here, when they do damage like they're doing in the suburbs, attacking people and everything, they send them for two months to Algeria. To prison there. They'll come back all square and all straight.

Rym and Lina agree:

> R: You send someone to Algeria for four or five years, the guy will come back, he'll say, "France is a paradise. I love France." You see? We know what Algeria is like, with all its problems, its scarcity, its injustices, all the corruption, we know what it is, we've lived there. Here is a country of rights. . . . Us, it's true we're grateful, really. The little we have, we're happy. But them, with all they have, they're lucky to be here. "Go suffer there. I'll send you for five years, you'll see what France is."

> L: Those who have had the experience, I know the son of a friend of my parents, he was sick of France, he saw everything in black: "They're bastards. They're racist. It's this, it's that." He went back, he decided to return for good. . . . He went back with the idea of staying permanently in Algiers because he was sick of France, disgusted. Well, he came back.

Respondents pointed out that members of the second generation do not know what the Maghreb is really like, and that they have expectations about North Africans that do not match reality. Many of these comments focus on some Beurs's holier-than-thou attitude despite frequently understanding little about Islam. Hayat shakes her head about girls who have adopted Islamic dress in France without understanding the basics of the religion: "The Muslim religion is not just pork, it's not just alcohol. Because there are a lot of good things in the religion. No, these people haven't studied the Quran, they don't know anything about Islam. Me, I say it like that. They take things that are well known from the religion, and that's it. The Muslim religion isn't that. You have to study the Quran to know."

Respondents like Amel, who married within the faith to a French man who had converted to Islam, became enraged when others told her how she should behave:

> These young people, I don't think they do Ramadan, or that they follow the religion. They're not interested. They're Muslim because their parents are Muslim. They smoke, they drink, they steal, and afterwards they come give me a lesson in morality because I married a French man — it kills me. It kills me. And they dare. They have the gall to come say to you, "Yes, but you're married to a French man; it's forbidden. You can't do that; it's not in the religion." And it's not even sure that they've read the Quran, and after they come give you a lesson in morality. I can't stand them.

Lina concurs, explaining why she does not have any Beur friends:

> They're intolerant. They're very intolerant. . . . We don't have any Algerian friends from here. We shock them. One time in a, I don't remember which job, there were French people of Algerian origin, born here, who lived here. It was Ramadan, I was hungry, I went out, I had a coffee, smoked a cigarette. The girl was shocked. She looks at me, she says, "Are you going crazy? You come from Algeria and you don't do Ramadan and you smoke?" I said yes, I said, "I can bring you dozens like that, masses and masses of people like us." She was shocked. She didn't talk to me anymore. . . . I said to her, "Why are you intolerant like that?". . . . My parents were tolerant, and we're tolerant. But people from here aren't tolerant. They're very, they have an obtuse mind-set. They're very closed. It's true that maybe I'm generalizing, but me, everyone I've met here is like that. We shock them.

The fact that we're from Algiers, we shock them by our way of thinking, by our way of living, by our way of talking, we shock them. We can't talk together.

Amel admits that she was surprised to finally meet a member of the second generation that she could get along with: "It was the first time I'd talked to a Beur, well, not the first time, but that I found a Beur nice. Because often Beurs here, I find, I don't find any affinity with them. We're too different."

Older women, including Souad, compared their children to younger second-generation members:

Young people today aren't like when my children were growing up. . . . Sometimes I talk to a neighbor, she says, "Oh la la! I remember when your kids were small, how they were respectful, how they were good. As soon as they saw me, 'Hello Ma'am,' they'd hold the elevator door for me, or if they saw me carrying groceries, they'd help." She said, "Now you don't find that." It's true, it's changed a lot. . . . Now children are adolescents and they fall right away into things that aren't good. . . . I see a little one now, how he talks, really it shocks me. It shocks me. At seven, eight years old barely, "You said something to me?" They start insulting you. It's changed a lot.

Mbruka worries that this type of behavior will affect perceptions of her young children: "When there's racism, they make an amalgam of everybody, and when you're a part of that community, if the image of the Beur is portrayed badly, your children will be part of it. . . . Because before knowing them, it's that image, and they don't always take the time to get to know you before having that image of you. So I hope they won't run into that type of problem."

Why Algerians Are Different

Respondents from all three countries faced the same problems in terms of being misidentified, encountering racism, having to fight to define themselves, and worrying about the image other immigrants and their children were giving them. Algerians, however, had some particular issues that were unique. Aside from the complicated history of colonization, Algerians were facing problems linked to the country's current civil war. Some participants, like Bahia, felt it necessary to defend the image of Algeria despite the bloodshed by pointing out that this type of situation is not unique to their country or to Muslims:

> There are problems in Algeria. . . . It's not Islam like that. It's not Islam. It's people who aren't nice, like drug users, bandits. It's like that in Algeria; it's not all the people. There are people, there are people like here — here, last week I heard three deaths, the boy was eight. There were three dead in the room. Who was it? [She is referring to the murder of a family of Dutch tourists in France.] Like us. There are a lot who are the same. It's like that the world, everywhere like that. Look at Kosovo, why? Before no problems, calm. They're sleeping in the street. A lot of things aren't good. Life is like that.

Houriya reminds French people about their own bloody revolution: "Sometimes when people see what's going on in Algeria, they say to me, 'Oh la la! It's barbarian where you come from.' I said, 'It's true that it's barbarian there, but be careful, a century ago, before France became a democracy, there was a big revolution. You cut heads too. You shouldn't forget that. There were people hung in the streets, you cut heads off with axes. It's the same.'" Nedjma, who is Tunisian, feels implicated because of the image given of Arab people. She agrees with Houriya:

> To have democracy in the United States or other western countries, or France when there was the revolution, to have democracy, when there are battles now in other European countries, um, wars, genocides, we're living it now with Kosovo . . . it's terrible . . . but I think it's a necessary step. . . . It's better to do things peacefully but . . . like everywhere else, I think Algeria has to make its own history, go through crises like all the other countries. . . . The media sometimes hurts it more than anything. I mean we show Algeria how we want to scare people, that's all, to say here is Islam, behind Islam are the Arabs, of course. . . . I'm against war, I'm against everything military, and I can't agree with what's going on in Algeria . . . it's a shame, but it had to live its own history. . . . The solution has to come from the inside and not from the outside.

The events in Algeria caused some women to emigrate to France. Five respondents fled imprisonment or the threat of bodily harm, and another two had come as students but stayed because of the situation in Algeria. "Contexts of exit," the conditions under which people leave their countries of origin, such as a carefully planned move or last-minute escape, affect immigrants' adaptation in the host country (Portes and Rumbaut 1996). Forced migration, in this case fleeing one's strife-torn country, has different consequences than more voluntary migration. Tinhinan explains why she left Algeria:

> I never wanted to leave Algeria; Algeria was my objective. I had all this ambition to do something in Algeria, to work, to serve my country, but given the situation, it wasn't possible, especially for a woman. It wasn't livable. . . . I saw that the situation wasn't evolving at all, so given that, I left, I made the decision to leave Algeria. It was involuntary . . . forced by the situation. It's never what I wished. . . . I decided to leave Algeria . . . we were out, we were stopped. The military stopped us in the middle of the road to search us. It was horrible. We were stopped several times, so, um, I couldn't stand that climate of terror.

Amel's situation was similar, but her mother was also personally threatened:

> In the beginning I didn't want to come. My mother wouldn't stop pushing me. . . . My mother was threatened because she was a mayor in the '80s . . . she dressed western, we lived, she was mayor of a little town, and well, everyone knew her and everything. I think she served two terms. And she didn't change her way of dressing; she smoked. It was viewed badly with the arrival of the FIS [Islamic Salvation Front]. It was badly seen, so we got indirect threats. Not like others, it was indirect, especially orally. And the death of Boudiaf, he was killed, I said to myself there's nothing left in this country, there's nothing left to do. So I was a little disappointed. . . . I was there when the FIS started threatening all girls who didn't wear the veil . . . they were going to be disfigured. I'd rather leave school than wear the veil. . . . I don't want to do it to make them happy; I do it because I want, not because I have to. . . . So, well, I didn't change my way of dressing, or my way of being. My mother didn't stop; she didn't put on the *hidjab*, and she still smokes.

Those who had children feared for their futures. Raised in a bilingual educational system in a country they hoped was making progress, women saw the schools become Arabicized and Algeria turn in on itself. Isma, whose mother-in-law was a French woman who had lived in Algeria all of her life, has a light-eyed, light-haired son. She became uneasy when she found herself insulted for marrying a Christian, even though her husband was Muslim, and felt her children were becoming at risk. On vacation, they came home one day to find their belongings inside the house burned and epithets written on the walls: "They burned my children's things. They set fire all over the inside of the house, and they wrote on the walls, on my mother-in-law's life, on my family, and for a month I didn't sleep at night because I felt they were coming to get us. So I said people who could burn children's things, they could burn my children too, and I couldn't see myself continuing there. I said to myself if they could do this it's because there's truly a lot of hate, a lot of intolerance." Yet the decision to leave was still a difficult one because they felt they were giving up on their country:

> My husband didn't agree. He didn't want to leave because his parents gave their whole lives to the country. His mother always fought, and she even accepted to hide, to not go out, to disguise herself to go out, but not to leave her country. So it hurt us to leave, but once she died, I really decided to leave. . . . I was born in a secular country, and then one day I saw people who spit on me because I didn't want to wear a headscarf or because I didn't want to go to the mosque on Fridays, or simply because I didn't think like them.

Deha, a journalist in Algeria, was imprisoned for her stories but also did not want to abandon Algeria:

> In the beginning, I didn't want to come. I came on vacation because my husband was on business. . . . I realized we were living a hell. In the beginning I didn't want to leave for the simple reason that I didn't want to leave and let the Muslim Brotherhood, all those people, get away with the country. . . . But finally, I had problems with the Algerian police. . . . The government did nothing for us, the military either, and the Muslim Brotherhood did everything against us. . . . When I think that I lived my youth very westernized, there was no problem. All of a sudden we were taking steps backward. So it's a little for that. . . . I realized on vacation, 15 days; we were invited to a picnic . . . people were laughing . . . and me, a lot of things didn't make me laugh because, I feel like I was only looking for what was blood. I felt like I was on another planet. There I understood I was losing it. . . . Anyway, I couldn't change much in Algeria. When I had

my problems with the police, I went before the court . . . no journalists stood up for me. . . . I said I'm not going to change things alone. But I still love Algeria, always . . . but it scared me. Finally, my trial, I hired a famous lawyer, human rights and all that. . . . There was only one journalist who took up what I had written. He was killed. You see?

Nour was also torn up about leaving, even after her husband was seriously wounded:

[My husband] was selected for a journalism internship in Europe, so we came for that, saying we probably wouldn't stay. But it was a chance to breathe. And I really think we needed it because we lived with the terrorism. . . . It was getting heavy. It was really starting to be heavy, and we said we have a life, we have a little girl. There's an expression from home that says, "God's land is vast"; we said "God's land is vast, let's go see elsewhere." . . . We couldn't do much more, it's not true that we couldn't do anything more for Algeria, that's false, but we weren't really capable anymore. We had no more motivation. . . . I believe we all feel a bit guilty for leaving Algiers. . . . When we lived there, daily life, it was normal. I mean we got used to it. It was eating us away inside little by little. . . . We got used to the shooting; we got used to the bombs. We adapted.

As a journalist, Nour's husband had received threats from Muslim fundamentalists. However, he was shot not by assassins but by soldiers who thought they had been fired upon when another soldier's gun went off. Because of the curfew, Nour could not go out to find her husband that evening. She spent all night thinking he had been killed, and she believed her fears confirmed when she found his car upside-down and riddled with bullets in the morning. Miraculously, he had only been hit once, and he recovered after undergoing abdominal surgery. Ten months after his accident, their daughter was born, and she became much of the reason for leaving:

It was the badly desired baby. . . . She symbolizes things. I don't want to put all that on her head, but finally she's the symbol of life. . . . I don't want to give her anything else but life. But she's conscious about what's going on in Algeria because she hears us talk. We haven't protected her from that either. She lived two years with the shooting; her childhood is colored by that. She was very, very afraid of firecrackers when, until just a year ago. She got used to it, but she lived that young. And I didn't want that to continue for her, you see?

The women who left Algeria not because they wanted to but because they felt they had no choice remained more attached to their home country and their identity as Algerians. Whereas other immigrants talked about missing the weather or the beauty or the warmth of their countries of origin, these Algerians spoke about their homeland in a different way. Nour is a prime example:

> When I decided to go back to Algeria in '88 [she had previously lived abroad at various times], I felt something I'd never felt before. It was the first time, a true love for the Algerian land. When there were demonstrations in '88, and everything changed there and everything, I really felt that love. It's land that if at the extreme you asked me to eat it, I would. It's interior. I love it. Really, I love it deeply. . . . Something interesting, even though we're binational, we still live in Algeria; we're residents in Algeria for the Algerians; we never matriculated at the consulate here, you see? And we don't want to do it. . . . We really have two lives in a sense. We don't want to let go of there either. . . . I'm looking for something that ideally would let me go back and forth. It's obvious we're very attached. That's our horror; that's our difficulty. We're very attached to the land, to the population, but we can't evolve in that system. It's like a betrayal that was done to us, you see? We don't have our place. . . . It's exile, and that exile, you feel it. . . . It's missing it; it's like a drug . . . we can hate certain aspects of our country, but we have a love of our country otherwise that is enormous. I don't know, I have American friends, they don't talk to me about their country with the love that I can give, I can describe talking about Algeria. Maybe it's because we're a young country. Maybe it's because we've had a particular history too, but, or because we've been so disappointed in our love, you see what I mean? We feel betrayed for sure.

Rym, who stayed in France after finishing her studies because of the problems in Algeria, feels the same way and describes how different Algerians handle the pain of seeing their country fall apart:

> We're sick for Algeria. It's an illness we'll never get over. . . . It stays the love of our lives. I think it's like a person who is ill and is condemned for life.

We're condemned to live with this regret. We would have liked to be able to return, live, live there again, but now it's clear that . . . two or three years ago I talked like that, unlike my husband. My husband is anti-Algerian, that doesn't mean he doesn't love Algeria . . . my husband and my father, I have two examples. They love that country so, so much, you see, they've carried that country in their hearts, now it's a rejection. They reject Algeria. My father has been here four years; my father did the Algerian war, he's a nationalist at heart and everything, he doesn't want to hear anything about Algeria, you see? . . . Lina and me, we've gotten over that. We said the events are what they are, we have to live with it. It doesn't prevent us from going back to Algeria, it doesn't prevent us from thinking about Algeria, it doesn't prevent us from talking about Algeria. But some people have rejected it, they've suffered so much; it hurts them so much to see the situation like it is. . . . You know we're in exile.

Mbruka's husband reacted the same way: "My husband went back only one time in seven years; he's never gone back since. He was so disappointed with the image that he found of Algeria that afterwards, for seven years he didn't go back, he'd kept the last beautiful image that we'd had, because we left when it was going very well, and he was so shocked to see how much things had gone downhill that he never wanted to return."

Conclusion

Mental health is better for all people, including immigrants, when they feel in control of their lives (Kim and Berry 1986; Portes and Rumabut 1996). Feeling like they did not make a choice to leave their country has left Algerians who fled deeply disturbed. Those who reject Algeria are in many ways attempting to reassert a feeling of control. Clearly the conditions of exit affect these identity processes. For all immigrants, in general, trying to control one's image is a serious endeavor with positive or negative consequences affecting identity. The context of reception is important in determining the success of these attempts. The following chapter examines other problems that immigrant women encounter in France, including a more in-depth look at racism.

FIVE

You Have to Be a Fighter

Coping with Problems in France

A number of factors affect the psychological well-being of immigrants. As we saw in the last chapter, "the conditions of exit" influence how people feel in their new homes, but "conditions of reception" also matter (Portes and Rumbaut 1996). Whether immigrants are made to feel welcome by immigration policies and the amount of social acceptance they receive influence their adaptation to the host nation. Early immigration researchers realized that poorly educated, lower-class immigrants suffered more negative mental health consequences (higher rates of distress, mental disorders, and hospital admissions) than those who came with more skills and status, and current work continues to support these findings (Srole et al. 1962; Portes and Rumbaut 1996). The greater the social adjustment, the more difficult the adaptation. Thus social distance matters more than geographic distance, with rural immigrants from nearby countries generally faring worse than their urban counterparts from further away (Srole et al. 1962). Overall, the mental health of immigrants is affected by their level of human capital and their socioeconomic status, the social support they receive, the material resources that they bring with them and/or that are provided in the host country, good health, problem-solving skills and a positive attitude, a bicultural orientation, and control over life events (Kim and Berry 1986; Portes and Rumbaut 1996). Immigrants who feel powerless and alienated are especially at risk for negative mental health outcomes (Portes and Rumbaut 1996).

Almost all immigrants experience downward mobility, at least temporarily, after migration. For some, difficulties earning enough and finding decent housing are persistent. Others face constant problems maintaining legal status for themselves or their family members in the country of residence. When asked what their main problem in France was, participants mentioned papers, housing, work, language difficulties, isolation, and racism. This chapter examines the challenges that North African women immigrants encounter, both structural and relational, and why they plague some women long after arrival while they are resolved for others.

Structural Problems

PAPERS AND POLITICS

One of the largest problems for immigrant women is obtaining and maintaining legal residence in France. Telja affirms this: "The hardest thing? It's the papers. To get papers is hard. Because there are a lot of people on the other side who want to come here, but who don't make it, yes, who don't have papers." Of the 45 participants, 18 had become French citizens, 19 had 10-year permanent resident cards (and 6 of these women were waiting to be naturalized), 2 had one-year resident cards, 2 had student visas, 3 had temporary papers, and one was vague about her legal status and had quite possibly illegally overstayed a visa. Some women, especially those who had a parent of French origin or who were born in Algeria before its independence, entered the country as citizens. Lina and Rym note that people hid their French nationality after the Algerian war of independence, but that in the past decade, they have been using these documents to come to France:

> R: There are people, like my grandfather, he was in the First World
>   War and the Second World War [for France]. My grandfather was
>   French. And before the '90s, before coming, it's clear that my father,

> it was out of the question to bring out all that. You see it was shameful. You couldn't talk about that, people were afraid.

> L: People didn't say that they had dual nationality. It was shameful. You couldn't say that. The country that colonized us, we couldn't be proud of having that nationality, so people hid it. We discovered a lot of people who after the events [in Algeria] brought out their dual nationality. Everybody who had a relative, a grandmother, a father, everything, they all took the old papers out and everything.

Other immigrant women typically entered France on student or tourist visas, or as part of the policy of family reunification begun in the 1970s. Family regroupment was designed to reunite working immigrant men in France with the wives and children they had left in North Africa. To qualify, however, men have to prove that they have lodgings large enough for the number of people they want to bring. Securing appropriate housing can take years and can either impede the establishment of the family in France or lead to a family living illegally in substandard conditions.[1] Women spoke in detail about the importance of having the right papers, how they received permanent resident cards and/or citizenship, and how difficult the situation is for those with a temporary or illegal status. As Fatima makes clear, "If you don't have papers, you don't exist in France. You have to have papers to exist, to last in France, but if you don't, it's like you are dead or something. . . . You're alive, but you're dead, standing up. You move around, but you don't exist."

As Joumana points out, immigrants who are in France illegally cannot leave to visit family members for fear of not being able to return: "Papers count a lot. People are afraid to go out, to get picked up by the police. It scares immigrants a lot, more and more. It's not a life. There are some I know here, it's been 10 years, 14 years, that their families are abroad and they can't go see them." Those, like Houriya, who finished school and who now has temporary papers, run into the same problem because of their ambiguous status: "I haven't gone for two years. Two years because I, I'm taking care of the problems with my papers; it's not very clear, so I don't take risks." Faroudja's (52-year-old Algerian) case is especially sad, and unfortunately not all that uncommon: "I didn't see him when my father died. I am here. Because I don't have papers to go there before. I'm sad. . . . I haven't seen my family in seven years. . . . I spent six years without papers. I received my papers, it's been a year, one-year residence card." Like Faroudja, others spent several years living in France illegally before finally obtaining papers. Nassima (50-year-old Algerian) spent over 20 years living with her daughters in Algeria before coming to France for medical treatment. Her husband asked her to stay, and she remained illegally for three years. She now has a one-year resident card. Djamila (39-year-old Algerian) spent five years in France illegally because her husband could not afford housing large enough for the family. After he finally obtained suitable living arrangements, they were able to get her a 10-year permanent resident card. Telja recounts her similar situation:

> For my papers, I had a lot of problems because I came in with a tourist
> visa. I stayed here a year and a half without papers. So I didn't go out much.
> I didn't take trains. And until, someone wrote a letter to my father-in-law
> congratulating him for 35 years of work. It was a deputy of France. And so
> my father-in-law said, "Me, the only thing I need, I need a residence card
> for my daughter-in-law who is here in France; she has no papers." And
> I had a one-bedroom, kitchen, at the time, but we applied, it was refused
> because we didn't have enough square meters. It was strict at the time.
> Nineteen-seventy, it was too much the law, very, very strict. They didn't
> accept because we were missing 10 square meters. And so thanks to this
> man, he contacted me, I was pregnant with my daughter, and he listened to
> me. He wrote a letter to the minister [of housing]. They agreed. I got from
> the prefecture . . . a card for three months, after the card for a year, and they
> made me the card for seven years, so that it lasted a minimum, the same
> time as my husband. And after they gave me the 10-year permanent resident
> card. . . . I hope I get the nationality . . . once we get those papers we're set.

Living in a perpetual state of not knowing whether one will be allowed to stay is not only stressful, but also prevents people from building their lives in the country for fear they will be forced to leave at any time. Amel lived this situation:

> From '95 to '97 I had a paper renewable every month that prevented me,
> I couldn't work with it, or go to school, so it was hell . . . I had my appoint-
> ment every two months, every month, but each time they said it might be
> the last time they renewed it. . . . It was a piece of paper with my name, date
> of birth, and everything, and a stamp, a time, appointment of the month; it
> wasn't even a temporary card, because a temporary card, had I been stopped
> there was no problem, but with this, if I was stopped, they could take me to
> the station, investigate. . . . One time I contacted an association about my
> papers, but they replied that they only took care of political refugees, and

in my case, well because we're Algerians they don't want to count us as political refugees because they're not fleeing the government, they're fleeing the terrorists, so it wasn't possible.

Mbruka and her husband almost returned to Algeria after finishing their studies because they could not renew their visas. An acquaintance knew the wife of a deputy and got them a meeting, and the deputy helped them get their papers. As she points out, however, her situation was fortuitous: "If he had respected the law, and if we had fallen on someone who was anti and everything, it wouldn't have gone through, not at all. And so a stroke of luck, a lot of luck, they accepted us and gave the authorization."

Other women had to find different solutions. As Hayat learned, "You just have to know how to get around things." Labiba agreed: "We try to get around [the laws]. We adapt to all the laws." The answer to Labiba's residence problems was a fake marriage, but this is a rare solution for North African women. A few, like Houriya, admitted that they prolonged studies they otherwise would not have continued in order to extend their student visas: "To stay in France, to be able to renew your student visa vis-à-vis the prefecture, you have to stay in school for a long time. So, well, I didn't really have a choice, and I did a dissertation." Amel's brother, on the other hand, truly did want to stay in school but was forced to leave anyway:

My brother was studying law. He was preparing his master's. He never had any problems with the cops or anything . . . he was serious. He went to his classes, he worked part time, he was a teacher at night, and his wife had to quit studying because she had a daughter, so she had to work. In part she was working so my brother could go to class. And one day they said to him, when he finished, after his master's he wanted to continue, plus his daughter was born here and was going to school, and they said no, it was impossible, that his masters was enough, that he had to leave.

So, well, it was that or stay illegally, so he decided to leave. . . . They said to him, "Yes, go back to Algeria to bring us another visa," even though he had a residence card. . . . Me I find it inadmissible, people who are here, I'll say a bad word, who fuck things up, they don't do anything to them. They let them do all that because they are French or have a 10-year residence card. Those that come for their studies, who are serious, they mess with them.

Leila admitted that the encounters with officials could be maddening, but argued that immigrants who are well informed of the laws and their rights, usually those who are well educated, stand a better chance of getting what they need: "It depends who they deal with. You know police officers, or people who work for the administration, they don't act the same with someone who, well, they can tell who knows his rights, and someone who doesn't know anything. Their approach changes. It's not the same." Nevertheless, even for prepared immigrants, the process can take a long time. Deha was able to get French citizenship because her mother came from a Spanish-Algerian Jewish family, but the problems for her husband and son took two years to resolve even though she hired a lawyer to help her:

> I didn't have all the paperwork, so they considered my son at the social security office as the son of my husband who is Algerian. . . . At the prefecture, when my husband and I went, we did things like they said; they screwed with us, like the husband can't work for six months, it went like that, he's not allowed to work, he can't leave the territory. So one day, the first time we said that must be the way it goes to do the application and everything. The second time they did that to us, we said okay, but the third time we didn't let ourselves be had. They took out the paper, I had a breakdown, I asked for the supervisor, I said, "How can you do this?" I said, "I'm not a second-class citizen," because it's true that my name is Deha and that I'm French by accident, because my mother was Spanish, but legally, if you play it legally, so I threw a fit, and I demanded my husband's papers. But I got a lawyer. It took two years.

The quest for papers is thus not only stressful but generally time-consuming, as Tinhinan found: "I spend most of my time dealing with the problems of my current situation in France. I look for work, I go to the unemployment office, it's what I do in general, I straighten out my problems . . . especially administrative offices to get information on a particular document, what you have to do, how to proceed to get, to know a little the laws that concern us in France. That's what I spend the most time doing." Many respondents complained that although they sometimes encountered helpful people at the prefecture, they often had to deal with racists who treated people badly. Yusra acknowledges that the situation is difficult for both the immigrants and the functionaries:

> Every year as a student, I have a student card that every year I have to renew, and since each year it falls in September, it's bursting, there's a lot of people, and you wait a whole day, and that's the minimum, otherwise it's

a week. In '97, I went for a week from 7:00 AM until 6:00 PM. . . . All the functionaries, you can't call them all racist, or people who don't like Arabs. . . . When I work I need a work permit, sometimes people arrive at the desk who don't know how to speak French, who can't even communicate, who are tourists here, who ask for a work permit, and it's not possible. And when you have 40 people who ask you the same thing in one day, I think it's something to tear your hair out about. So I understand them. There are some who are really bad, who have bad faith, very hard, when you say hello they don't answer, or who think of you right away as the immigrant who came to eat the French people's bread, but honestly, the majority are okay. . . . Everybody is stuck in a small room, you're number 300, you're the 300th person, and they have to say the same thing to people, to check, I don't think it's possible for functionaries like that to stay nice. There's a moment and they explode; it falls on you — well, you're not lucky, but that's the way it goes.

Bahia, among others, thought that the situation had worsened in France: "Before it's not like now. It's easy before the papers; '86, '85, '86, it's a little easy, under Mitterand." This also appeared to be the case for getting visas. Four women complained that they were unable to get tourist visas for their family members. Amel had not seen her mother in two years and was still trying to get her a visa. Mbruka wanted her mother to come for her child's birth, but her request was refused: "It's gotten very difficult, I can't get visas, unfair things in life. . . . Two years ago I tried to get a visa for my mom. Yes, it's not fair, given that there's no real danger. I tried the last time I gave birth. I would have liked my mother to be there because she came for the first one. It was easier to get visas. Because it's always nice to have a member of the family, especially since we don't have any family here, just friends." Of course the danger the French state sees is that immigrants will come in with tourist visas and not leave, as Soraya (25-year-old Moroccan) points out: "There's always a problem of visas. Especially my mother because she's still young; she's not 50 yet, and to get a visa you have to be 50 or older. Yes, I tried to get a visa for my mother, and they refused." The French worry especially about Algerians because they are concerned that people will try to flee the situation there or that terrorists themselves might come into France. Oumniya (50-year-old Algerian) believes this is why her son has been denied tourist visas: "He comes sometimes on vacation, before visas, but now I don't believe any visas. They will close the visas. Before visas, but now with the FIS

[Islamic Salvation Front] and all that, it's been three, four years that he hasn't come. I don't think they give visas."

For those who have secured a 10-year permanent resident card, the question becomes whether or not to ask for French nationality. The majority of women who currently have permanent resident cards have not taken steps toward naturalization. As Fouzia puts it: "What's the point? It's not necessary. . . . What does it change anyway? For us, it's too late. If we do it at the beginning, it's good, but we didn't do it. For the children, it's normal, they're born here, they're used to it, they're born here, but us, French citizenship, we're born in the Sahara. What does it change? We didn't think in the beginning. It's too late." Chafiqa agrees:

> There are a lot of papers to do; they ask for too much. I tried, but they ask for too much, I dropped it. You have to get your brother's papers, parents, so that's why I dropped it. I have the forms, with my husband, because we were both, we were colonized by the French; they were there when we were born. We can ask for our citizenship if I want to be French, but I don't see how it's going to help me much. It won't help me much. It's just a paper. I said to myself, it's not worth it. I'm happy like this; why change? I have my residence card; my [Algerian] passport, my residence card is enough. My papers are in order; I go where I want. The passport is for home, but when you have the residence card, the passport is just a thing to get stamped, that's all. The residence card is the most important of all.

Many women disagreed, however. They noted that French citizenship helps them be treated better and affords a higher degree of security. Warda explains, "Not having French nationality, it really reduces your advantages, even if they exist on paper, they don't give them to you because you don't vote, because you're not interesting, you don't have a voice." Khadija (44-year-old Moroccan) explains that this is why she became naturalized: "Now I have French nationality, since '91. Before I had the residence card, and now I have French nationality because sometimes I want to vote. I know that we foreigners don't have the right to vote, and I want to vote. Um, for administrative things, sometimes when you don't have the nationality, you can't do it. And like this I can say here, I have the nationality." Joumana became a citizen to make finding work easier: "I asked them to do nursing-aides' training. Afterwards they said to me, 'If you were of French nationality you'd keep working with us, but if you're Moroccan, you're not allowed.' So I had to go to the consulate to ask for the papers, to be hired permanently. Otherwise they take advantage of a person doing an internship." Nedjma stated that as a citizen she was protected: "By having my French nationality, I've been defended compared to others who don't have it. I was defended as a Tunisian French citizen, if someone, a Tunisian, for example, I had a problem with Tunisians, it's rare, but it happens, but it was them against me, and then I was defended as a French citizen against the others who were Tunisian."

Asked when she decided to become a citizen, Nedjma's answer leads in another direction: concern for her son: "I did it at a certain moment maybe, I don't know, for my son. I thought that maybe for the child it would be a better security for him to have the nationality given that he didn't have it; he was born in Tunisia." Other women, including Oumniya, also wanted citizenship to ensure stability for their children: "I'm going to ask for nationality because I want to have Algeria/French, dual. Me, I haven't started [the paperwork]; my children, yes. But I was thinking, I asked my husband. My husband, he wants me to stay with the residence card. Me, I like both. That way, if ever they come for my children, there's no problem." Others, like Rachida, believed that citizenship would ensure that they could remain with their French children even if the political climate in France changed for the worse: "I'm afraid of problems. That yes, that they say one day, 'Go home.' That no, I'm afraid, I tell my children. I'd regret leaving my children." Because children were often the priority, many women, like Fatima, took years before they asked for citizenship for themselves:

> I submitted my papers, because my children, they're all French, from the biggest to the smallest, there's only me that's still not. I submitted my application. We'll maybe get it this year, because they said, "You have to wait a year and five months." . . . It's been a long time. Even the woman when I submitted my application, she said, "It's now that you come to get it? All this time, you didn't have a metro ticket to come submit it?" I said, "Well, with the children, I took care of the children, work." She said, "But still, you have to take care of yourself a little bit." I said, "Yes, but the essential thing is the children first."

LODGING AND WORK

One of the common stereotypes about immigrants is that they live in crowded housing in poor neighborhoods; unfortunately, this stereotype is too often based in truth, as Joumana, who herself lives in one of the most dangerous sections of Paris, points out: "Often people, immigrants I'm talking about, there are some who live four or five in a room." The government provides some public housing, but the wait is very long. Zhora is a case in point:

> Me, I have seven people who live in a two-bedroom. And the children are fragile. And I have to find something, housing, for example, that has some ventilation, a little bit. For us, we asked, but we're still waiting. It's been 20 years that we've been waiting. We have a small apartment, but it's not enough because I have children who are older; there are small ones. The others can stay up until midnight. It's complicated. We have to fight. Where do we put our things; there are the children, the clothing. It's true it's important. . . . There's a backlog in housing, I don't know. It's long to wait 10 years. The children need to find some room, where do they sleep, all the room, read, if they don't have their things. That too is important. If we don't have good health, a good attitude. Something is always missing. If we want to work, we don't find a chair or room, where do we put our piece of paper, or pieces of paper, the notebooks, things.

Faroudja is in a similar situation: "I have a problem because I'm badly housed, I have a little room. . . . I asked for housing. My husband doesn't work; he's unemployed now, on sick leave. If you don't have, he doesn't receive a lot, to have good housing. It's a shame. We wait. It's difficult. We wait for the answer to the applications, but we wait."

Young, single women are not eligible for government housing aid, and when they live on small jobs, adequate housing is very difficult to find. Over 25 percent of foreigners in France live in lodgings with no interior toilet, 25 percent have neither a bath nor a shower, and 19 percent do not have hot water (Taïeb 1998). Hayat found herself in this situation:

> It's true it's very hard, for example, to have housing. I'll give you a little example. At one point I was babysitting, but I did that under the table. So at the same time I was a student. I was looking for a studio, to find a studio, you have to have pay stubs. There weren't any. You have to, to prove, even 20 hours, doing 20 hours a week, meaning making half of minimum wage, with half of minimum wage it's very, very hard to find a studio, because you have to earn three times the rent. So it's always very hard to find a small room for $200. And even so, 15 square meters, having the minimum, hot

water for showering, a kitchenette, that's all. And me, at one particular time, I had a room that I paid $200 because I was paying for my studies on the side. I had a room for $200, I didn't even have hot water. . . . I showered at the place where I babysat.

Even women who make a larger salary struggle, and to find a good deal, as Leila did, people often go through friends: "To have a studio, you have to have a salary bulletin that is four times the rent. So how are you going to earn four times the rent if, even an office worker, she'll earn $1,200 and that's not four times the rent. Never. That means you have to go through friends, acquaintances, things like that. Otherwise you can't make it. It's very, very hard, housing in France and work."

Difficulty finding suitable work, or work at all, was one of the most common complaints among the participants, including Labiba: "Not having work and not having one's papers, those two things, the worst things that can exist." The rise in unemployment in the 1980s and 1990s has severely affected all French people, and immigrants are the worst hit (Gourévitch 1998). When asked what the hardest thing being an immigrant in France is, Yusra responds, "Finding work. It's true, it's difficult. Finding work, trying to live decently . . . because one law, well, it changes your whole life. It changes everything. Now, for work for foreign students and everything, I find it ridiculous because I never find work, so it prevents me from finding work. So I have to find solutions, small jobs, you see. But, well, you do it because I don't say no to work. I work, anything, secretary, operator, everything, everything. I say, well, that too I've learned with time to detach myself from the work, from what I do. I do it for what it brings in." Houriya highlights one of the difficulties for immigrants without resident cards who are looking for employment: "It's a vicious cycle because to work, they ask for you to be French, and for the prefecture to give me a work permit, they ask for a contract. The company has to sign a paper. And the company refuses to sign because it wants the authorization already. The prefecture wants the company to sign, and the company wants the prefecture to give the authorization, so it goes in circles. It's done on purpose. It's like that."

Many women, like Fatima, combine two jobs in order to make ends meet: "In the morning I serve the meal at a nursery school . . . and the afternoon I do cleaning. I start work at 11:00, I leave at 2:00, and I start at 4:00 until 8:00 in the evening. It's true when I think about it, it's difficult for me." Joumana compares the situation of immigrants in France to that of Moroccans and relates how she had to begin helping her family out as a teenager, despite suffering from asthma and other health problems:

> Here, work, you have to fight. [We] earn more than them, but they're better off than us because of the climate, they're among themselves, even though they're lacking money, but they make it anyway, and life is cheaper too. Here people don't live well, all the foreigners, yes. . . . If, for example, the papa works for $800, you have to, we see the papa who suffers, and the mama doesn't work because she takes care of the house, so obliged to, it was my case, I had to do things, and do any sort of work, and to help. . . . Little by little I looked for work, babysitting. I have to work like a slave. I was very badly paid, too. Oh yes. The dust and eight hours standing up in a big store. I can or can't, nothing doing, I don't have a choice. I've worked a little at everything, for example, working in people's homes, babysitting, taking care of a handicapped old person, doing the shopping, making the meals. . . . I'm still without work, work that I like. The work I don't like is there, it's not lacking, like housecleaning, like babysitting, it's there, but you have to have, you have to be strong. . . . Nursing aides. . . . Difficult work, it's not easy. You have to be strong. It's unpleasant work. I like hostessing, computers, receptionist. I like sales too.

The easiest work to find, private housecleaning or child care, is often the most exploitative because it is unregulated. Some women did this type of work when they first arrived, and others continued to do it because they were lacking work permits or other skills. Amel talks about her first job: "This man I worked for, on a certain level he helped me. I agree. I've always been grateful to him; he housed me for a while, he helped me. But, I mean, making me work like that: 'Me, I help you, but you, you get exploited.' I didn't agree. Especially because he said he was a friend, a friend of my father's." Labiba was hired to work illegally in a restaurant but soon learned the consequences: "Someone told me they were looking for a waitress, and I lived there. After a month, the person exploited me, from 6:00 in the morning until 1:00 in the morning without paying me. The day he said he'd pay me, I go in, there's no pay, nothing." Yasmine related a series of underpaid jobs:

> I did cleaning; it was my first job. She said 30 francs [$6]. I preferred housecleaning to other things. And I worked once, the second day, the third day

I saw that an hour here is paid 40 francs [$8]. She said no. I said too bad, I won't work. . . . I worked making cakes. . . . I like cooking cakes like that. I worked for two months, and after . . . the woman called me, they wanted my recipes. I said, "No, they're my recipes." I didn't like to work there, and anyway she only paid me 75 francs [$15] a day, that's nothing. . . . I made a dress, I was paid 375 francs [$75]; it's nothing. All the hours for [$75]. I said forget it, I'm not staying. I can't stay, make two like that. I said, "Oh well, it's better than nothing."

Even women who were willing to take the worst jobs were sometimes excluded because of a lack of language skills or for other reasons, as Assia found out: "Especially looking for work, they always need someone who can read and write. I asked to work in a school cafeteria, and they said you have to know how to read and write, to work in the cafeteria, to find work." Djamila took the only kind of work she could find: "I clean for a lady. Because when you can't read and write, what can you do?" Zhora noted that the process of looking for work in and of itself is difficult for illiterate women: "Because we don't understand the language, we don't understand, we don't know how to read or write. It's a little complicated for us. And then we're stuck. We don't manage to speak French well in life. I look for work, you don't know the addresses, you don't know how to speak well, you don't know how to get around, take the metro, find work far away. We have children. It's very complicated for us foreigners."

Women's responsibility for child care affects their employment options, as Zhora experienced: "I've been looking for work for a long time. I haven't found because I find a job that starts at 5:00 in the morning, me I have children at home." As a single mother, Amina found she had no choice but to work. Each day she worries about her daughter because she does not have enough money to hire someone to care for her:

I have a big problem, it's the little one. To have her watched, there's no one to look after her, and I can't get a spot in child care. I'm all alone with my daughter. The father dumped me. I've found myself with the little one, so I don't know what to do. Every night I'm thinking where am I going to put my daughter because I work. I take care of children for her. Feeding a baby costs a lot. . . . Tomorrow, for example, I have no one to watch my daughter. I start work at 9:00 in the morning and now I don't know who is going to look after my daughter.

Jawahir's solution to the child care dilemma has been to leave her youngest child with her parents in Tunisia while her older two live with her in France.

In response to the economic situation, French companies have shifted to hiring people on short-term contracts with fewer benefits, and many women, including well-educated women like Leila, thus move from job to job: "I haven't succeeded in having a regular job all the time. I've worked as a temp, I had short-term contracts, I did things like that. It's not a regular job. . . . Work now is very difficult in France. You can surely see that yourself because the short-term contracts, six months, three months, people who live on aid, homeless people in the street." Joumana also faced this problem:

> I worked six months in a social center as a receptionist. Luckily it's not hard work, luckily for me. They took advantage to the maximum for six months, and after they said, "Good night. A Dieu." They don't hire you. And normally they should hire me because they took me as an intern. They should hire me, or part-time work, better than nothing. I said, I'll work hard and after I'll change to full time. No way. They take advantage as much as possible and then they say, "A Dieu. Good-bye."

In part because of these employment practices, and also because of other factors, including problems with job equivalences and sometimes racism, the majority of highly qualified, university-educated women were unable to begin or continue their careers in France. Whereas students and illiterate women were often grateful for low-paying domestic work, those with diplomas and skills were disillusioned with employment opportunities in France. Mbruka noted that her university studies did not lead to the type of career she had hoped for in France, "so I'm rather frustrated with the professional life." Houriya, who had completed a doctorate in the natural sciences in France, had been looking for work for over six months: "I have to fight on the professional level. I have to find a way to get going professionally." Keltouma, who did a doctorate in the social sciences in France, has become depressed over her inability to find a job that matches her credentials and is considering going back to Morocco: "Unfortunately, finding work is a bit hard. It's really hard, actually. . . . I'm not sure I'm looking in the right way because it doesn't seem normal that after three years I haven't found anything. . . . It's a stressful life here, especially professionally speaking. When you look for work and after a certain time, which is really a long time, you realize it's a vicious circle really, and you don't have a way out. It's true it's stressful. And very demoralizing."

Those women who had or were on their way to successful careers in Algeria before having to leave also suffered. Deha, who was a radio journalist, realized she would not be able to continue her career in France: "Here there's not just radio. Because I don't know the French codes, I don't know how to function for a French public." Nour, on the other hand, is still fighting to make it in the television and film business in France:

> I'm in an infernal circle, if you don't have contacts, you don't find jobs. . . . Especially because I'm atypical, which means that if the person has 20 CVs, she's not necessarily going to stop on mine, because I'm Algerian and I had a lot of professional experience in Algiers, so that scares them a little. There's racism in regards to that. . . . So it's a problem finding work here. . . . And I seriously ask myself the question, I know I have abilities, I'm good at certain things. . . . I speak several languages . . . but I have a lot of difficulty because I don't fit in their system. I don't fit their norms. I know the last internship I had, I got along with everyone. They didn't hire me. After I left, they hired someone else. It really posed me problems, you know. I thought a lot about it, and it's not because I'm incompetent. . . . You have to correspond to their norms . . . talk a certain way, you have to fit that. Because it's their codes. They thought I was nice. I could have evolved following their codes. . . . I could have evolved professionally and everything. . . . But, so finally, in French society the only place where I'm at ease is the musical artistic milieu, or in certain production houses that are really healthy, very cool, very independent, you see? And you have to know people to get in. So there. It's really complicated.

Both Lina and Rym had been trained as veterinarians in Algeria and had come to France to do specializations in veterinary medicine. Because their diplomas do not correspond exactly to French medical degrees, and because they do not have contacts in French veterinary medicine, they have been unable to find work that matches their level of education. Rym chose to be a veterinarian haphazardly, and although she wants a better job than her current employment, selling tickets to a park amusement ride, any decently paid white-collar work would be fine with her. Lina, on the other hand, is still coming to grips with losing her dream of practicing veterinary medicine:

The failure here in Paris for me is the fact that I haven't been able to work in my field. You see a lot of my friends have gotten over that. And me, no. I haven't gotten over that because I love the studies that I did; I did it for love, I love animals, and I don't see myself in another vocation. Everyone says to me, "Lina, change, you have to convert yourself into something else," and I can't do it, you see?. . . . I spent several years unemployed. . . . I worked because I had to work, I had to pay rent. Working in the school, I stayed two years. I liked that because of the social aspect . . . but at the same time everything that's office work, me, it's not my thing. Me, it's being on the terrain or in the lab or, you see, the pharmacy or something . . . being in my field. . . . I took my equivalencies once; I failed it, but us it's a closed milieu. The veterinary milieu is a hermetic milieu. I applied, I was listed for five years at the unemployment office. I applied to be a veterinary assistant; I wasn't asking to be at my status. I was asking to make $1,000 a month, be in an office, get back on track, you see? Get with it again because you lose it when you don't practice. It was a closed milieu. You need someone's help to get in; you have to have it.

A couple women have been successful doing what they wanted in France. Isma was a teacher in Algeria. When she arrived in France she worked in a store, but within a year, she had found employment as a teacher. Malika, who did advanced studies in France, changed fields and still managed to become an executive producer for a large production house. Malika had not only gotten training in France but, more importantly, had lived in the country for 16 years and thus started her career before the economic crisis worsened. Yet even so, she mentioned that being Tunisian had sometimes been a disadvantage and that some men objected to working for a Maghrebin woman.[2] Malika was not the only woman to note racism in employment in France. Leila finds that racism has worsened with the economic situation:

There's no work, delinquency, um, I think now they live, they live a situation much more difficult, I see, than in the '70s and '80s. It's a lot harder now. With the economic crisis, people suffer much more. And with the rise in racism; the French they think that foreigners came to take their jobs, and I don't know, it's increased problems among people. The selections that businesses make, of course, well, they prefer to hire a French person than a foreigner, and that's created problems among people too.

Telja also believes there is discrimination in hiring: "By Arab first names. It's hard to find work. By skin color. By frizzy hair." Nour mentioned a recent study: "There was a study done recently . . . about people with Maghrebin names, and they have a lot more difficulty finding work, it's more difficult for them to find both apartments and work." Yet immigrant women understand France's dependence on foreign labor, as Bahia made perfectly clear:

> I know an old woman, an old woman near the pharmacy, always mean to people, especially an Arab: "But why do you come here to France? Go, get out! Go, get out!" After I say something, I say, "Madame, please, look the Arabs, they work here the shit," excuse me, I say it like that, "They work here in the metro, they work in the ground, they work everywhere. Who is it? It's Arabs, it's the foreigner. Excuse me, the French don't work like that. Excuse me. The French they work the pen and paper, nicely, no problems. The foreigner works a lot of things not good. In the sewers he goes, in the sewers like that, you find men black, dirty. Who is it? For who? So France lives. So France is good. It's like that. . . . And if there aren't Arabs and blacks here, you find France on the ground."

WHY SOME MAKE IT AND OTHERS DO NOT

As Malika's case, among others, illustrates, the time of arrival in France plays a role in how successful immigrants have become. Immigrants generally tend to improve their situations with time in the host country; women who arrived in the 1970s or 1980s escaped some of the brunt of the current economic crisis. Leila, who came in the 1970s, returned to Tunisia, and then moved back to France, noticed this: "The first time, I didn't have problems. . . . But when I came last time, first of all with the unemployment crisis and everything, there's not a lot of work. It wasn't like that in the '70s and '80s." Fatima agreed: "Then [in the 1960s] life was easier than now for work." Luck also mattered for success, such as Isma's teaching application being accepted almost immediately and Mbruka's finding a deputy to help her solve her residency problems. Participants also mentioned the impact of social support, being able to rely on others when times were hard. Lina explains how she has survived her problems: "Difficult moments, money problems, housing problems, mental problems, work, et cetera, but since we came, there's four of us, we did our studies together, and we came together, and when one flinched, the others were always there." Friends helped not only psychologically but also materially. Labiba's friends established a rotating credit system to help themselves rent apartments and get papers:

> Everything that was administrative — well, when I was a student, it was fine. We always managed among ourselves to slide the quota of money that you had to have in the bank. We had all saved, and each one passed from one to another. So when my date at the prefecture had passed, I took out the money, I gave it to someone who had a date, I took it out. And housing, we all housed each other. Then you would have thought there were 100,000 people living in the same place. With the same papers we went morning and night to the prefecture. But, papers, honestly, I didn't suffer much.

Many women, however, had little social support because they were without family members or friends upon arrival. For these respondents in particular, the secret to surviving in France seemed to be learning how to fight. Thirteen women, including Hayat, mentioned fighting in their responses to problems in France: "You have to be a fighter in this country. You have to be a fighter. The one who sits back, well he won't get anything." Malika concurred: "I feel like I've fought a lot. And I feel like had I stayed there, I'd have fought less. . . . Today, a long time later, I say to myself it would have been easier for me there. If I had put up the same combativeness that I put up to stand up for myself, if I'd have been the same there, it would have been much easier. I have the impression that I set myself a challenge, very, very, very hard. But I did it to myself." Besma realizes that facing these challenges changed her: "You reach a level of maturity in spite of yourself because of the trials you have to face, making your way on your own. I think you don't have your family's support anymore, you don't have your markers, you don't have the same environment, so, um, you make your way on your own. And you do it, I mean it's a battle from day to day. It's not something that happens overnight."

Several other women, like Yusra, talked about the effect living in France has had on their personalities.

> *CK:* Being demanding, being stubborn, has that changed over the years or were you always like that?

Yusra: Yes, there was a predisposition, so afterwards the character was affirmed, or reaffirmed, became more, well it was a question of survival. If I didn't do it, I can't achieve what I want. So I had to.

Tinhinan feels positively about herself as a result of learning to fight: "I'm a rebel. Yes, when I compare myself to a lot of other women from home . . . despite the hardships, I think I've grown, so I feel like a rebel. I say life is a combat, we're called to, it's that we struggle." Houriya, however, views her change in character more negatively:

> Difficulties in my life have made me aggressive. And that's what I reproach, that France made me this way. . . . When I say France, I mean the difficulties that I've run into in France. It's the little annoyances, daily annoyances, the difficulties, the racism that we encounter, the rejection we encounter, has made us become, there's a feeling of revolution; there's a feeling of rejection that we have to deal with in our daily lives, with all the difficulties. Um, it makes us a bit aggressive.

Yet this aggressiveness is adaptive, as Hachmia affirms: "Some have trouble getting their claws out, as they say, so for some it's true that it's difficult. Others it goes well; it depends." Labiba agrees that those who stay in France are those who have learned to stand up for themselves: "It's natural selection. We'd be selected to leave."

Some of those who do not learn to cope may indeed return, but others remain in France in poor conditions. Those who do not learn to fight suffer from a host of material, physical, and psychological problems. This was the case for Zitouna, who was 48 years old, divorced, and the mother of four children: "When I arrived, after a month I was so sick that I spent almost three years without leaving the hospital, going in and out of the hospital. I had difficult adaptation problems and bad health problems because everything changed for me." Twenty years after arriving in France, she has never worked and still has not learned to speak French. Since her divorce, she has relied on associations to help her deal with French administration and get aid. Zitouna is a good example of the effects of social distance on immigrants' adaptation. As an illiterate woman coming from a rural area of Algeria, Zitouna did not at first believe she was in France when her husband brought her to Paris. Having never been to a large city in Algeria, and seeing Arabs out the window of her apartment in an ethnic enclave in Paris, she remained convinced for a month that she had been lied to and taken to Algiers instead of Paris. It was not until her father visited and told her she was indeed in France that she believed it. Given the distance she traveled, not geographically but rather socially, in addition to her health problems, Zitouna was one of the most taxed participants and in one of the worst situations because of it.

Another example of a participant's difficulty making it in France is the case of Amina. Amina was sent to France at age 23 by her parents to help a sick uncle with his business. He made her work all the time without pay, and she eventually stopped living with his family. Having finished high school, but without having passed her baccalaureate, Amina has only found domestic employment during her 10 years in France. She is cut off from her family in Tunisia, with whom she already had strained relations growing up, and is now unable to tell them about her child, conceived out of wedlock with a French man.[3] Her younger boyfriend left her after three years, upon the birth of their child and under pressure from his parents, who did not want an Arab grandchild. More than a year and a half later, she has not gotten over this relationship. Having a child has left her with financial burdens beyond her means, and she relies heavily on her one good friend, Jawahir, for child care and financial help. Whereas Jawahir, who lost her husband at a young age to cancer, describes herself as loving life and being hopeful, Amina admits that she is nervous, scared, and "always sad." With little social support and constant struggles to make ends meet and care for her daughter alone, Amina is depressed.

When we compare Amina to Yasmine, who is also 33 years old, and who has also gone from job to job and has had to depend on others' help, we find a difference of attitude. Although her material circumstances are similar to Amina's, Yasmine perceives herself to be in control and consequently exhibits more well-being. Despite her problems with the French language, she has stood up to men who wanted to take advantage of her and to exploitative employers alike: "You have to work, you have to succeed. You can't trust anyone. It's like that. If you want something, you have to resist. You have to work, you can never let your guard down. Yes, it's like that. Never. You can never say that there's no hope. There's always hope. Me, I always have hope." As Kim and Berry (1986) point out, a positive attitude is one of the characteristics associated with better mental health among immigrants.

Finding work is hindered by language problems and by racism, but these two factors also cause problems that are not material but rather relational. Both language barriers and the experience of racism and rejection can lead to feelings of marginalization and isolation. Women thus talked at great length about how their language difficulties and racism affect their lives and adaptation in France. For some, these problems led to further withdrawal from social situations, but most try to ameliorate their difficulties by being proactive.

Relational Problems

LANGUAGE

Two women, Nassima, who has lived in France for seven years, and Zitouna, who has lived in France for 20 years, have never learned to speak French and can only understand a little bit. For any important interaction, they have to rely on translators. Soraya, who works in an immigrant aid association, helps women who do not speak French:

> I have young girls who come from Morocco, that didn't go to school there, that their parents didn't let go to school, that now have difficulties. They don't even know, I have to go with them to do shopping, to accompany her, or for little things like that . . . even for all their papers, for the prefecture, I go with them. I make an appointment, and I go with them, because if they go to the prefecture, they can't speak, they can't communicate. . . . There's always the language problem because it's true that in Morocco there are even people who don't speak Moroccan at all. There's Berber and a lot of other languages. It's difficult. There's still a lot of work to do given that.

Joumana, who came at age 13, explains why despite moving to France so young, she still has difficulties speaking French more than 20 years later:

> Sadly, I didn't learn a lot because of finances. I helped my parents . . . to help I worked as a cleaning lady. I worked babysitting children. And I didn't go to school much because of financial means. . . . A little bit. I couldn't follow the level. . . . I did elementary school in Morocco, here it's junior high, but the level was too advanced for me. I couldn't keep up, and I left. . . . Now I think that in the beginning, despite my age, I go into elementary

school, learn well, to follow. . . . I don't have the bases, nothing. Very diffi-cult. That's why I didn't continue. I didn't continue, I quit; it discouraged me, so it's a shame. Especially that. I'm still without work, work that I like. . . . I didn't find anyone to help me learn French in the beginning . . . and I didn't perfectly learn the French language. Because, really, had I learned the French language arriving from Morocco in France, then I'd be a Miss Joumana, another, not like now. It's a shame. That's what I was missing, someone who could help me. My father doesn't know anything of the language, my mother either, since she was at home. Had I known French girls, had they told me, "Start in elementary school," I would have had the basics in French. Yes, so I was really a foreigner. I don't know anything, I couldn't, one year, two years, I lost like that. And after I said, "Forget it. I'm not going. I'm going to look for work," and little by little I looked for work.

Several women are actively trying to improve their French and to learn how to read by attending free language and literacy classes in Paris. Like Hachmia, they do not want to be dependent on their children or others for-ever: "For the children too, not needing them for something or to under-stand what's going on." Djamila does not speak Arabic, only Berber. She is trying hard to learn French because

You're not every day with your daughter or your son. It's good to do things alone, the metro, know everything. It's good. . . . First we're going to learn to write like that, understand, it's going to go into our heads. Even in the metro, we don't take it alone because we can't read and write. That's life. We like to read and write. We're going to go work, earn a little money. It's like that. But it's a shame, in Algiers, never I went to school, I don't know. No, never. Never I went to school. That's what I say to my children, studies are good. Oh yes, I say to my children, continue the studies; studies are good.

Yet mastering French is difficult, especially for older women, including Fatima, who put off classes until their children were grown: "Trying to learn to read and write French. Well, I write not bad. Writing is okay. But to enter the things, French in my head, to write, well I speak, difficult for me . . . but now, it's going well. And now for writing, to get it in my head like that, with-out copying, to see the word, copy, I copy from my head here. It's that that's difficult a little, but I hope it will go better." Bahia is tired of relying on her sister and being embarrassed because she cannot speak well: "Me, I don't understand anything, and my husband works. There are papers, come to the social security office, and the doctor, I bring my sister. She always comes. Always I'm ashamed. 'Come, you speak, with me, come.' After I don't talk, and my sister talks. Me, I stay like that, I look, and my sister talks." Yet she struggles with French and is unconvinced that she will make much progress: "I say to my husband, 'You have to speak a little French to me.' He said, 'Me, I speak a little, then the children, you have to speak with the children and you learn French.' And me, now it's too late. It's not like before, young people. Now a lot of things in my head, even I understand like that, after I forget. Almost 40 years old now. It's too late." Despite the difficulties, improving one's comprehension and learning new skills contribute to a sense of increased control and make immigrant women, like Hiba (43-year-old Algerian), feel proud of themselves:

> Me, I need to learn to read and write. I'm very happy now, okay. Before I didn't even know [how to] sign my name. Oh yes. Now I know my address. I write my address, my name, the name of my children, my husband. I took classes twice a week. . . . We need to learn, because before it's not it. We were busy with children at home; now the children are big. We need this . . . because before we didn't know, everything here we didn't know. I don't know my own letters. I wanted to know what was written inside. Now I get up in the morning, I go down, I go to the mailbox, there's mail, I take the letter, I know where it comes from. In the Maghreb, I didn't know how to write much, but I know where it comes from. I'm proud. I know where it comes from. Me, I know, in my head. Before, I open the mailbox, I give to my husband, I don't know what's in it. But now, yes. It's me. My husband also, he doesn't know how to write or read, just his name, he writes a little bit, the alphabet. But now I know how to read; but I hope it will continue.

Even when women know how to speak French, they sometimes have a Maghrebin accent that continues to mark them as outsiders. Fatima realizes that people's perceptions change when she begins to talk: "It's the accent that can give you away. But if you don't talk, well, it's a European. They say, 'Madame, please,' but when you talk, 'Oh no, her, she's not European.'" Having done her studies in French in Tunisia, Leila noted, "Us the French language wasn't a problem, other than that I have an accent. I still have my accent because, after all, I'm North African. When I talk, people know I'm not French . . . because it's not our native language, we still have that little accent, we can't lose it, impossible. It's rare that a North African, any foreigner, I'm not just talking about North Africans, who comes to Paris after adolescence, and he loses his accent; he can't." Jawahir also has an accent; she talks about this and other language problems that give her away as an immigrant and make her uncomfortable communicating:

> My accent, I got it here because I was hanging out with Turks in a workshop, and they didn't speak French. Not a single word of French. So I had to, before coming I spoke perfect correct French, literary French I spoke. And when I got to France, since I hung out with foreigners, Turks, they didn't speak French; they had just arrived from Turkey, and I speak Turkish a little because of them. So I said, "You — there — come — here," and it's really, I couldn't, because of that I have an accent. . . . So I mixed up the familiar and the polite, and the feminine and the masculine, and I mixed up the grammar, the conjugations, and all that. I had a mix in my head. Yet I was perfect in French in high school, all that. It was perfect for me. And when I came here I used the informal with people that I shouldn't have used the informal with; I used the polite form with people I shouldn't have used it with, and it was horrible for me. Horrible.

SOCIAL ISOLATION

Language problems were a large factor contributing to a feeling of isolation for immigrant women in France. Not being able to speak French well meant not just problems at the prefecture but also an inability to meet people. As mentioned in Chapter 2, women were at a disadvantage compared with men in terms of learning French and making friends in France. Men's jobs often force them to learn French and to meet others, even if those others are immigrant laborers from different countries. Women's relegation to the home and to domestic jobs that they perform alone, such as cleaning an office building at night, do not foster progress in these areas. Women who knew some French were still often embarrassed by their poor skills. Mimouna (44-year-old Tunisian) explains,

> In the beginning it was the dream to come to France, but after, when I stay in the house all week all alone, I wait for Saturday and Sunday to go out. In

the beginning, I didn't know anyone. My children went to school, and me, I stay in the house all alone, and I get bored. I tried in the beginning, I try to talk, but afterwards, slowly, understanding and going out a little. The children, luckily my children are a little big, to help me, explain things to me. Sometimes when you don't know, it's difficult when you don't know the language, if you can't read and write; if I go a little far I can't get back home. . . . If you can't talk, you can't call a French person for help or something, you can't; they can't help us. You stay like that in a corner. If you don't understand the language it's sad. . . . I have a few French friends now; when I talk with them, I feel, it's not like before when I didn't talk at all, you understand? When you don't talk, it's very bothersome. Sometimes you want to say something, you can't. And I feel, I feel that I'm not good, or that people are making fun of me, or, people because I don't speak French well, or, you understand? And sometimes I'm ashamed.

Even for those who spoke French well, like Houriya, the differences in attitudes and communication styles and the difficulties making French friends made it hard to adjust and find social support:

There was something I did there that I don't do anymore here, I go home at night, I talk with my mother, my father, my brothers, something I don't have here. I go home, I'm all alone. There also we talk with the neighbors . . . we were always with the neighbor talking. Neighbors here, everyone shut in his house, communication-wise, it's catastrophic. If you're not in a party, a social event, if there's no party, for example, there's no communication. There is no problem of communication. People come up to you, even if you don't want to talk, they make you talk. Even if you don't know each other, in the bus, the train, the street, communication it works. It's part of human warmth. . . . For example, [in France] when there's a party, a birthday or something, they come to you, it's true, they ask you questions, "What's your name? What are you studying? When did you come to France? What do you want to do?" and everything, everything, everything, and the next day, you meet her in the hall, you say hello, she doesn't even answer. . . . I have the impression that there's a rejection. When you come from Algiers, a third world country, they reject you right away; you're not interesting.

Besma also felt "enormously rejected" when she first moved to France: "It's distrust right away. They don't open their doors. I spent three years [in

Dijon]; I had a lot of friends who were from Dijon who were with me at the university. I never went to any of their homes, their parents', they lived with their parents. It wasn't even something that happened naturally, or spontaneously. It happened to me maybe one time, and to wait practically outside the door, it wasn't even, it was really cold. It's a mentality like that."

Given the difficulty creating new social networks, the distance from family members is especially trying and becomes magnified, as Hayat realized: "I think a lot about my family now that I'm in France. I don't know if it's because I miss them or, but it's true that I think about my family all the time." When asked what the hardest thing about living in France is, Najet answers that it is being far from her family: "[In Morocco] there is family, a lot. Here there is nothing. Here there is no one. Total solitude." Salima agrees: "We need the family from time to time. . . . When I came here the first time, I was sad. I was very, very sad. How to put it, a big change. Made a big change. Made a big change . . . because there we live, we grow with the family, and here I was all alone. That's why I was sad, very, very sad. I don't know anyone, and on top of it, I don't go out. That's what hit me the first time when I came here. It's a big change, a big change. It's very difficult."

In addition to the solitude and missing relatives, immigrants like Labiba realized that their lifestyles and personalities were changing as a result of living in France:

> Here people have lost their relationships, um, I've lost my family relationships. Whereas before I was very family oriented, here no. And since life is very hard, you're running all the time, you don't have the time to consecrate yourself to others, whereas there everything was family. You got up in a family, you ate with the family, you went with the family, you snacked with the family, you spend your heart in families, that's it. People here become too materialistic automatically. Everything that's human relations, they don't do it anymore, they don't see it anymore.

Telja concurred: "Between Algeria and France, I find that we don't live the same life, because we live shut in. So in Algeria we have a lot of space, we see the family often, we have a lot of human warmth. Here in France there isn't that. Everybody at home, shut in." To remedy this situation, Soraya purposely moved to be closer to her in-laws: "When I came to France I lived in a different suburb; it was hard because my family, my husband's family lived in another suburb, so I wasn't happy. He went to work, he came home at night, and me, all day I didn't know anyone." Other women have few or no close relatives in Paris. Searching for friendship and a sense of home leads some immigrants to try to recreate a sense of their native communities in France, as Cherifa points out:

> What [immigrants] are missing the most is contact, that permanent contact with others. Um, they don't understand that on the same floor [French people] don't talk as if they lived in a voodoo neighborhood; therein lies the connection to some African communities that group themselves in the same neighborhood, in ghettos. It's because there's this ambiance that they want to recreate in France. It's instinctive to want to create a little the same ambiance. They want to find their products, they want to find their way of cooking, they want to find the smells. It's a permanent search for their roots. Go to the African neighborhoods, there are lots of African products. Go to the Algerian neighborhoods, there's everything that reminds them of Algeria . . . you'd think you were in Algeria. Go to Chinatown, the Chinese community has created the ambiance, the products, the smells, to have less, a less radical, less change. I think it's like that all over the world. I think that people who come from the same country try to group themselves in the same neighborhood. I think that is what they must be missing.

Few respondents, however, indicated that they had been successful in reestablishing a coethnic network in France, probably in large part as a result of French housing policies that sought to disperse immigrants of the same group in different areas.[4] This is problematic in some ways because living in an ethnic enclave when possible not only gives an automatic sense of community but also provides a haven from another problem in France: racism.

RACISM

When specifically asked whether or not they viewed the French as racist, Lina and Rym were the only respondents to say that they were not. According to Rym, "It's a welcoming country. They say the French are racist; it's not true. The French are not racist; they are very, very tolerant." Lina concurred: "I find that the French are, contrary to what is said, racism and everything, they are tolerant. . . . The French are tolerant. They recognize the value of the person. They don't judge you on your origins, they judge you on your way of being, what you are at the moment." Yet Isma, on the other hand, reveals that her biggest problem in France is being seen for who she is: "The most difficult thing honestly, honestly for me, it's to be accepted as an individual. It's not because my name is Isma, because I have darker skin. . . . It's not because I come from a country called Algeria which is North Africa, which is a country that was colonized. That's the hardest. The hardest thing is to be accepted as wholly an individual, a human being."

Lina, insisting she has never been a target of racism, continues, "I never had any problems. I never had any problems with them. You go into a bakery, 'Hello, Madame, I'd like some bread,' like we were in Algeria, like we are here. And I never had any trouble." Yet of course, racism does exist, even in bakeries, as Keltouma recounts: "One time I bought, my sister bought some bread, and they gave her a loaf burned all over. And I didn't entertain the idea that the woman . . . could sell a loaf of bread like that. So I went to see her, saying — I put it badly, so instead of saying to her, 'You gave my sister a burned loaf that you shouldn't sell,' I said, 'You gave a black loaf to my sister.' And she said to me, 'Have you seen yourself? What are you?' So for me, that's a racist act." Why do various respondents hold such different perception of racism in France? Lina, Rym, Isma, and Keltouma are all young, well-educated women who speak French fluently, so these factors do not explain the differences. What does?

Participants described racism in various domains and for different reasons. Several women related blatant incidents of racism that they had experienced. In addition to the comment at the bakery, Keltouma had received racist letters from a neighbor who was unhappy about having a Maghrebin live in his building in an elite arrondissement of Paris (she was living as a companion and guest in an elderly white woman's apartment). Houriya, among others, spoke of being "treated like sheep" and receiving racist comments at the prefecture. She also related one-sided, blaming conversations she had with French people about the Algerian war for independence. Besma experienced several anti-Arab incidents during the Gulf war in the early 1990s.[5] In particular, she faced a man in the Paris metro who systematically insulted all the Arab passengers. Warda related how a North African woman she knew was cut in line by a French woman, who, when her friend resisted, countered, "You know for us, you don't even exist. You don't count, so I go first." Amina expressed her dismay that the parents of her ex-boyfriend could reject their grandchild simply because she was half Tunisian. Soraya realized she had been discriminated against in a job-training program where, despite her good grades, the professor set up internships in companies for her three French classmates but not for her or the other student, a sub-Saharan African woman. Despite these numerous examples, just as many women swore that they had never been a victim of racism.

Many women, like Najet, admitted that the French were indeed racist, but that they personally had never experienced racism: "Me, I haven't had problems like that. Maybe others have." Mbruka realized that what happened to others could potentially affect her: "I feel that feeling when I, um, live situations even if they don't concern me, when I see a situation of racism towards my community. But again, directed at me really, I've never felt that. I feel concerned when there's an incident directed towards my community. I say to myself, 'Shoot, it can happen to me.' . . . When they say 'Oh, dirty Arab,' I say, 'Shoot.' But me personally, no." Several participants, including Telja, admitted this because of what they see in the media: "Maybe it's happened to other people, but not to me. . . . We see things that happen on TV. It touches us when we see testimony, people who are mistreated, we feel affected." Souad agrees: "No, I don't feel welcome; I know there's a lot of racism. There's a lot of racism. They make us feel that, watching TV." Khadija gives precise examples: "Not in my family, in immigrants, yes. For example, the affair, I don't know what it's called, the one who was killed, who was thrown in the Seine. There was the affair of the student who was killed in the demonstration. There are lots of acts like that."

Recognizing that racism occurs but insisting that it has not happened to oneself can be explained in two ways. First, there are issues of defining racism. For example, Yusra states the following: "When I got here, I was confronted with people; we get comments sometimes. Well, I was never the object of a racist act or anything, never, but you see on others, or all the newspapers." Thus it may be that she views acts as examples of racism, but not comments. She may also compare what she has experienced to the dramatic type of events described by Khadija, and thus may not view her experiences as serious enough to truly constitute racism. Similarly, Djamila says, "Never, I don't have problems. Never. I don't know the commissary, or the police, never me." For Djamila, racism may only equal police harassment and arrest, not minor incidents like dirty looks in the metro. People may also be reluctant to define more subtle incidents as racist if they are not absolutely sure about what occurred. Amel is a case in point: "I never got a comment,

'Go home! What are you doing here?' No. Well, one time, I don't know if you can call it that." She goes on to describe how she did not get a babysitting job from a French family and suspected it was because of a fear of Islam. Unable to know for sure, however, she is reticent to label it racism.[6]

The second impediment to recognizing racism is not simply an issue of definition but rather one of control. Labiba's case is a good example. She has repeatedly had police officers come to her store and ask her about permits, questioning her right to be there, yet because she stands up to them, she does not feel wronged by what others might consider harassment:

> *L:* I've never suffered racism. . . . Yeah, I always feel welcome because I don't bother them, they don't bother me. Let's say it's that. It's true, when you're not looking for it, they don't come bother you. It's when finally someone passes a certain limit of the law, the other starts reacting to you. You saw this morning when the police came?
>
> *CK:* Oh yes, the three of them.
>
> *L:* Well, I sent them away. You'd think it was me who was at home and not them.
>
> *CK:* Yeah, but you said that they've already come three times.
>
> *L:* They came because they don't know. It's normal. But I had to explain that, that, that, and all the rest, that's all. But I didn't have to feel small or, or to be afraid. Really, I wasn't afraid to stand up to them. I let them know indirectly that they didn't know the laws; they left. It's good.

Nour expressed a similar view: "Racism, I never, I think that I've never been a victim of racism personally. Um, I never heard, I heard racist comments that I reacted to, but personally I've never been a victim of racism, maybe because my way of talking, people can't take advantage of me, often, in prefectures or anything." Yet, interestingly, Nour had mentioned at an earlier point in the interview that she felt racism had prevented her from finding a permanent job.

Thus, despite being exposed to racism, some women feel they have not experienced it if they do not suffer from it or if they do not feel like victims. This form of psychological protection was also used on a more passive level by Fouzia. She simply refused to pay attention to what may be happening around her:

> *F:*   I don't care. I've been here 23 years; I don't have problems with that.
> I don't think about that. In all countries there are bad people, and
> there are good people. That's all. No, I don't think about that.
>
> *CK:*   So you've never had an incident where people were mean or racist?
>
> *F:*   No. Not at all. I don't bother people, people don't bother me.
>
> *CK:*   I spoke with a woman who [also] wears a headscarf, and she said that
> sometimes people look at her meanly, and she thinks sometimes it's
> because of that. Have you had that problem?
>
> *F:*   No. I don't think so. I don't look at people how they look at me. If
> they want to, they'll do it. I don't pay any attention to that. No, not
> at all.

By not defining racist incidents as such, and by feeling that they can control racism by being assertive or refusing to let it bother them, women made themselves less vulnerable. Mbruka notes that her husband deliberately did not want to consider discrimination as a reason for his unemployment, because racism was something he would not be able to control:

> You ask yourself the question when you're facing a situation where you
> wouldn't have to ask yourself that question if it didn't have that aspect to
> it. And as my husband said, he went through a period of unemployment
> and was out of work a year and a half before finding a job, and he said,
> "Honestly, although I rationalize, I don't see anything else. . . . I ask myself
> the question. I don't want to enter into that reflection because," he said to
> me, "otherwise I won't go look for a job, if I start saying to myself, well,
> with the racism I can never find anything."

This need to feel in control explains why so many women insisted that they had never been subject to racism because they obeyed the rules, were polite, and so on. Souad was proud of the positive comments she received about her children and firmly believed that "when you respect yourself, everyone respects you." Joumana attributed her lack of problems to her personality: "Already on my side, I'm nice, so people have to be — I'm someone who is very welcoming, um, friendly; people automatically they see that I'm really nice, so they are nice." Najet also felt that racism could be prevented by how one acted: "It depends on you yourself, meaning you have to control yourself to control it." Yet, obviously, those women who admitted experiencing racism were no less friendly or well-behaved and in no way at fault for bringing racism upon themselves. In a study of North African men's reactions to racism by Lamont et al. (2002), they found that a strategy used by one-third of the respondents was to distance themselves from "bad Arabs." This group insisted that they, on the other hand, minded their own business, followed the rules, and tried to stay invisible. As Lamont et al. point out, however, "In doing so, they blame the victims of racism for their situation, often justifying French racism by the fact that immigrants are intermingling with French society in a way that they should not" (2002:18).[7] Ultimately, whatever the means, believing that one can control racist reactions is a fallacy, but a psychologically useful one. This in turn explains why some of these women may have been unwilling to label racist incidents as such for fear of breaking down their belief in a personal shield against racism.

As we saw in Chapter 4, when, despite trying to prevent racist incidents from happening, they do occur, respondents who fought back were the least emotionally affected afterward. When Rachida was unable to stand up for herself because of the high status of the person insulting her, and when Mimouna was unable to talk back because of a language barrier, they carried their pain with them for years. Those who asserted themselves, on the other hand, felt in control and sometimes even managed to change the person's behavior as well. Leila relates an event at the prefecture:

> The woman at the desk received me very badly, but I put her in her place. I didn't let myself get taken advantage of. So I answered her, and I was really aggressive with her verbally because she really had a condescending attitude. First she acted badly with an Algerian lady and her child. I looked at her sideways; that didn't please me at all, and maybe she saw that in me, and when I went up for the information, she answered me aggressively, and I didn't let myself be had. I wanted to see her superior and everything. But one of her colleagues, she calmed everything down. . . . She said to her, "Yes, you can't talk to her like that. You should apologize and everything". . . and since that day in fact, when I go to the prefecture, it's always that woman. When she sees me, "Hello! How are you?" But it's hypocrisy. I know it's not sincere, but when I put her back in her place, she understood.

Chafiqa also stood up for herself when she took her six children and the two children of a friend to the park in the suburbs of Paris: "A woman walking saw them. She said to me, 'Oh, there's a lot of them!' I said 'Listen, Madame, it's not you who feeds them at night, in the morning. You have nothing to say. It's my children, and I take care of them. You don't come to my house to wash their clothes or feed them . . . it's not your business. . . . They have their father and mother who take care of them. I didn't call you to wash their things.' After she looked at me. . . . I left. I left her."

Hachmia swears she has never had a problem with French people, but that if she ever did, she would respond: "I have good relations with French people, with people. If I have a problem, they help me a lot for my papers and things. I've thought, I've said sometimes, I don't like racism, even if there's a little, I would dialogue with them to say we have the right like people, we're here because we're here. Otherwise, it goes normally, good." Respondents like Hachmia and others who fought back when faced with racism are not those we need to worry the most about, as Nedjma points out:

> I don't have problems, in any case, particular problems. It's true that in the beginning I lived some verbal aggressions, true, real, some verbal aggression, or mean, to let me know I was a foreigner, that I wasn't welcome, and to which I never gave in. I always stood up for myself. Even when others were disrespecting me, I didn't give in. I say, "There's rights, and it's not because you're French or I'm Tunisian that you can," so I always stood up for myself. But sadly for those who don't, those who can't defend themselves, you have to think about that, not me.

Even when immigrants do not experience racism directly aimed at them as individuals, they still face another problem: being a party to comments made about other North Africans in their presence. Nour has had this happen frequently: "No one has ever said to me that I came to eat the French's bread, um, no, other than racist comments made by people who were talking about Arabs without knowing that I was Arab myself, or Algerian." Passing as a member of a higher-status group is one strategy available to those who are not easily categorized (Hogg and Abrams 1988). However, when people feel attached to their ethnic groups, they may instead choose to set the record straight, as Nour did. The situation becomes more complicated for those who own up to being a minority and try to correct the stereotypes but meet with a comment such as "Maghrebins are — , but you, you're different."

Five respondents noted that they had been in situations where racist comments were made, but the speaker assured the respondent that she was not implicated. After a long, heated interchange about Algerians with a woman she knew in her first job in France, Isma found that all her comments were dismissed: "She was being aggressive towards me, um, she really thought she could calm me by saying, 'Me, what I see here,' and I told her that that was enough. At any rate, I didn't let myself be had, but I gave her arguments to which, after she finished by telling me, 'But you, it's not the same.' It's always like that, me, it's always like that. People say to me, 'But you, it's not the same.'" Isma was irate in this situation because she not only felt that she was being told by a French woman what Algerian women were really like, when Isma, having lived there, should have been the expert, but on top of it, her comments were discounted because she was supposedly not like other Algerian women.

Mbruka and her husband have encountered similar situations: "No matter how long we've lived, we've had funny situations, especially my husband at work; they don't consider you anymore as, because they've gotten to know you, they don't think of you as the Arab. And my husband has often corrected people, saying, 'Watch it, you're talking to an Arab. I'm Arab, and I'm more Arab than the Arabs you're talking about when you're talking in a pejorative manner.' And the person in front of him says, 'No, you it's not the same.'" Another particular incident fascinated her. "The mother of a close friend votes for the National Front . . . and when we ate over for the first time, she loved us so much; she still votes for the National Front, she says to us that we're not the same. And the young black guy who came, the friend of her daughter who came to dinner is a black guy from Martinique, he's not the same." By making each individual person of color she meets an exception, this woman can maintain her schema that minorities and immigrants are bad and can continue voting for a racist, anti-immigrant, right-wing party. The adamant maintenance of schemas in the face of evidence to the contrary is one of the reasons that stereotypes and racism are so persistent (Fiske and Taylor 1991). Thus, this situation — where individuals are told they are different from the groups they belong to — is not only difficult for the person in question to deal with, but also has a large impact on society.

Help in France

Although life is very hard for many immigrants in France, not everything, of course, is negative. Respondents related not only acts of racism they had experienced, but also acts of kindness. As several women, including Mimouna, noted, "There are bad and good [people] in every country."[8] Although they found the French racist as a group, most mentioned individuals who were hospitable and helpful. Many, like Oumniya, managed to make acquaintances in their buildings, if not close friends: "There's a very good lady . . . very, very nice, and the neighbor. . . . But in the building very, very nice to me. Even I speak bad, I ask correct to me. 'No, me I speak bad. I speak bad.' 'No, Madame, you speak well.' Sometimes she comes over, not a lot. Me, sometimes I go up to see the woman, more by the stairs. That's it. Talk about children, vacation, how are you." Mimouna also found neighbors who were willing to help her: "Yes, I know some, who helped me, neighbors, neighbors who showed me a lot to do my papers . . . a lady, she even came with me to do my papers. . . . I was very happy because I can't take the metro alone, and my husband can't come with me because he works . . . so she agreed to help me."

Respondents were pleased with some of the services the French state provided to aid them and took advantage of translators and social workers. Zitouna discussed her interactions with French administration: "The French here always respected me. In the beginning, to talk to me, they always brought someone to translate, to try to help me understand. And even now they say that I have to learn to speak French, try to understand to get along. They always helped me." Amina was first assigned a case worker who wanted to classify her as homeless and wanted to put her child in foster care, but she met another social worker in the hospital when her daughter was sick who helped her get her permanent resident card:

> I landed on another [social worker] now. She is really very nice. It's thanks to that social worker that I got my papers. . . . I had my papers in a month, I got my papers. It's thanks to the social worker. She could do it right away. They sent the convocation, she helped me for my daughter's papers, all that. In regards to, because the grandfather is French, and since I don't talk to the father, his parents don't want me, I can't get the grandfather's papers. She had to send another letter and everything to get the papers for the little one's nationality. And it's thanks to her that I got all that, the social worker.

Although many women had negative experiences doing domestic work for pay, some worked for families that treated them kindly. Amina raved about both the fairness and kindness of her employer:

They are too nice to me. You believe it, I didn't have my papers, I worked for her and she pays me, she gives me my days off and everything, and she pays me. She's always proper. When there's a holiday for them, she gives me presents. When there is a holiday of mine too. She even came to my place and everything, and she buys me presents. She bought me a washing machine and everything when I got the apartment. For my daughter and everything, always presents for my daughter. I even gave my daughter her name as a middle name. She has two names, and the second is my boss's.

Hayat also thought fondly of her employer and mentioned how touched she is that she always receives a present on her birthday. Other respondents, like Nour, received help in finding housing in a suburb of Paris.

The apartment, we lived for eight months at my mother's. It's an older man, a French man, who asked for us, and didn't say anything to us. So it's by his help, who didn't even talk to us, we didn't ask him anything. He knew what situation we were in; he got us an apartment. So that's the sign of hospitality, really, clearly. . . . So we had a lot of luck and lots and lots of help coming here. Especially because people looked at us and said, "Oh la la, good thing you came, it's horrible what's going on there and everything."

Keltouma actually lived with a French woman for free in the center of Paris and become almost a member of her family:

A French woman welcomed me, opened her home to me, really thought of me like her own daughter. So she trusted me, she left her whole home, she lived in a five-bedroom; I lived in it with her without giving her anything in exchange. . . . It's true that with words I can't tell you the gratitude I feel towards that woman. . . . There are other people who helped me a lot. Especially the family of that lady who helped me, who I've always considered like a real family, like a second French family, with whom I continue to maintain very good relations. The woman died, the woman who took me in, she died. Really, I didn't live with her for very long, then she had a cerebral hemorrhage, she went to a nursing home, and her family, out of kindness, they didn't close the apartment. They let me live there alone, and I was able to benefit from the housing for the duration of my studies. So until the lady died, she died just around the date of my defense, so it's a funny coincidence, as if, as if she wanted me to finish my studies.

Finding French people who fight with them in their battles for papers and housing makes immigrants' lives easier. Positive interactions and the establishment of friendships with French people also go a long way toward making them feel at home in France. This is especially fortunate because the majority of Maghrebin women in France admit that they are remaining in the host country permanently.

Conclusion

Although all immigrants face challenges, some cope and make strides faster than others. Having an education and therefore a good grasp of the French language makes it more likely that immigrants can learn to work the system and protect themselves from isolation and even abuse. Yet participants of all educational levels who learned how to fight for themselves feel more positively than those who view themselves as powerless and vulnerable, regardless of their actual material circumstances. Reacting against racism or feeling capable of protecting oneself from it likewise protects psychological health. It is important to remember, however, that although the belief that one can control racism may be beneficial at the individual level, it indirectly places blame on victims of racism who, according to this logic, must not have behaved appropriately and thus prompted the attack. Illusions of control, therefore, are not only false, but they also are potentially damaging to others.

The next chapter looks at the primary reason why North African women have elected to stay in France despite the difficulties and stress: their children. How do immigrants go about raising children who are French citizens? What are they trying to pass on from the Maghreb, how are they trying to help them fit in in France, and how successful are they?

SIX

You Can't Transplant a Flower Twice

Children and the Future

Many immigrants originally planned to return home to the Maghreb, and some even built homes there in the hopes of moving upon retirement. As they have watched their children grow up in France, however, they have come to realize that a permanent return to North Africa is unlikely. This chapter examines immigrant women's hopes for their children and the difficulties involved in passing on cultural traditions to children who are ethnically North African but who are legally, and often affectively, French.

Respondents' changing life plans support the temporal perspective approach proposed by Roberts (1995). Roberts argues for looking at how life events such as the birth of children affect immigrants' decisions to return home or remain in the host country. Socially expected durations in turn influence how likely immigrants are to orient themselves to the host country, acquire property, build new social networks, and request citizenship (Roberts 1995).[1] When North African men came to France by themselves as migrant laborers, they often returned to the Maghreb after a few years or at retirement. Those men who remained in France alone often continued to live in boarding houses cut off from the French population.[2] When wives began joining their husbands in the 1970s under French family reunification laws, families became increasingly likely to remain in France permanently. The arrival of women and children facilitates settlement as families become "enmeshed" in community organizations (Hondagneu-Sotelo 1994). Immigrant women also help shape the communities they live in through their influence on their children's self-identification and cultural behaviors.[3] Despite playing this role in anchoring families in France, respondents often took years to understand the implications and to reframe their expectations for their own lives and those of their children.

Staying in France Because of the Children

When asked about returning permanently to North Africa, a few young, single women mentioned that they would consider it. The majority, however, planned to stay in France. As Jawahir put it, "You can't transplant a flower twice." Eleven women, including Hiba, stated that they had always planned to return to the Maghreb but now admitted that they cannot because their children will remain in France. "We're stuck now. Especially with the children who grew up here. We can't do anything about it. There was a time we wanted to return home, but to live there, with the children, we can't leave the children here alone. Yes, we'll stay here." Assia and Hachmia concurred:

> CK: Do you think you'll stay in France forever now, or do you think you'll go back some day?
>
> A: Especially the children, they're born here. We always need the answer, because normally they stay here. They take classes here, they are big here, so . . . they want to stay.
>
> H: For them, their future is here. The future of the children is here, so, because the children will find a job, the children's work too.

Lina and Rym, who do not yet have children, recognize that despite their plans now, their attachment to their home will have to take second place to the desires of their children down the road:

CK: Do you see yourselves staying here permanently?

L: For now. In the short run, yes.

R: For now, I think that for the next 10 years we're here. I'd say 10, 15. Later maybe we'll do like immigrants, we'll finish our retirement there, if it gets better. But you know, you say later, then you have children, and kids, it's over. Life is here now, that's it.

L: The children won't react like us about Algeria because they'll be born here. So they won't have that love, that need for Algiers, that we have. Them, no. I don't think so. And we'll have to stay here because of our children, I think.

Some women say they will compromise, visiting the Maghreb for longer periods of time and traveling back and forth more frequently upon retirement, but that they cannot move there definitively. When asked if she plans to return to Algeria permanently, Chafiqa responds yes without thinking and then backtracks: "Oh yes! No. Not permanently, but I do three, four months there and then I come back here. When it's nice, I go there; when it's winter, I come back here because it's warmer inside than there. I have my children too. Can't forget that. All my children are here, so I can't. And my house too, I can't." Souad agrees: "No, I don't think I'll go back permanently because my children are here; they're established here. Um, I can't go back. Even later, when I'm retired, I'll do the shuttle between Tunisia and here. But go back to live permanently there, no. Because of my children. I can't be that far from my children." Oumniya is willing to spend half the year in each country because she has one adult son who lives in Algeria and the rest of her children are in France: "I like half here, half there. That's it. Even six months there for my family, my son, six months here." When asked about her plans, Fouzia replies that it is up to her husband, but she is careful to draw the line at returning to Morocco permanently: "It depends. When my husband is retired, I don't know. We don't know. We haven't thought about that for the moment because my husband works. After we'll see. If he wants to stay here we stay. If he wants to stay there a little bit, a little bit. We can't stay there permanently because the children are here. It's impossible because the children won't go. I don't think the children will follow us."

Realizing that she has already uprooted her young children's lives once, Isma is reluctant to do it again:

I say to myself that as long as the children need to be, to have security, to be in school, I don't think we're going to move them much. I don't want to upset them too much . . . take them out of a context and then reenter them in another context. I see for example my son . . . in Algeria, he'll go back to school . . . he's going to feel even more like a stranger, and I don't want to make him live that because it's very, very hard. . . . It would be truly very hard for my children, so I don't see why I'd want to return to that. I go back for vacations because I want to, but that's all.

Isma recognizes that even after a year in France, her son would feel like a stranger in Algeria. Women whose children had been raised almost entirely in France were also aware of the fact that their children would have a hard time fitting in in the Maghreb. Khadija would love for her children to return: "[I'd like] them to return to the county one day because Morocco needs young people, young people from here. Me, I'd prefer if they made plans there because Morocco there always needs it." When asked if she thinks they will go, however, she admits that they probably do not want to and will stay in France.

Only three women had children raised almost entirely in France who wanted to live in North Africa. All of the other respondents acknowledged that their children would make their lives in France. Although many of their sons and daughters liked to go to the Maghreb for vacations, they stated that they could not live there because they have a French mentality, do not speak Arabic well, and stand out as foreigners. Najet explains: "They like Morocco, but only for vacations. Because they're born here, they've grown up here, they have a different mentality, a different way of life here. Morocco is for vacations. For all the Moroccans, Algerians who live here, living there isn't easy for them. Already the language, they speak Arabic badly. They don't understand much about Morocco; they don't understand their laws, their lives there. They don't know anything." Fouzia agrees: "For example, when they spend the month of vacation, they want to come back here right away. Like it's a tourist because they're happy to go, they're happy to come back. For them, staying there, it's like foreigners. For them, their country is here because they're born here. It's normal." Bahia's children cannot even last a week on vacation with their father's family in Tunisia: "In Tunis, after a week, 'Mama, I want to go home.' They don't want to, they aren't used to it."

Soraya's husband was born in France of Moroccan parents, and she realizes that he could never make his home there: "I can't return to Morocco because [my husband], he doesn't know Morocco. He's Moroccan, yes, he knows Morocco because he's gone two or three times in his life, but, well, he can't live there. To begin with he doesn't even speak Arabic. He doesn't speak Moroccan, not at all; he only speaks French. No, I think we'll stay here." Even for children who did speak Arabic, immigrant women like Telja understood that their sons' and daughters' allegiance is to France: "Them, they're French. They consider themselves as French. Their land is here. Their homeland is here. They're French, so I don't see why they'd marry there or live there, never. Maybe one day they'll go to see the family, that's all." Warda's son had expressed this himself: "My children feel Franco-French. . . . My son said to me not long ago, 'I only have genetic ties to Algeria.'"

Participants also appreciated the opportunities in France for their children that they often perceived as better than in the Maghreb. Hachmia and Assia talked about what they liked in France; what were new opportunities for them were taken for granted by their children:

> *H:* Coming to France, it's really something nice, to change, to learn things. Doing things we couldn't do.
>
> *A:* For the children too.

Mimouna recognizes that her children have grown accustomed to the benefits of living in Paris and is happy that they will have better employment opportunities in both France and Europe than in Tunisia:

> They like France, because there, Djerba is too small, [it's] for retired people. You understand here in Paris, it's big, there are a lot of choices, there's everything. For young people it's good, sports and everything, but there a small island, there isn't even a gym. It's true . . . it's not like here, activities and all that for young people. It's good. . . . I'm happy for my children, for my children's future, because I was right to, I'm happy for my children's future because here is France, a big country, and Europe, able to work later even in Europe, not even France, especially with the nationality and all that. Over there, there isn't a lot of work and all that, you understand? If they stay there, even if they do studies, there's not much; they won't be able to find good work.

Hopes for Children

When asked about their hopes for their children, all the respondents wanted to see them pursue higher education, get married, and find good jobs. Education seemed especially important to those women, like Zitouna, who had not been able to attend school in the Maghreb: "I didn't go to school, not me, not my parents, not my brothers, not my sisters — we were in a village where there wasn't even a school. For me, the dream when I came here was to have children who can have an education, have diplomas, and to be able to work." Women were just as concerned with their daughters' education as they were with their sons, as Khadija demonstrates:

> *K:* My oldest daughter is in her second year of law. The boy is also at the university, and the girl who is 18, she works. She didn't like school very much. . . . I want my children to all have good jobs, do advanced degrees, since I can't do it.
>
> *CK:* Do you think your daughter is going to be a lawyer?
>
> *K:* She wants to be a journalist.

Maghrebin women, like Bahia, have high hopes for their daughters' careers: "My daughter is big. I hope later on she'll be a dentist." Zhora was pleased that her daughter was studying medicine. Souad is thankful that her girls pursued degrees and are able to support themselves:

> They all work, except my son. He didn't do long studies like the girls . . . and he works a little bit. . . . All three of the girls passed the baccalaureate. One did two years of law . . . she stopped after two years because she got sick. She stopped, and then she continued to work. The other . . . she did two years in England; she got her degree in English. . . . I always hoped they would continue their studies, be independent and have good jobs. And God rewarded me.

Telja cannot wait to have grandchildren but understands that her daughter's education comes first: "I dream of it, but sadly my married daughter continues her studies in law, so she's not ready to have babies. . . . I wish them success in their studies. I wish happiness for the girls and boys, both. And I hope they find a job at the end of their studies."

Naidoo (1986) found that Indian and Pakistani women immigrants in Canada hold traditional views on family, marriage, men and women's roles in society, and religion, but espouse Canadian values regarding castes, dowries, and schooling and careers for women. North African women in this sample also believed in schooling and careers for women, even when they were very religious. Although mothers ideally preferred for their children to follow certain customs, particularly religious practices, they gave them a great deal of leeway. Eight participants specifically stated that their children of either sex were free to marry whomever they chose, Muslim or not, and the vast majority of younger, less religious women who were not asked the question probably also agreed. Fatima believes that what matters is her children's happiness: "They have their choice. They do what they want. I gave the freedom. I said, 'You do what you want; it's not my business. When you are happy either with a Moroccan, or an American, or a French person, or a Dutch person, or a Belgian person, I don't care as long as you're happy. That's what counts.'" Souad expresses the same sentiment: "I didn't force them like a lot of mothers, 'No, you can't be involved with French civilization,' or 'You can't marry a French person.' No, I let them choose. Even to marry a French person, or an American, or a Dutch person, I, the principle thing is that they're happy. That's what I wish."

Chafiqa noted that even if she said no to a prospective spouse, her children would not listen to her: "Well, they'll get married to whomever they want. Me, what do you want? Even if I said no, they won't listen to me. It's their choice. It's not mine. . . . They chose their happiness. . . . I'll be happy to just throw the party and that's all; I'll be happy with them, that's all. It's not up to me to decide who they marry, no. I'm not like that." Djamila admits she prefers Kabyle spouses for her children, but she knows that it is not up to her: "Whatever they want. I don't know if they'll get married to a French person or an Arab. Me, I'd like for them to marry a Kabyle. Me, I'd like it, but I don't know what they'll say." Hachmia stresses that you can't decide who people will love and notes the changes in marriage arrangements over time: "My children, I give them the choice what they want to do, because it's not the parents who will marry the children; I don't force, can't force a love of someone. It's daily life. Getting married is not a game. Because before parents married their children; it's not the same. Life changes."

The insistence on children's personal happiness and their ability to make choices is a surprising finding given that in Islam, children's religion is determined by the father; thus as long as the father is Muslim, the children are Muslim, even if the mother is of another religion. Muslim men are consequently allowed to marry women from any "people of the book" — Jews, Christians, or Muslims. Muslim women, on the other hand, are only permitted to marry Muslims. Yet only four women specifically mentioned placing restrictions on whom their children could marry. Telja and Fouzia both stressed that although their boys could marry anyone, their girls must marry Muslims. Najet wanted her children of both sexes to marry Muslims, "so there won't be problems later." Bahia, however, was the only respondent who planned on trying to pick a spouse for her girls herself. She argued that he did not necessarily have to be Muslim, but that she wanted someone who would treat her daughter right and felt that she was better qualified than her daughter to evaluate this:

> B: I say to my son, the big one, 18 years old, "If you find a pretty girl, there's no problem, even French, even African, even black, even Chinese." If he finds a nice, calm girl, and a good family, he can marry her. It's him; it's not me. . . . He finds an Arab, maybe she's mean. It's not good. . . . If he finds a good woman, he can get married. . . . The girls, it's me who chooses . . . with their father, because girls aren't like boys. . . . Here girls it's hard. Even in Algeria like that, the parents choose. If [the girl] finds a husband, he's not good for the girl; he hits, he doesn't give food, he doesn't bring home the food, lots of problems for my daughter and for me too. Why? If I choose for my daughter, a good boy. . . . It's better for my daughter; it's better. Even in Algeria like that. If we don't find a boy for the girl, she stays at home.
>
> CK: But can he be French or is it better if he's —
>
> B: Whatever.
>
> CK: As long as he's good?
>
> B: Right.

Soraya was critical of the immigrants she met in the association where she worked who ran their children's lives to this extent: "They have to learn to let their children decide. Because most people here . . . even if their children are 30, 40 years old, married, they decide for them. I'd like them to learn to control themselves, to say that's it for me, now I'll let my son or daughter. . . . I have people who are unhappy because their parents forced them to get married, they chose the husband or wife of the children." Few participants expected to have this much control over their daughters' lives. Most also wanted their daughters to benefit from the freedom of life in France that they themselves had come to appreciate. Karima (43-year-old Algerian) was an exception. She, and especially her husband, strictly monitored their daughter's whereabouts and friends. Yet Karima expressed some regret about her daughter's lack of freedom:

> My daughter is living this right now; she knows, she got invitations to go to the stadium, she went once with her brother because her brother intervened with her father, saying, "Papa, I'll take her to the stadium"; so he closed his eyes. But the whole evening, he didn't stop: "Well, this is new — a girl who goes to the stadium now." He didn't stop all evening. I said, "Listen, you had the choice to tell her no in the beginning" . . . and the poor thing, she knows. Sometimes she is called, invited, and she says to me, "Mama, it's not worth it to tell him. You know he won't let me." She already knows the things that her father — um, for example, her friend invited her to Normandy. She said to her, "Listen, you know Papa won't let me go with a French family," that they don't know, they have two older boys, he'll never let her, you see. . . . But sometimes it hurts me when she says, "Mama, it's not worth it that I tell Papa. I know." So she already sorts things, even though she was born in France. I mean she was born in France, but we always raised her with our culture also, our religion, our interdictions.

Rachida, on the other hand, stands up to her husband on her children's behalf: "Always we don't agree, but don't agree. Even the children, they, they don't agree with my husband. Me, I'm always with the children. He says, 'No, you do this, you don't do that,' and I say, 'No.' I want freedom for my children." Hayat also argues that it is important to give children room to make their own decisions:

> People say it's a question of education; you can't let children get away with too much, you need authority. But I think, me, I think that you have to give a minimum of freedom to your children so they know how to find themselves, you see? Because when you have confidence in them, I think your children give it back to you. You can't oppress them too much. When you say all the time, "You have to do this. You have to do that," they don't know what to do anymore. You have to know how to listen to them. That's very important. Me, maybe I, I revolted a little bit because my parents

talked to me too much about virginity. . . . "Don't do this. Don't hang out with boys. You shouldn't" — it annoyed me. Maybe if they hadn't talked to me about all that, I'd have stayed in Algeria.

Souad took this tack with her children and is pleased with the results: "They've all succeeded, and that's what I wanted. Because I raised them well; I educated them well, and, um, I had confidence in them. Yes, I had confidence in them. Never I, if for example, my daughter says to me, 'I'm going out,' I say, 'No, don't go out,' or, well, I gave her all her freedom. And I had confidence in her, and they have confidence in me. They haven't betrayed me." Lacoste-Dujardin's (1992) study of girls raised in France by immigrant parents supports Hayat's and Souad's contentions. She found that girls with very strict parents were likely to rebel, sometimes even running away. Girls who had more open communication with their parents were more likely to listen to them, have fewer problems, and do well in school. Paradoxically, then, having good family relations may lead to children who choose to uphold certain North African traditions, while those who feel forced and constrained may abandon everything they have come to associate with their parents' control. Many respondents seemed to understand this. They related the difficulties in transmitting what they feel is important in Maghrebin cultural traditions to children growing up in France. Most believe that it is better not to push too hard.

Passing on Culture

RELIGION

In the United States, where turn-of-the-century white immigrants quickly lost cultural traditions and assimilated, religion remained the one acceptable domain of difference. Parents who realized that they were unable to teach the language of origin and other customs from home often concentrated on transmitting their religion (Warner and Wittner 1998). Although the French are less welcoming of religious diversity than Americans, as the law banning the headscarf in school attests, this pattern is also evident in France.

Passing on religious beliefs and practices to their children is very important to many respondents, like Tinhinan: "Traditions matter a lot to me . . . especially what's linked to religion, maybe." Some, including Salima, believed that being religious would keep their children out of trouble: "For example Ramadan. We do Ramadan already. We try, the children, they do like us. . . . It's important for us that they follow the religion. They don't forget the religion; they don't forget. No drugs, no violence. That's it." Women tried to encourage religious behaviors by setting a good example and by talking about the importance of being Muslim. Telja relates her attempts to influence her children: "Religion, sometimes, you can't; for Ramadan I always talked about it, for prayer I always talked about it. I hope one day or another they will, they'll make the choice. It's up to them to make their lives. But I talk about it all the time. I always try to talk about religion, what I know, that's all. But they're smarter than me because they look it up in books, so they discover themselves." Assia felt doubly guilty for not praying, first because she felt she owed a debt to God and second because she wanted to set an example for her children to follow: "I need to teach the children too. My son, too, he says to me, 'Mama, why don't you do the prayers?' I'm old enough now; at 36 years old, I should pray."

Respondents seldom put direct pressure on their children to practice, however. The majority, including Souad, did not believe in forcing their children to pray or even to keep Ramadan: "I have two daughters who don't practice. For that, I don't force them. You can't — they do things if they're, if they're aware they want to do it. But to force, have to do this, or not do that, I, I don't force them to do something they're not, they're not ready to do." Amel said she would do her best to set an example while her children were growing up but that in the end, the choice is theirs: "There won't be pork at home; there won't be alcohol. And then after if they want to choose another path, well, they'll choose. But, well, I, I'll raise them the way I was raised, meaning they do what they want, and afterwards either they follow or they go toward other religions, or they don't believe in God, and that's it." Fouzia also believes that the motivation for religious acts should come from within:

F: Traditions that they follow, celebrate holidays, celebrate Eid, Ramadan. Prayer too.

CK: Do they do Ramadan?

F: Ramadan, yes, but prayer, some do it, some no.

CK: And you don't eat pork or alcohol?

F: No, that no. Neither me, nor my children. Not at all. Not at all. Even when they stay at the cafeteria, I ask that — well, they know that.

CK: And your daughters, do they wear the headscarf?

> F: No. I don't make them, but if they want to, they do it. But it's not me who's going to say, "You do the headscarf. You do this and this." No. The day where she wants to, she will do it.

Religion is both one of the most important cultural aspects to pass on to the second generation and at the same time one of the things participants worried about the least. Like Fouzia, many women indicated that if they provided their children with a basis, they might choose to become more religious later in life. Rachida herself admits that she did not start to pray until she was an adult: "I'd like for the children to do Ramadan and prayer, and otherwise, the rest, I don't ask for more. The children, no one [prays] but me. Normally, I do the prayers, so — me too, I started praying late. I didn't do it before. The children do Ramadan." Respondents were also unconcerned because they assumed that their children will self-identify as Muslim regardless of whether or not they practice, as this exchange between Najet and her daughter, Mounira, reveals:

> N: You're born Muslim. You have to follow that culture by any means. That's all.
>
> CK: And the children?
>
> N: They'll follow.
>
> CK: Do they do Ramadan?
>
> N: Yes, yes. They see the parents, already they do it, have to do it.
>
> M: We don't have to do it.
>
> N: You don't have to, no. If it's forced, it's shameful, it's —
>
> M: No, I mean you, you and Papa don't force us. We know we're Muslim; we should do it.
>
> N: Automatically.

Only one respondent was seriously worried about her child's religious identity, and this was because he was in a special situation. Unhappy with the poor quality of the public school in their heavily immigrant neighborhood located in a poor northern suburb of Paris, Mbruka and her husband had made the difficult decision to enroll their son in a private Catholic school. This was causing some confusion for the six-year-old, confusion his mother was trying to deal with:

It's coming little by little. So we discuss. When he talks about Jesus, I talk about Mohammed. When he talks about Easter, I try to find . . . the equivalent. When he says, "Mama, can we go to mass? The teacher said we could," I said, "No, you know honey, I'm Muslim, so are you." "Oh no, no, no, me, I'm Catholic!" "No, honey, you know you're not Catholic." . . . We came back to the discussion one day, he'd understood, I think without accepting it really, because he doesn't want to be different but, um, at least he doesn't insist anymore, "Mama, I'm Catholic." He says, "Oh, okay." So I don't know, we recently bought a children's version of the universal declaration of the rights of man where they talk about different religions, and that was a way to also talk about that, well, religious wars, and everything. There, so it's a little bit difficult. But, well, but it's an important choice for me because I think that he'll live here. . . . I prefer for him to have a good education and resolve the religious problem myself than for him to have a poor educational base and that he'll be Muslim, for example.

LANGUAGE

The majority of respondents also planned to or had tried to teach their children Arabic or Berber. However, a number of these women were unsuccessful. Studies have shown that bilingual children score higher on a wide variety of intelligence tests, and thus the loss of the parental language negatively affects both cultural competence and general achievement (Caplan et al. 1991; Portes and Schauffler 1994; Zhou and Bankston 1998). Why did some women not care about passing on Arabic, and why were so many of those who did care unsuccessful?

Only five respondents were not trying or did not plan to teach their children another language besides French. The two women whose children had non-Muslim French fathers were making no effort, despite the fact that these children were being raised without their fathers.[4] When asked what language she talked to her daughter in, Amina replied, "I speak French more, because my daughter, when we speak Arabic, she doesn't understand." Cherifa only speaks Arabic in front of her son when she is annoyed: "When I speak to him in Arabic because I'm upset, he says, 'Mama, stop saying swear words.' He must think that everything that's strange, for him, it's a swear word. . . . He doesn't speak a word." A few other women planned to expose their children to Arabic but did not want to insist on it. Asked whether she would speak Arabic to her children, Yusra responded, "Not necessarily. Not necessarily. It depends on, I'd give the means, in the beginning, to my child to learn a little, but then it would be up to him or her to choose. It's not mandatory." Isma believed that her children could learn Arabic at any time if they wanted to and that it did not have to come from her:

> I don't speak with my children because, because I don't think about it. It's not really that I refuse, but because I don't think about it. . . . I don't feel obligated to. I don't say, "Oh yes, I have to, I have to speak to them because, because it's important." I don't think so, I don't think so. They live in a totally French context. . . . My son did a year of Arabic at school in Algeria. He was good at it. I mean, a language, when a child wants to learn a language, he learns. . . . Honestly, I'm not worried about it.

Finally, Soraya was afraid that her daughter's language skills in French would suffer if she introduced Arabic at the same time: "For my daughter, I speak French because she's too little to learn, I think. I think she's still too young to learn a second language. She hasn't mastered French yet."

The vast majority of participants, however, did have an investment in teaching their children Arabic or Berber. Mimouna explains some of the reasons why:

> The people I see around me, they're all, they like to do the traditions, they like to speak their language for the children. It's for one reason, it's not that they don't like the French, no, it's the opposite, but so that their children don't forget, lose the tradition when they go back there. Because when they go back even for vacation two months or a month, and they find here we're foreigners, and there they become foreigners. That's why. They don't like for their children, they don't understand anything when they go home, or even to talk to grandparents, if the grandparents don't speak French, the grandparents, the poor things who wait all year to see the grandchildren.

Other women argued that learning another language was important for other reasons. As Amel puts it, "It's always a plus to have an extra language." Keltouma agreed and spoke about her love of her native language:

> It's essential to teach them the Arabic language. To begin with, learning a language is a gift, and it would be a shame for my children to not know their language of origin. It's very, very important for me. I can't even imagine that

my children couldn't speak Arabic, so, um, the day I have a husband and kids, at least one needs to speak to them in Arabic, from the beginning. Not only talk, but it's essential that they go to institutions where they have Arabic classes and religion. Read and write. I love the Arabic language; I'm proud of the Arabic language. I find it's a shame if my children don't take advantage of that knowledge. And it's important for the family in Morocco, if I translate, if I take the children and I have to translate to my children, I find that would be catastrophic. It would be sad.

Besma was not as concerned about family as she was about how her own children would feel if, as adults, they did not speak Arabic:

> I'm convinced that it's necessary to transmit what we are and what we've inherited, and all the memory, all the history, all the civilization that is, that is more than important because I'd be afraid that he holds it against me someday. Because I see around me, I have friends who have children, their children hold it against them to have not taught them Arabic. And I understand these kids because they're in an identity dilemma, in conflict with themselves. And also, it's really, it develops so many capacities in a person to have access to other languages.

Many participants, though, found that despite their best intentions, they were largely unsuccessful in teaching their children Arabic. For some this was because they themselves had grown up speaking French or were so cut off from Arabic that using it was difficult. Malika explains that this is the case for her sister: "My sister, so there are two boys, well, she never speaks to them in Arabic. They don't know how to speak Arabic. Us either, among ourselves, we don't speak in Arabic, so she says it would be artificial for her to talk to them in Arabic." Mbruka found she had the same problem despite her original commitment to teaching her son Arabic:

> For my children it's very problematic — for example, I didn't succeed in transmitting my maternal language, my Arabic language, to my son because, um, I'm so imprinted because I spoke French at home in Algeria. . . . When I had my son I really tried to make an effort to speak to him in Arabic so that he'd learn Arabic first, that it became a nonnatural act, and I had a hard time. So I had to force myself to speak only Arabic, to be able to speak to him only in Arabic, and the French quickly won out. And when I was

frustrated, I said, "Okay, stop now. That's enough!" and I spoke in French. So my son speaks very, very little Arabic. And it's something that for me is a real problem. So he practically doesn't speak any Arabic; he understands very few words.

Warda also noted that being cut off from others who spoke Arabic made it impossible for her children to learn to speak, even though she and her husband did frequently use Arabic at home:

> My children, sadly, with all the efforts I tried to make, don't speak Arabic fluently. They understand, of course, but they are incapable of having a conversation in Arabic. Um, first of all because I lived in a neighborhood where we almost never ran into, but never, there weren't people who spoke Arabic. Now, for the past few years, we come to this neighborhood where people speak Arabic, where I meet people who speak Arabic, but sometimes I'd go a whole year without speaking Arabic. And my children too. So despite teaching them, they didn't practice. The practice was missing. Even speaking it at home, we didn't succeed. My mother, when she comes, she speaks to them in French. My brothers and sisters, it's the same. Which means that us, um, me, I continue speaking Arabic with my husband as well as French, but I realize that as soon as we want to have a more elaborate conversation, it's always in French that we have it, even if for daily things we speak Arabic. . . . And since at school, in preschool, in kindergarten, and in the immediate environment people only spoke French, the little friends were all French, my daughter never had a single Maghrebin classmate, and my son either. So it was very hard for them; they never had an opportunity to say words.

Even women who barely spoke French, however, had a difficult time trying to teach their children to communicate in Arabic. Often their children, like Khadija's, could understand but not speak: "We speak Arabic, but the children speak French. Meaning we speak to them in Arabic, they respond in French. They understand, understand but don't speak." Assia is ashamed that her children do not speak Arabic and is trying to find a way for them to learn:

> I have my son who doesn't know how to speak Arabic. I have my children who don't understand Arabic. I speak a little bit, but always when I speak in Arabic they answer in French. When I want to say something, always they

answer in French. I'm thinking about signing them up for an Arabic class. I'm ashamed they don't speak Arabic. I'm going to sign them up; I started for my daughter. I have my son, the little one, who looks at songs in Arabic, and he says, "Mama, I don't like it. I can't understand. You have to change it." He says, "Why do you understand? Me, I don't understand. You have to change it." He wants songs in French. That's why I was thinking to enroll them to learn Arabic.

Several of these primarily Arabic-speaking women, including Fouzia, have some children who speak better than others:

> CK: Do they speak Arabic well?
>
> F: A little bit. Not a lot because the French is stronger. Because here there is school and everything. Even if we speak a little bit of Arabic with them, no, they understand, but to speak it's difficult for them. A lot of problems for answering. There are some who speak well too. Yeah. It depends.
>
> CK: Is it because some tried harder, or is it because some go more often? Why do some speak better than others?
>
> F: Um, because some studied Arabic here too.

Usually, those children who spoke better were the older children. By the time the youngest came along, older brothers and sisters were using French around the new arrival. Latifa, Rachida's daughter, thought that all her brothers and sisters spoke Arabic, but her mother made her reconsider:

> L: We all speak, yes.
>
> R: No, don't speak good, good, good, but—
>
> L: Yes, the youngest one has trouble.

The pattern was the same in Chafiqa's family:

> CK: And so you speak Kabyle at home?
>
> C: Yes. Yes, I speak, me. There are some who understand, there are some who don't understand. With my husband I speak, yes . . . with my children I speak. They understand, but they aren't able to answer. There are words they say in Kabyle, but my oldest son speaks a little

better, my oldest daughter. The youngest, he doesn't want to speak. There are three who speak well, and three who don't speak well.

Fatima's youngest also had the most trouble because he had had less exposure to family members and fewer trips to Morocco than his older siblings:

> If I find myself with friends or with my sister, we speak our language. Even my children, they speak Arabic. My son, my son speaks Arabic, my daughter. They speak Arabic because they listen to me when I speak with friends or with their aunts when they came to the house. . . . And when he's in Morocco, there he hears people; he talks with the aunts, the uncles, the nieces, so obviously, at the beach or in a restaurant, and everything. But they speak Arabic. The little one understands, but he can't answer. But the others, yes.

Fatima's example provides some clues to why certain respondents were more successful at transmitting their language than others. Having family members visit frequently and spending a lot of time in the Maghreb helped, as Hachmia noted: "Mine speak fluently. They go to the country every year, and they speak really well." Jawahir's sons visit Tunisia at least twice a year:

> *J:* Me, with my children, French. But when they go there, my children, they arrive at the airport, they see my parents, it's over. You'd say they left the French language at the airport.
>
> *CK:* The children speak Arabic when they're there?
>
> *J:* Yes. Fluently. They understand, they speak. But when they arrive in France, they speak French. When they arrive in Tunisia, they often go on vacation to Tunisia, often, they arrive at the airport, they speak Arabic. It's over. The French they leave in France, okay. When they arrive there, they speak Arabic.

Hiba's son had also learned Arabic from periodically attending school for short periods of time in Algeria: "Mine speaks Kabyle, Arabic, French, and English, so that when we speak over there he won't be sad. That's why he's interested over there, he speaks well. And since we go there, he goes to school there. He goes to school. Even here, I pay, I pay the Arabic school."

The children who not only spoke Arabic the best but who could also write and read were those who had indeed attended Arabic classes in France. This factor was in many cases as or more important than parents' use of the language. Karima highlights the importance of both:

> We said when the children were born, at home it's Arabic, because I always wanted them to learn the maternal language. So, um, when I was pregnant, I always listened to, when at the time it was the fad to make the fetus listen to music, it was *chahabi* on my stomach. . . . Yes, so at home, now, really always, it's always been Algerian music. So I always wanted the children to imbibe a little the Algerian culture. . . . We always spoke Arabic. . . . I was already an Arabic language teacher in Algeria. . . . My children speak Arabic very, very well. They even did it as a second language in high school. So language, culture, everything, there I think I didn't let anything get by. I inculcated everything in them, the basis.

When asked whether her children speak Arabic, Souad's answer is similar: "Yes, yes, all of them. They speak. They did, when they were little, they did a little bit of Arabic studies because there are schools that give, they did it for two, three years I think, yes. Well, they don't know how to read very well, but they know the letters; they can write a little bit. But they speak Arabic very well because at home when they were little, I spoke Arabic with them."

Although some women without children believed it would be easy to pass on their native language, Labiba was aware that it is more difficult than it seems. She also realizes that if she does not establish a basis for her son while he is young, it may be too late: "I would like for him to learn Berber and Arabic before he enters school because I know French is inevitable. The French structure is already there to ensure it. . . . But, on the other hand, if he's six, seven and doesn't have the maternal languages, I can't make up for it." In addition, some respondents, including Najet, recognized that even if they succeeded in making their children fluent, language use would probably not survive into the next generation.

> *N:* They only speak, they don't write. Not easy. They weren't, they don't have school here, they don't have Arabic school here, so they learn to talk, that's it, not read and write.
>
> *CK:* And do they speak Berber well?
>
> *N:* Yes, yes, yes, okay, a little bit.

> *CK:* Do you think they'll be able to pass on, to give Arabic to their own children?
>
> *N:* Oh, that's a little bit difficult because they already speak Arabic badly, so for later, if we're not here, I don't think so. Already between them they speak French, between brothers and sisters, automatically they speak French.

Portes and Shauffler (1994) argue that even in Hispanic enclaves in Miami, Spanish-language use will die out after a few generations. More than half of children in these enclaves prefer English to Spanish. This is likely to also be the pattern among Arabic speakers in France.

OTHER VALUES

Although respondents learned that transmitting Arabic was difficult, they did expect to be able to pass on other customs and values. Deha, who admitted she did very little to uphold Algerian traditions at home, spoke about what she has taught her son to appreciate: "The food; he adores [an Algerian dish]. . . . And music." Other women also mentioned food and/or music. Yet other customs, including wearing traditional clothing or painting one's hands and feet with henna, were harder to convince children to follow, and participants like Chafiqa recognized that they had to make compromises: "We do a little French, a little Algeria, for the children we do it. We make them happy, and us, we make us happy. They follow the culture that's here. Because I can't force them. They do like I do, but I don't want to force them, insist with force to do something they don't want to do."

Although traditions and customs often went by the wayside, respondents insisted that they could at least pass on important Maghrebin values. When asked what mattered most for her daughter, Soraya answered, "That she be generous, because people aren't very generous here. Niceness also. And contact with people because there's a lot, there we love contact, we love to go see people." Cherifa talked about the qualities she had fostered in her son:

> Politeness, that's important. Being a good listener, um, communication. Being family-oriented, that's primordial. The fact that he gets up in the morning and comes to say, "Good morning, Mama. Did you sleep well?" Or before going to bed, he instinctively comes to say, "Good night, Mama."

"Good night," to all the people there, that he doesn't go up to his room like
a lot of Europeans, like a lot of French kids who go up, you look for them
for 10 minutes and you find them in bed, for example. I absolutely care
about that.

Mimouna agreed that encouraging family closeness was what mattered most:

> Values, yes, to stay, to think, always be close. There are people who don't
> think about their brothers and sisters and all that; they don't like to. So
> that they love each other, that's the best thing. It's not money; that's noth-
> ing. It's more than money that, because money is nothing when you don't
> have love . . . that's the wealth to leave for my children, attached to the
> family. Even the family at home, in the country. I always call; I say, "Pass
> me"; I always pass my children to their grandfather, to my brothers and all
> that, so that they don't forget, even the year they don't go back, and always
> they have good relations with the family, don't forget, you see? There they
> don't forget my children, and my children don't forget their family.

The focus on making children family-centered is also a form of insurance for
North African women in France. Shocked by seeing elderly parents left in
nursing homes in France, Cherifa worried that if her son became too French,
she also might find herself abandoned one day.

Warda noted that living in a neighborhood in the center of Paris without
a large concentration of Maghrebins made it harder to transmit traditions. In
an attempt to balance out his attendance at a mainly white Catholic school,
Mbruka has purposely chosen to enroll her son one day a week in a day care
center in their suburb that is largely composed of second-generation children:

> We're in France; their country will be France, it's clear. Even if they go on
> vacation regularly, it will still be the country for vacation. And that's why all
> these problems result — because we're not very traditional, and that limits
> the things we can transmit. On top of it, what's annoying is that we're cut
> off from the Maghrebin community. We don't have family, so we don't have
> North African friends, not by choice, but because life worked out that way.
> Which means that [the children] don't have a lot of contact with Maghre-
> bins to see that even if we don't do it, that they know that it's done, that
> they see how other families who are different from us live. . . . So it makes
> a little bit, not a big difference, having him spend a little time in child care

with his old friends . . . with the kids he was with in kindergarten. So he sees them on Wednesdays.

Despite realizing that vacations alone will not do it, Mbruka, like the majority of other participants, regularly takes her son to North Africa to visit his relatives: "I send my son to make the link, so that he'll know the grandparents."

Children's Names as Compromise

Parents were in control of one custom that their children have no say in: the choice of a name. What Maghrebin women in France are choosing to name their children is telling about their cultural positioning. Names are markers of identity for others and for self. According to symbolic interactionists, children begin to see themselves as objects when they recognize that, like other objects in their environment, they too are named. The choice of a French name, a Maghrebin one, or something in between thus sends a powerful message that can have both personal and societal implications. Isma said she would never really feel French in part because she does not have a French name. Karima noted that this is not just a matter of how you view yourself, but how others view you: "The fact of having an Arabic name, I assure you, that catalogs you." Being cataloged leads to assumptions about behavior, as Nour found: "My daughter, one day because her name is [typical North African], a teacher who didn't know said, 'But you, you don't eat pork.' My daughter said, 'Yes, I eat pork, me, I eat pork.' And the teacher almost didn't believe her, you see?" Being cataloged also leads to discrimination, as several respondents, including Telja, pointed out: "There's racism by Arab first names; it's very hard to find work."

Cognizant of this, some women took advantage of ambiguous-sounding or French names. Nour preferred her maiden name in part because it was less identifiable: "I kept my maiden name; I had always kept it, even in Algiers. My married name is [typical Arabic last name]. Maghrebin sound. It's already hard to spell, because they [pronounce it wrong]. So it's already a problem. Me . . . here they don't realize where my name is from; they don't know, it's not common either. So I kept that name on purpose." From her bogus marriage to a French man, Labiba had gained not only a French last name, but also a title: "I still have the husband's name on my card, my permanent resident card. I haven't changed my name yet. . . . He was a French noble. It's true. I had the title of countess for five years. Yes, I have it now, until I take it off my permanent resident card. It's true. Each time I go to the prefecture, they find, [noble last name], Labiba. They look; 'Dark as she is, she's a countess, that one?'" Warda's son found that by changing the order of a few letters in his first name, he could pass it off as French. This served him well:

> He was called for a week of national service. . . . He went with his original first name, his original first name is an Arab first name, typically Arab. The last name doesn't show; people don't know what it is. . . . He gets to [the military base], there were two lines, not two lines, but there were groups; the officer who greeted them said, "You, go there; you, go there; you, go there." They took him for a young immigrant . . . they put him with the immigrants. . . . He said, "I wasn't in my usual intellectual category; I found myself with the little hoodlums from the suburbs." There's a minimum of, because they don't take the same tests, they don't do the same things, really. So he said, "We're really treated like dogs." And the next time, he swore to, he said to me, "I'll change my first name; nobody will know who I am anymore." He had an easy-to-change name. . . . He said, "At home I'll still be [original name], but there I'll be [French name]." He changed his first name. He said, "They called me with the students, with the teachers" . . . and he got through like that. He said, "It's crazy the consideration you get for a simple first name."

Despite the recognition of racism based on first names, only two women chose to give their children typical French names, and these were the children of Amina and Cherifa, both of whom had French fathers. All of the older immigrant women had given their children traditional North African names, such as Hafida, Fathiya, Hind, Soumia, and Rafika for girls, and Mohammed, Hassan, Abdermalek, Djamel, and Azouz for boys. For some younger women, like Labiba, a traditional North African name was also important: "He has an Arabic first name and a Berber middle name." Several young, well-educated women, on the other hand, attempted to find names that worked well in both French and Arabic. They sought to prevent discrimination against their children without losing the heritage carried in a name. They thus picked North African names that either sounded French or were common in other languages, such as Maya and Nadia for girls and Ryan and Yannis for boys. Lina and Rym have noted a pattern for young children born recently in France, and they intend to follow it:

> R: Sometimes we discuss first names and everything, that we'll give our kids, we've already had some friends, it's clear you're not going to call them David or Laurent, that's obvious. Despite the fact that it would be very good for them because they're going to live here, and they won't have the same problems as us. My husband, when he goes to apply for a job . . . he's French, but his name isn't —
>
> CK: Jean-Marc.
>
> R: Right. His name is [typically North African]. . . . And us, with our children, already the first name, well, we aren't going to call them, as I said, we're not going to give them French names, but we're going to give names that sound French, you see?
>
> L: No, meaning easy to pronounce. No "Kh" or with a "Rrrha" or with a —
>
> R: Wait, Lina, easy to pronounce and harder to catalog. Like the guy, when he sees your name, he's going to dig in his head to figure out where you come from. He won't know right away.
>
> L: Me, people say to me very often, "What origin are you?"
>
> R: You see, it's a neutral name. She has a neutral name.
>
> L: Lina. It works everywhere. So they ask us. And we'd like it to be the same for our kids, that they're not cataloged by their names.
>
> R: Like Mohammed, Abdelkadir, Karim, Fatima, you see? We have friends now, all our friends who had kids . . . there's several named Ryan; it's popular, Ryan. You have it in the U.S., and it's an Arab name. It's also an English name, but it's an Arab name. It means the seventh door of paradise. Yes, Ryan. If he's in Algeria, it will be Ryan, and if he's in France it will be Ryan [she pronounces it two different ways]. There are a lot of first names like that. People, we want to, they have to live here, they shouldn't be classified. But, well, it's hard because there aren't a lot of first names; you really have to find them.

Although Nadia is a common name in North Africa, Maya, Lina, Yannis, and Ryan are not, and yet they are being used extensively for children born in France to Maghrebin parents. Both Isma's and Mbruka's sons had the same uneasily identifiable name. Soraya chose an Egyptian name that sounded French for her daughter. Women are also looking for Arabic words that sound good in French, even if they are not actually traditional Maghrebin names. This allows a compromise: remaining connected to the language and traditions of the country of origin without marking their children with names that will elicit negative reactions. Nevertheless, last names remain a problem. Mbruka was sorry to find that her young son already had a preference for French names over Arab ones: "It's difficult for him. 'Oh, [last name], I don't think it's nice.' And his first name is [an Arab/Mediterranean name with a French sound], so he likes his first name, but his last name, he thinks it doesn't denote the same thing. 'I don't think it's nice.' What we do, with my husband, we choose names, other names that are typically Arab or foreign or French names, Duval, Durand, and he found Duval, Durand prettier." Thus, despite some control over how their children are perceived, Maghrebin women, and their children too, realize this only goes so far.

Conclusion

The compromises women are making in terms of names are one indication of a strategy for making their children bicultural. Various social scientists argue that teaching bicultural competence promotes the success and mental health of minority children (Harrison et al. 1990; Hill et al. 1994). A couple of respondents, including Nour, spoke explicitly about their wishes to have biculturally competent children: "My main preoccupation is not to make an Algerian, it's to make someone who will be at ease wherever she goes, in the whole world, there where she lives." Nedjma elaborated about the differences between immigrants and their children and how best to help children of foreign origin in France. She concludes on a positive note:

> We've lived that schizophrenia; we still live it. The choices are sometimes difficult. . . . So you have to try your best to help the children grow without, try to make that culture a richness, and not something that creates a dichotomy in them. You have to be this or that. Or this, not that anymore. And why can't we be both? Now the world is full of mixing. So mandatory you have to teach your kids to accept that mixing, and not only to accept it, but also to tell them that it's a richness. It's a wonderful richness.

Closed Doors and Opened Doors

This research addresses questions of cultural choices and identity negotiation among North African women immigrants living in France. Despite the
differences among women, several important patterns emerged. I examined
the impact of gender on Muslim, female immigrants' experience of leaving
the Maghreb and living in France. As other studies of immigrant women
have shown (Andezian 1986; Kibria 1993; Hondagneu-Sotelo 1994; Espiritu
1997), North African women in France take on new roles, including dealing
with French administration and often engaging in paid work. This leads to
increased independence, both mobile and financial, and helps offset the disadvantages of underpaid and unstimulating jobs. All the women interviewed,
regardless of how much they were able to take advantage of it, appreciated
the freedoms they found in France. Yet participants had radically different
definitions of freedom. For some, it means making decisions independent of
husbands; for others, it means liberation from traditional responsibilities at
home; and for still others, it simply means being able to go out shopping
alone. The experiences of immigration differ for men and women. Women

who did not work, rarely went out, and were far from relatives experienced a great deal of social isolation, something that working men are less likely to encounter. On the other hand, participants insisted that as women, they were treated better in France than Maghrebin men who faced more racism. Although state aid for women and children reached everyone who knew how to get it, only French-speaking women in western attire garnered benefits from being female in daily interactions with French people. Thus life in France is easier for North African women than it is for men, but only if they are willing to play the game by making an effort to fit in and do gender in a culturally appropriate way.

This book also looks at the cultural choices North African women made, what they kept from home, what they took from France, and how they felt about adaptation in their lives. Despite different levels of exposure to French culture and education, participants were unanimous in what they disliked about France. In addition to missing their families and the warm weather, Maghrebin women found the French cold, uncommunicative, and individualistic. This points to the influence of culture on preferences and the drawing of symbolic boundaries between groups. After a period of time in France, many North Africans also became critical of certain aspects of the Maghrebin "mentality," such as the lack of work ethic and the machismo. They learned to appreciate the opportunities France offered them in terms of education, work, and cultural enrichment. Participants also incorporated different amounts of French culture into their own behaviors and values. Although some maintained Maghrebin traditions to a high degree, others spoke, cooked, and dressed French. Nevertheless, all the respondents were engaged in selective acculturation, picking and choosing various customs to keep, add, or change. Even religion was affected by the move to France. Although some women were not at all religious, even those who were very observant had modified their practices to adapt to France. They moved celebrations from holidays to the weekends and manifestations of religious observance from the public domain to the private. They redefined what it meant to be a good Muslim woman, focusing not on norms they grew up with in North Africa, but rather on the purity of their hearts. The shift in religious practices and numerous other cultural behaviors from weekdays to after work and from outside to inside, what I have termed "culture on the weekend," demonstrates the flexibility of people in situations of migration and is evidence of the alternation model in practice (LaFromboise et al. 1993; Killian 2002).

An important part of this work is exploring how Maghrebin women construct and manage their identities in the midst of a foreign context. When asked how they self-identify, the majority of respondents feel either Maghrebin or both French and Maghrebin; only seven identified primarily as French only. What is interesting is not only the labels they chose, but how they arrived at those designations. Participants used the same criteria to arrive at different conclusions. For some women, obtaining French citizenship was determinate for self-identification, whereas for others, the document was only a piece of paper that did not change how they viewed themselves. Some used the extent of maintenance of North African cultural practices to evaluate how French or Maghrebin they were, but others felt that place of birth prevailed over everything else. The varying criteria point to the fluidity of personal definitions of identity.

Misdesignations by others were the cause of stress, and women engaged in different forms of identity work resisting these meta-perceptions. Several argued that the split between Arabs and Berbers was at least partially artificial and reflected an attempt by the French to manipulate identity politics for their benefit. The continued infighting in Algeria between these groups leads to a tension around these labels that highlights the effects of history and social context on individual identities. Surprisingly, a number of women even rejected classification as immigrants, arguing that because of their socioeconomic level or because of their reason for migration, the label *immigrant* did not apply to them. In dealing with French people, respondents fought to be seen as individuals rather than simply as foreigners, Arabs, or Muslims. In general, Maghrebin women were better off when they felt they could manage others' reactions to their image.

Information for analyzing how immigrants are faring can be organized by looking at the structural and relational problems North African women face in France. The primary structural problems are getting legal residence papers, finding work, and obtaining housing. The main relational problems have to do with communication, isolation, and racism. Women have various strategies for dealing with racism, including denying that it has ever happened to them. Some women believe that by monitoring their actions, dressing nicely, and behaving politely, they can prevent racist occurrences. This strategy, however, puts blame on those who fall victim to racism. Others perhaps overlooked minor incidents, defining racism as only severe, physical attacks rather than as comments or discrimination. When faced directly with racism, those women who defended themselves verbally fared the best. In general, women who felt like they took action to control their lives, be it standing up to racism or fighting the system to obtain papers, were doing better in terms of mental health than those who felt surpassed by life events and unable to take care of themselves. Finally, numerous participants found that French people would make racist comments in front of them about Maghrebins, yet assure them that they were different. This support for the idea that schemas are hard to change even in the face of contradictory evidence helps us understand the persistence of racism.

This book concluded by looking toward the future: examining North African women's expectations for their children and their efforts in raising them. Participants held the same expectations for their sons and daughters — that they would continue in school and then find work and get married. Although the women interviewed all want their children to take advantage of the opportunities in France, this has paradoxically forced mothers who wanted to return to the Maghreb to remain in France permanently. They have realized that their children are more French than North African and will live out their lives in France. To be with their children means that they too must stay. Although they know that their children are French, they have also tried to transmit the customs and values from the Maghreb that they find worthwhile. Passing on culture is difficult, however. Many women were not successful teaching their children to speak Arabic, and even those who did recognized that Arabic will not survive into the third generation. When trying to foster religious commitment and other cultural traditions, respondents believed it best to expose their children to their values and behaviors without forcing them to follow. They hoped that if provided a good base of knowledge, children would one day choose to actively practice Islam. They did not expect, however, to influence their children's choice of a spouse, and many were open to allowing both their daughters and sons to marry non-Muslims. On the other hand, they worked hard to inculcate their values, especially generosity and a commitment to family. Participants generally recognized the need for their children to be actively bicultural. A current trend among young women, the choice of a French-sounding Arab name, reflects their commitment to facilitating their children's integration in France without abandoning their heritage.

Theoretical Implications

This study is based on the experiences of North African women in France, and as much as possible it attempts to reflect their perspectives on their lives. Thus, instead of focusing on testing macro-level questions, I strove for "grounded theory," encouraging women to tell their stories in their own words so that the salient issues in their lives emerged naturally (Glaser and Strauss 1967; Blumer 1969). By allowing them to do the talking, I heard the same terms repeated frequently, but I also found that various immigrant women defined the same concepts differently. What does it mean to be an immigrant? How do we determine who is French and who is Maghrebin? What is freedom? Recognizing the different responses immigrant women have to these questions allows us to examine their cultural choices and implications for identity negotiation. It also points to the difficulties that governments have when they attempt to treat immigrant groups as a monolithic block.

Despite assumptions that the first generation will continue to identify primarily with the country of origin and the lack of an acceptance of hyphenated identities in French public discourse, 20 of the respondents said they felt both Maghrebin and French, and 7 reported feeling more French than North African. As members of a recognizable minority group, Maghrebins should be socially constrained in their choice of an ethnic identity (Waters 1990). Yet participants often used flexible criteria, such as their level of cultural behaviors, rather than fixed biological categories to determine their self-identification. However, because French people are likely to base ethnic identity on physical attributes such as skin color, conflict frequently arises between self and meta-perceptions. Women tried to control others' perceptions by engaging in a variety of identity work strategies (Snow and Anderson 1987), including managing their appearance (for example, not wearing North African clothing, making an extra effort to look well put-together) and choosing particular groups of people to interact with, those who were less likely to be racist. When racist incidents did occur, they often argued with the offender. Whether or not they succeeded in changing the perception, taking action helped mitigate against later stress. This is an important addition to Burke's (1991) work on stress and identity processes. In the future, research needs to look longitudinally at identity feedback loops and how the level of stress varies on the spot and over time for those who do not attempt to correct others' misperceptions compared with those who try to change the appraisals, and to compare these people in turn with those who not only try but *succeed* in positively influencing others' appraisals and behavior.

Recognizing that immigrants are low status, several women refused to apply this label to themselves. Passing as a member of a higher-status group is a common strategy predicted by social identity theory. This finding is nevertheless surprising because "immigrant" is generally accepted as a clear-cut category not open to negotiation. In order to reject this label, respondents reformulated the definition of immigrant from someone who has moved from one country to another to someone who has come primarily for economic reasons or is having trouble adapting, thus inserting issues of class, motivation, and psychological adjustment. Although at the individual level this may seem like an effective form of resistance to an identity imposed by others, ultimately, this self-distancing from the immigrant label may serve to reinforce negative stereotypes of immigrants that keep them below natives on the status hierarchy. Nevertheless, all of these findings point to the high degree of identity work among members of low-status groups, and the fluidity of personal identity, even among visible minorities whose self-identification choices were previously thought to be more tightly constrained.

Differences among the participants affected not only how they viewed themselves, but also how they felt about their place in France. These differences did not result from country of origin, but rather broke down along lines of education and social class. For example, well-educated women struggled more actively with decisions about how to raise bicultural children in France. The differences between women of different backgrounds have important ramifications for the successful integration of immigrants into the host society. Although previous research often focuses on the greater problems of deprived immigrants, less attention is paid to the difficulties highlighted by those who are better off (Portes and Rumbaut 1996). Poorly educated, rural women and well-educated women from cities had different perceptions and problems. The former suffered from the greater social distance traveled, and they often lacked the skills to effectively fight for their rights in France. They also suffered more from social isolation when family members were not present because they had fewer contacts with French people. The latter did indeed feel more comfortable in France, but they were also more hurt when their expectations about work opportunities and relationships with French people were not met, and these disappointments could have critical effects on self-esteem.

Portes and Rumbaut (1996) report the unexpected finding that Mexican and Cuban immigrants who speak English well and are better educated develop more negative views about the United States, particularly in terms of racial discrimination, during their first few years in the country. On the other hand, as expected, they are more satisfied with their lives in the United States and more likely to plan to apply for citizenship than less well-acculturated immigrants. My findings on well-educated Maghrebin women's disillusionment in France may be a part of this phenomenon. More research along these lines needs to be carried out to determine whether this is an example of alienation or rather, as Portes and Rumbaut argue, just a "realistic appraisal" of realities in the country of residence (1996:186). Thus, in thinking about whether particular immigrants have adapted well to life in a new country, we must remember to consider not only material success, but also perceptions of acceptance or rejection.

Participants from all backgrounds did have much in common, however, pointing to more general patterns of acculturation. Rather than being either the "bearers of 'tradition'" or "the agents of 'modernity,'" all women practiced selective acculturation, preserving some customs and adopting new French ones, albeit to different degrees (Freedman 2000:15). Often traditional behaviors, including cooking and wearing Maghrebin dress, were practiced "on the weekend," a natural boundary between the private and the public (time for self versus time for work; home versus street). The traditional practice of veiling in Muslim countries demarcates men's space, or public space, from women's space in the home. Thus, in the Maghreb, women put on the veil to go out into the street and take it off at home. In France, where the street is no longer men's space but rather French space, the relegation of headscarves to the home demonstrates a case of cultural adaptation where the behavior is modified to fit a new context but is not lost altogether. In comparing France and its law banning religious dress from public schools to the more religiously tolerant yet still deeply racially divided United States, we can question whether the state should force immigrants and their children to change their behavior in the hopes that this will make everyone get along better, or whether they should be allowed to acculturate selectively even if their choices may make others profoundly uncomfortable.

Despite the popular perception that North African immigrants do not take their daughters' education seriously, all the respondents voiced the same dreams for their children, both male and female: success at school and in work, and a happy family life. At the same time, they want children to maintain Maghrebin values, including practicing Islam. These desires, however, may be undermined in part by their children's decisions to make exogamous marriages, a choice that surprisingly many mothers approved of, even for their daughters. Perhaps the willingness to allow daughters to marry non-Muslims stems from the belief that forcing children is not an effective means of accomplishing one's goals and from a realization that a marriage to someone outside of the group is better than no marriage at all. All the participants appreciated the greater range of freedoms for women in France, even though their definitions and experiences of freedom differed. They also identified the same negative and positive aspects of France, and this recognition of differences was a first step toward picking and choosing from the best of both worlds.

Regardless of social class and educational level, those women who learned how to fight for themselves (for example, navigating French bureaucracies and standing up to racist remarks) reported lower levels of psychological distress and were more hopeful about the future. Portes and Rumbaut (1996) identify a sense of control over life events as one of the important factors influencing the mental health of immigrants, and the findings here support this assertion. On the other hand, immigrant women who believe they can control situations they cannot set themselves up for disappointment. Those who think they are able to prevent racism by dressing nicely, or that any qualified person can find a suitable job despite a tight labor market compounded by racist hiring practices, can also end up blaming the victim. A fine line exists, therefore, between taking one's life in one's hands and recognizing constraints that are beyond one's control.

New studies should look at immigrants from different countries to determine whether or not patterns of identification and acculturation hold up across groups. For instance, are different racial minority immigrants more or less likely to self-identify with the host nation than Maghrebins? Lalonde et al. (1992) point out that the greater number of Haitians in Canada makes them more visible in the host country and less likely to identify as Canadian than Indian immigrants. How have September 11, 2001, and the recent wars in the Middle East affected Muslims' adaptation in western countries? More research is needed to examine visibility, world events, and other factors that may affect the social identification of members of various ethnic groups.

The idea of selective acculturation is a relatively new one in the immigration literature (Portes and Rumbaut 1996). Participants in this study provided numerous examples of selective acculturation. Do Asian or sub-Saharan African immigrants in France practice selective acculturation to the same degree as North Africans? Are they as unanimous about what they appreciate and what they dislike in the new country? It is also vital to compare different contexts of reception. The United States, which prides itself on multiculturalism, for example, has a different immigration history and different expectations about how immigrants should fit in the country than republican France. At the same time, however, policies for admitting immigrants have been changing worldwide in response to terrorist attacks in western nations. Attention to the wider social context in which immigrants experience cultural adaptation and identity negotiation is crucial for understanding how these personal processes work.

A particularly intriguing question concerns the acceptance or rejection of the term *immigrant*. Are some groups more willing to accept the immigrant label, or does this always vary by class and the motivation behind immigration? One study has examined immigrants' reluctance to label themselves as such. Gold (1997) found that Israelis in the United States rarely classify themselves as immigrants. Moving to Israel is a highly valued religious act, and consequently, moving away from Israel is looked down upon. Even Israelis who left decades ago and raised children in the United States thus continue to state that they will return to Israel in the future. Other groups who might have reasons to view immigrants in a positive rather than a negative light, perhaps because of socioeconomic advantages or being labeled as part of the "brain drain," may be more likely to incorporate the term *immigrant* into self-descriptions.

Finally, by focusing on immigrant women, I have ignored half of gender's effect on these processes. North African women in France believed that they were better off than their male counterparts because they are seen first and foremost as women and consequently experience less racism. I did not, however, ask men their opinions on this subject to find out whether they agree that woman have it easier. I also cannot compare how these dynamics affect men's self-perceptions and levels of acculturation. In addition, it is important to find out how male Maghrebins' experience of being men changes during immigration. Do they, like women, feel a degree of liberation from the restraints of certain gendered expectations, or do they experience changes in gender roles as a loss in status? How are they reacting, for instance, to their reduced control over female family members? Kibria's (1993, 1994) work on Vietnamese families in the United States suggests that male immigrants cling to their traditional roles as men in an effort to offset the losses they experience in status as socioeconomically deprived members of a minority group. Lamont (2000) has studied working-class North African men's reactions to racism in France, and future research is needed to look at various class levels and compare male and female immigrants' perceptions and success in adaptation.

Immigration places people in a profound situation of personal change and forces them to question not only taken-for-granted cultural assumptions, but also their own sense of self and place in the world. Although moving to France did not usually signify an end to all ties to North Africa, the women I interviewed did realize that their migration had a great impact on their lives. As Amel phrased it, "I think coming here closed some doors for me; maybe it opened others." That the majority of women planned to stay in France signifies that they are happier going through the new doors.

Methodology

I conducted semistructured interviews with 45 women in Paris between January and July 1999. All of the participants are first-generation immigrants from the Maghreb. They are all Muslim, but they differ on other characteristics such as age, employment history, marital status, and number of children. Theoretical sampling led to a rich sample rather than a truly representative one (Glaser and Strauss 1967; Nippert-Eng 1996). I sought a sample that varies on time spent in France, socioeconomic level (education and profession), country of origin (Algeria, Morocco, and Tunisia), ethnicity (Arab and Berber), and legal status because there are empirical and theoretical reasons to believe that differences in these characteristics are especially likely to influence identity processes (Platt 1986; Lalonde et al. 1992; Waters 1994; Roberts 1995; Bozorgmehr 1997; Schulz 1998).

I recruited subjects through organizations such as neighborhood associations, literacy classes, and personal contacts. I attended numerous North African social events and conferences dealing with immigrants and Maghrebins, and I spent time hanging out in an Algerian boutique and sitting in on literacy classes. These strategies sometimes led to contacts and/or interviews. In addition to being generally informative, they also allowed potential participants to observe me in different situations before agreeing to be interviewed. Starting with multiple sources from different backgrounds (university students, professionals, homemakers, women enrolled in literacy classes, cultural association employees) helped me avoid becoming trapped in one type of social network. The interviews were conducted at the interviewees' homes and workplaces, in association locals and classrooms, and in cafés. Most of the interviews lasted between 45 minutes and two hours and fifteen minutes. I conducted 43 interviews in French, and two were done in Arabic with the help of a translator. I interviewed eight pairs of respondents at the same time because it was more convenient for them. The women interviewed in pairs were either close friends or members of the same literacy class. All of the interviewees were read a letter explaining the study and their rights as participants. Although I gave the letter to the participants to keep, I purposely read it to them because several of the women were illiterate. I then obtained verbal consent before tape recording the interview. In addition to recording, I took systematic notes during the interviews. I also wrote field notes about physical appearance (skin color, regional tattoos, jewelry), nonverbal communication during the interview (pauses, tears, facial expressions), and my feelings about the interviewing process. I noted issues and themes I thought were particularly relevant and that I should highlight, as well as ideas for new questions. These field notes were usually written immediately after each interview on the way home in the metro. In my notes and in the final product, respondents are referred to by pseudonyms, and certain identifying details about them have been changed to protect their anonymity.

The interviews contained open-ended questions about general topics such as cultural behaviors (dress, cooking, language use, religious practices), children's socialization, beliefs about gender roles, racism in France, and view on assimilation. I asked respondents about pressures and challenges they have faced in terms of their position as female, Muslim immigrants from North Africa, and how they respond to these dilemmas. Although I do not know what the women in this study were like before immigration to France, I was able to ask them how they think their lives and views would be different today had they remained in the Maghreb. Participants discussed the meanings and importance attributed to their various identities: religious, racial, immigrant, and female.

The questions I pose are best met by in-depth interviews because they involve the exploration of choices, values, and beliefs and the description of processes. Survey methods would be inappropriate for understanding the complex dynamics of identity negotiation and acculturation, especially given the paucity of information on these topics. One of the greatest strengths of qualitative methods is that they reveal the respondents' perspectives (Jayaratne and Stewart 1991). Interviews allow respondents to generate themes and categories themselves (Lamont 1992). This method helps to ensure that respondents allow the researcher to see into their worldview instead of the other way around (Patton 1990). The interviews were guided by the participants' responses to the open-ended questions, and although the majority of original questions were posed to all interviewees, new questions and topics arose during the course of each interview. This flexible approach to data collection is advocated by Glaser and Strauss (1967) and Blumer (1969). For Blumer, the question must be approached "through the eyes and experience" of those who live it, and the "directions of inquiry, data, analytic relations, and interpretations arise out of, and remain grounded in, the empirical life under study" (1969:139–40).

As a white, female, American researcher, I am a member of the outgroup in terms of everything but gender. In some ways, my being American may actually have been an advantage in asking immigrants about their experiences. Respondents were not always sure that I was familiar with either Maghrebin or French culture and therefore sometimes felt it necessary to explain assumptions they would normally take for granted (Lamont 1992). Given that I was not French, they may also have felt more comfortable discussing problems such as racism in France that they might not have broached as easily with a French researcher (Silverstein 2004). Nevertheless, my outsider status in terms of race, and, in the majority of cases, class, affected the data collection. For example, I found that the way I posed certain questions varied depending on the French-language capacity and particularly on the educational level attained by the interviewee. It is also possible that participants tailor their responses to what they think the interviewer wants to hear (Rude-Antoine 1997). Given the history of colonialism and orientalism, interviewees may be anxious to present a picture of themselves as modern in order to deflect commonly held stereotypes, as we see Deha discuss in Chapter 4.

Although I was interested in the participants' identity construction, maintenance, and change, I found that I too had to negotiate my identity. One participant in particular labeled me the "reporter" and introduced me to her friend this way because this was her frame of reference for someone who does an interview. At the end of another interview, a respondent joked with her husband about getting her session with the "analyst" for free. Another women whom I interviewed in a literacy class was under the mistaken impression that I was a supervisor in charge of the building there to talk to her about the drafts of air and smell of paint. When she found out my real reason for talking to her, she continued with five minutes of complaints about the building before participating in an interview that lasted an hour and fifteen minutes.

Qualitative manuals include several pages on how to negotiate entry into the field. They are less loquacious on how to leave it. After working hard to establish trust and rapport, disengaging can produce anxiety and guilt concerning the participants (Snow 1980). Taylor (1991:244) explains the reasons for these feelings: "Because the success of qualitative research often depends on personal relationships with informants, leaving the field can place the researcher in an awkward or uncomfortable position. . . . The better the rapport and the closer the relationships, the more likely people will feel used when the researcher starts to leave the scene or disappears altogether." Even though I rarely spent more than a few hours with respondents, this problem arose. Two women, interviewed together, explicitly told me that they felt uncomfortable about never seeing me again after spending an entire afternoon talking about their lives with me. As Stebbins (1991:250) notes, "[s]emistructured interviews . . . tend toward the development of interpersonal relationships as the interviews unfold." Several of the women I interviewed were close to my age and equally well educated. Our similarities and the conviviality of many of the interviews, talking in cafés or over lunch at their homes, led to a blurring of the line between research and friendship. Although I was tempted by this relationship, I remained wary, knowing that the self-disclosure had not been equal. I was concerned about the ethics of developing a friendship that had begun for different reasons and would likely end after I returned to the United States. After much reflection, I decided it was best to try to keep contact to a minimum after the interviews. I did, however, see a couple of the respondents in social settings where I had been invited to make new contacts, and I also attended a talk by an immigration specialist with another participant. All of the interviewees had my home telephone number and were free to call me after the interviews, but I usually only called participants afterward if they had specifically told me to get in touch with them for a contact or an address. I did make a few phone calls and one attempt to visit to say goodbye in person, as Lofland and Lofland (1995) recommend. I also sent a postcard to a respondent who asked for one.

Many qualitative researchers struggle with issues of reciprocity. Some pay the participants, some give gifts, and others perform services such as running an errand or watching a child when asked. Most agree, however, that interviewing is not a one-way process. The researcher takes away coveted data, and the interviewee has the opportunity to talk about herself and share experiences and opinions with someone who is hanging onto every word with undivided attention. I often felt this to be the case, especially with older, lesser educated women. These women are more likely to feel isolated in France and to have few friends. They work primarily in domestic service jobs, if they work outside the home at all. Despite their frequent difficulty in speaking French, they opened up and talked at length about what concerns them. Certain younger women were also clearly pleased to be interviewed. A few worried that they had gone on too long because they enjoyed talking about themselves. One asked to make a copy of the tape because she wanted to be able to reflect on her life and thought our conversation was beneficial. The joke about the free session with the "analyst" also points to this aspect of interviewing. Finally, one participant told me directly that many of the things she had said she had kept to herself for years. She repeated several times how much she had needed to express them. For this woman, unable to confide in her family and even her best friend, an interview with a stranger was a cathartic experience.

Even though I felt positively about this facet of interviewing, I still worried about taking up the respondents' time. I thought it appropriate to give each interviewee a small gift (a stone or wood carved box or a small ceramic vase) at the end of the interview to express my appreciation for her willingness to participate and all that she had shared with me. Frequently, however, my gift-giving backfired, particularly when the interview was in the respondent's home. In these cases, participants often accepted my gift and then turned around and took something off a shelf in their living rooms for me. Despite my vigorous protesting, I was not allowed to leave without taking their gift. Although I willingly accepted a tin full of delicious homemade Moroccan cookies "for my husband," I felt terrible when given jewelry and decorative objects from the Maghreb. Clearly, I had not thought enough about the cultural differences in gift-giving norms before deciding on my strategy. For these respondents, etiquette meant giving a gift in return after receiving one. They did not share my view that I had already received a gift: the interview.

My background, of course, affects not only the data collection, but also the analysis. I chose the questions, translated the answers, and decided how to present the ensemble. Rude-Antoine (1997:101) cautions that when researchers interpret interviews, they "inevitably intensify a certain normalization" (translation mine). I would like to view myself, as Lofland and Lofland (1995:3) phrase it, as the "witness and instrument" of the respondents' stories about themselves. Yet the process of selecting and organizing the participants' words is a difficult task that in many ways confers more power on me as researcher than I ideally would like to have. As hooks (1990:151–52) argues, "Often this speech about the 'Other' annihilates, erases: 'no need to hear your voice when I can talk about you better than you can speak about yourself. . . . I want to know your story. And then I will tell it back to you in a new way . . . a way that it has become mine, my own. Re-writing you, I write myself anew. I am still author, authority.'" In a study about constructing one's own image, I realize that my presentation creates yet another image that the participants contributed to but did not control. The location (feminist, sociologist) from which I write this text is imprinted in every decision at every step of the way. Because this cannot be avoided, the next best solution is to be aware of these parameters and to acknowledge their effect on this work.

I purposely talk about Maghrebin women's experiences of acculturation and identity negotiation because there is no one unique immigrant experience. We must be careful, therefore, about suggesting that the information highlighted here is applicable to other women in different situations. The benefit of qualitative interviewing lies in its groundedness in the lived experience of people (Glaser and Strauss 1967; Blumer 1969). What this method loses is the capacity to generalize; what it gains is internal validity. We can, however, begin to highlight patterns and point to larger implications of this work, especially when the analysis of the events that compose everyday life is tied to knowledge about the larger social structure (Raissiguier 1994). Comparisons between the findings presented here and those of researchers studying other groups of immigrant women in different contexts, and more generally triangulation of methods and sources, allows us to make progress toward theoretical generalizability.

Participants

Participant Characteristic Totals

Age (years)		Time in France (years)	
25–26	2	1	2
30–34	13	1–4	3
35–39	9	5–9	8
40–44	9	10–14	9
45–49	4	15–19	7
50–54	7	20–24	9
58	1	25–29	3
		30–34	2
Age at immigration (years)		35–37	2
13	1	*Country of origin*	
14	1		
17–19	11	Tunisia	8
20–24	11	Morocco	11
25–29	11	Algeria	26
30–34	7		
35–39	1	*Marital status*	
40–45	2		
		Single	11
		Married	25
		Divorced	5
		Widowed	4

(continued)

Participant Characteristic Totals (continued)

Number of children		Legal status	
0	13	French	17*
1	8	Resident card, 10 years	19
2	5	Resident card, 1 year	2
3	6	Temporary permit	2
4	6	Student visa	2
5	2	Waiting	1
6	4	Illegal?	1
7	1	Applied for French citizenship	6

Education		Employment[†]	
None	9	Full time	13
Some	13	Part time	14
High school	5	Housewife	11
College	6	Unemployed	2
Master's	2	Not working	1
Beyond master's	10	Student	1

* Plus one European woman.

† Of the 27 women employed full- or part-time, 11 are doing cleaning or child care and 4 work for associations.

Participant Characteristics

Name	Country of Origin	Age/AI/ TimeFR*	Marital Status	Children	Location	Legal Status†	Education‡	Job
Amel	Algeria	26/20/6	Married	No	Suburb	rc	t	Child care
Amina	Tunisia	33/23/10	Single	1	Paris	rc	t	Child care
Assia	Algeria	36/19/17	Married	3	Paris	rc	s-12	Housewife
Bahia	Algeria	38/26/12	Married	6	Paris	rc/F	s-8	Housewife
Besma	Tunisia	34/18/16	Widowed	No	Suburb	F	p	Association
Chafiqa	Algeria	50/14/36	Married	6	Suburb	rc	No	Child care
Cherifa	Morocco	44/30/14	Widowed	1	Suburb	F	d	Secretary
Deha	Algeria	34/31/4	Married	1	Paris	F	1	Temp work
Djamila	Algeria	39/27/12	Married	4	Paris	rc/F	No	Cleaning
Faroudja	Algeria	52/45/7	Married	1	Paris	rc-1 yr	s-8	Sewing/housewife
Fatima	Morocco	54/17/37	Divorced	4	Paris	rc/F	No	Cleaning
Fouzia	Morocco	42/18/24	Married	7	Paris	rc	No	Housewife
Hachmia	Morocco	40/20/20	Married	4	Paris	F	No	Cleaning
Hayat	Algeria	32/23/8	Single	No	Suburb	temp	d	Small business
Hiba	Algeria	43/26/17	Married	3	Paris	rc	No	Cleaning
Houriya	Algeria	34/26/8	Single	No	Paris	temp	p	Unemployed
Isma	Algeria	36/35/1	Married	2	Suburb	temp	1	Teacher

(continued)

Participant Characteristics (continued)

Name	Country of Origin	Age/AI/TimeFR*	Marital Status	Children	Location	Legal Status†	Education†	Job
Jawahir	Tunisia	33/18/15	Widowed	3	Suburb	rc	t	Child care
Joumana	Morocco	36/13/23	Single	No	Paris	F	s-13	Cleaning
Karima	Algeria	43/22/21	Married	2	Paris	F	t	Translator
Keltouma	Morocco	35/25/10	Single	No	Suburb	F	p	pt-center
Khadija	Morocco	44/19/25	Married	4	Suburb	rc	s-16	Association
Labiba	Algeria	35/25/10	Single	1	Suburb	rc	p	Small business
Leila	Tunisia	43/20/16	Divorced	No	Paris	rc	d	Teacher
Lina	Algeria	32/26/6	Single	No	Paris	F	p	School aide
Malika	Tunisia	38/22/16	Single	No	Paris	F	p	Manager
Mbruka	Algeria	33/19/13	Married	2	Suburb	F	m	Technician
Mimouna	Tunisia	44/34/10	Married	3	Paris	F	s-12	Housewife
Najet	Morocco	46/19/27	Married	3	Suburb	rc	s-16	Housewife
Nassima	Algeria	50/43/7	Married	2	Paris	rc-1 yr	s-8	Housewife
Nedjma	Tunisia	52/31/20	Divorced	1	Paris	F	p	Artist
Nour	Algeria	34/31/3	Married	1	Suburb	Euro	d	Unemployed
Oumniya	Algeria	50/29/20	Married	6	Paris	rc	s-14	Housewife
Rachida	Morocco	47/24/23	Married	5	Paris	rc/F	s-11	Cleaning
Rym	Algeria	32/26/6	Married	No	Suburb	F	p	Service job

Name	Country of Origin	Age/AI/ TimeFR*	Marital Status	Children	Location	Legal Status†	Education‡	Job
Salima	Algeria	38/19/18	Widowed	3	Paris	F	s-13	Housewife
Soraya	Morocco	25/20/5	Married	1	Suburb	rc/F	b	Association
Souad	Tunisia	49/18/31	Divorced	4	Suburb	F	s-16	Not working
Telja	Algeria	44/17/27	Married	6	Paris	rc/F	No	Child care/cleaning
Tinhinan	Algeria	34/30/4	Single	No	Suburb	sv	m	Teacher
Warda	Algeria	58/20/34	Married	2	Paris	F	p	Association
Yasmine	Algeria	33/32/1	Single	No	Paris	?	s-16	Sewing
Yusra	Morocco	31/20/11	Single	No	Paris	sv	p	Student
Zhora	Algeria	51/29/21	Married	5	Paris	F	No	Housewife
Zitouna	Algeria	48/28/20	Divorced	4	Paris	rc	No	Housewife

* Age/age at immigration/years in France.

† Legal status is as follows: ? = illegal?; Euro = other European; F = French; rc = resident card (10 years unless noted 1 year); rc/F = applied for French citizenship; sv = student visa; temp = temporary card (*récépissé*).

‡ Education is as follows: No = none; s-(age) = some schooling; t = *terminale* (finished high school); b = baccalaureate; d = DEUG (college diploma); l = license (graduate studies); m = *maitrise* (master's); p = DEA/*doctorat* (beyond master's or Ph.D.).

Notes

1. The Maghreb comprises five countries: Libya, Tunisia, Algeria, Morocco, and Mauritania. Maghrebins in France come primarily from the three countries of the Central Maghreb — Morocco, Algeria, and Tunisia — and thus the term is used to refer only to these three groups. Differences between the women come less from their country of origin than from level of education and class differences.

2. On immigration policies, see Wihtol de Wenden (1984, 1988), Weil (1991, 2005), Fassin et al. (1997), and Sassen (1999). On Islam in France, see Kepel (1987), Etienne (1990), and Césari (1994, 1997, 1998). For interviews with first-generation men, see Sayad (2004) on Algerians, and Lamont (2000) on working-class Maghrebins. The voices of second-generation women have recently begun to be heard (Lacoste-Dujardin 1992; Raissiguier 1994; Gaspard and Khosrokhavar 1995; Souilamas 1999; Venel 1999), but those of the first generation remain neglected. The qualitative study by Weibel (2000) includes first-generation North African and Turkish women in France and Germany, but the sample is composed only of religious women who wear the veil.

3. Geisser (2003:119) urges researchers to study "the diversity of 'ways of being' Muslim in France and in the world" (translation mine).

4. Gordon (1964) identified seven subprocesses of assimilation: cultural/behavioral, structural, marital, identificational, attitudinal receptional, behavioral receptional, and civic.

5. Alba and Nee (1997:828) point out that not every early proponent of assimilation used the term to mean an end to all ethnic behaviors. They quote Park and Burgess's 1921 (1969:735) definition which describes "a process of interpenetration and fusion." In examining contemporary immigration patterns, Alba and Nee (2003) also argue that the situation of many of today's nonwhite immigrants is not as different from that of European immigrants a century ago as recent arguments lead us to believe; although assimilation in terms of language use and economic mobility is occurring at a slower pace, it is still occurring, and thus the classic assimilation approach is neither archaic nor irrelevant.

6. In much French work on immigration, *assimilation* is used to mean cultural assimilation, and *integration* is used to mean structural assimilation, social acceptance, and economic mobility. Lionel Jospin, former socialist prime minister, has said, for example, "We want to integrate immigrants; the Right wants to assimilate them or eject them" (cited in Rude-Antoine 1997; translation mine). Sometimes, however, integration is used in reference to culture, and insertion is used for economic incorporation; the ambiguity in meanings of these words is advantageous for politicians (Kastoryano 2002). Writing on the French context, Sayad (2004:301) asserts that "*adaptation, insertion, integration* . . . are all more or less euphemistic variants" of assimilation.

7. Other terms for immigration processes include *accommodation, adjustment*, and *incorporation*. These words are used differently by different authors.

8. Said (1979), among others, critiques the trend of conflating together all Muslims, and even all Arabs, from various countries, ethnic backgrounds, and class levels. As he points out, there is no one Arab psychology because one hundred million people cannot be summed up succinctly nor made into one whole. Said argues for the need to see the Orient as various "geographical spaces with indigenous, radically "different" inhabitants who can be defined on the basis of some religion, culture, or racial essence proper to that geographical space" (322). Although defining groups along more specific and accurate dimensions may be a step in the right direction, we continue to reify and essentialize ethnic groups by making them our unit of analysis (Dominguez 1989). For discussions of this phenomena among social scientists in Algeria, see Amselle (2003) and Silverstein (2002b, 2004).

9. Raissiguier (1999:439) points out that the "lack of concrete knowledge [about immigrant women in France] is partly due to the fact that there is still very little research focusing on women *per se* or using 'gender' as a critical category of analysis, but it can also be traced to the fact that within immigration scholarship, 'immigration' itself has traditionally been constructed as a male experience." Gaspard (1998) notes, for example, that the history of immigrant women coming to France alone in search of work was ignored until recently.

10. In seeking to give immigrant women, and Muslim immigrant women in particular, a voice, a problem is posed. I realize that I am attempting to enable subjectivity while at the same time arguing that the self is constructed. (See Raissiguier's [1994:24–26] discussion of the problems of subjectivity in a postmodern era.) Additionally, while calling for much-needed studies that allow immigrants "direct and free expression" about their own lives and families, Rude-Antoine (1997:100–101) points out that participants may be responding to what they believe the interviewer wants. Given these caveats, the interplay of the self and others, including the interviewer and the interviewees, cannot be ignored (see Appendix 1 for a more in-depth discussion of this problem).

11. See footnote 2.

12. Gaspard (1998:169–70) notes that women may indeed serve as "bridges" or as "mediators." Their role in integration is thus not entirely baseless, but this view

rests "on a traditional conception of the division of masculine and feminine roles, a conception according to which it is men's role to make laws and women's to make morals, men's to run society and women's to transmit those values which are considered immemorial" (translation mine).

13. Raissiguier (2003:3) writes that "[w]hether bearers or breakers of tradition, women are called forth precisely to raise the specter of 'Tradition' that stands in the way of the successful integration of African and Muslim immigrants and their children." See also Silverstein's (2004) discussion of girls born in France and the headscarf affair.

CHAPTER I. NORTH AFRICANS IN FRANCE

1. In private government papers, Charles de Gaulle wrote that "Mediterranean" and "Oriental" immigration should be limited and Northern European naturalizations favored (Noiriel 2001).

2. Although first-generation immigrants of various origins have historically faced prejudice, this is not true of second- and third-generation European immigrants who are seen as French (Noiriel 1988, 2001). Despite being targets of public disfavor, even Poles and Armenians eventually saw their children become accepted in France (Amselle 2003; Noiriel 2001). Second-generation North Africans, on the other hand, continue to be viewed by the French as Tunisians, Moroccans, or Algerians, even when they are French citizens, and consequently continue to face discrimination and anti-immigrant sentiment (Auslander 2000).

3. In addition to changes in legislation that encouraged family reunification, norms in North Africa were also changing. Whereas previously family emigration was generally viewed as a shameful act, so much so that families sometimes left their villages in the middle of the night, by the 1980s, moving one's wife and children to France was tolerated as part of the general shift toward smaller, more nuclear families (Sayad 2004).

4. Quiminal (1997) argues that these policies are inherently sexist because they automatically view women as dependents rather than as additional wage earners for the family.

5. Almost 42 percent of these immigrants have become French citizens.

6. In their examination of the philosophical and political hypocrisy of French colonies, Bancel et al. (2003) highlight the contradictions between the principle of equality of the French Republic and the classification of colonial subjects into different groups with differing rights. They also situate the origins of modern France's position on cultural difference within the colonies: "[S]ince [the Republic] hates cultural differences, it does not know what to do with individuals who have beliefs, ways of living and doing that are not European but mixed [*métissé*]. These individuals will thus have to pass through the gauntlet [*fourches caudines*] of republican pedagogy. Their ancestors are the Gaulois, their history that of the kings of France. From minorities, they must disappear in the majority; from visible, we dream of making

them invisible" (125–26; translation mine). At the same time, of course, French colonial officials and ethnographers were working to count and categorize various ethnicities, thereby creating minorities. On this point, see Amselle (2003) and Silverstein (2002b, 2004).

7. With the creation of the Council of Muslims of France in 1995, the state has tried to gain some control over and nationalize "French Islam" (Kastoryano 2002).

8. See Khellil (1991) for individual and systematic examples of prejudice and discrimination against Maghrebins in France. Body-Gendrot (2000:80) discusses continued discrimination in hiring, including the example of employers specifying a preference for native French employees ("BBR — Bleu, Blanc, Rouge"). Geisser's (2003) book, *La Nouvelle Islamophobie*, is devoted to the mix of anti-Arab and anti-Maghrebin racism combined with a fear of Islam.

9. Some argue, however, that the increasingly elderly French population needs a large workforce, including immigrant workers, to pay their pensions. Weil (2005) notes that France needs a total immigration of 5.5 million, or 110,000 people a year, to maintain its current working population.

10. These include students without financial aid, some spouses of legal immigrants, and parents of French children (Raissiguier 2003). See Fassin et al. (1997), particularly the chapters by Danièle Lochak and Nathalie Ferré.

11. Other differences concern voting rights and the type of conditions that must be met before being able to bring family members into the country (Rude-Antoine 1997).

12. Stopping people for identity checks because of race is known as *controles au faciès*.

13. Some Maghrebin writers and researchers have objected to using the term "second generation" for the children of immigrants (Khellil 1991; Begag and Chaouite 1990). They argue that the point of reference for these children should not be their parents' immigration, but rather their birth in France, thus making them the first generation. Noiriel (1998, 2001), Auslander (2000), and Césari (1997) all note that the term *second generation* was not used historically in France for the children of white immigrants from Poland, Italy, Spain, and Portugal. I have chosen to follow conventional norms in the immigration literature referring to these children as members of the second generation while recognizing that the term is politically problematic.

14. French politicians in favor of banning the headscarf in school argue that the law will help solve the problem of insular communities and "ghettoization" in France. Instead of fostering integration and the mixing of different ethnic groups, the law may in fact have the opposite effect, particularly for the girls who are expelled. See also the informative chapter in Rude-Antoine (1997) on the veil in France.

15. Interestingly, despite months of study on the issue of religious clothing, schools, and secularism, the government commission failed to consider the Sikh turban, probably because the Sikhs are a small population in France and are not portrayed as troublemakers. French Sikhs tried to argue that their turban is a cultural, rather than religious, symbol in the hopes of preventing its inclusion in the ban (Sciolino 2004). Their arguments failed, however, and three boys were expelled from school after the law went into effect in the fall of 2004, even though they had agreed

to wear simple hairnets to tie back their hair rather than wearing the traditional turban (Amiraux 2004).

16. See Charrad (2001) for an explanation of how precolonial history, especially tribal organization, affected state formation in the three countries after independence.

17. Algeria is 2,381,740 square kilometers, Morocco is 712,000 square kilometers, and Tunisia is 163,610 square kilometers.

18. Moroccans are increasingly immigrating to other European countries, including Italy, Spain, Portugal, Germany, Belgium, and the Netherlands. Tunisians and Algerians, on the other hand, migrate predominately to France. France remains the primary choice for university students pursuing degrees from all three countries because of the common language. See Sayad (2004) for an analysis of the power relations that make it more likely for Algerians to "choose" France as a host country.

19. Charrad (2001) puts the figure at 13 percent European in Algeria, compared to half that percentage in Morocco and Tunisia.

20. As many as 100,000 *harkis* (Algerians who fought or worked for the French) and their families were massacred when they were disarmed and left behind by the French army. The 1968 French census counted 85,000 *harkis* and 55,000 of their family members who escaped to France. They were often parked in isolated military-like camps where their children received a substandard education, and little attempt was made at social integration (Stone 1997). Many eventually moved to the outskirts of large cities where they continued to suffer from discrimination by both French people and other North Africans. In 1998, their number in France plus their descendants was estimated at 450,000 (Couvreur 1998).

21. The votes on the left were split among the numerous newly created parties, some of which decided not to participate in the elections at all.

22. L'Office des Migrations Internationales and L'Office Français de Protection des Réfugiés et Apatrides keep records of admissions by refugee status. The number of Algerian asylum seekers has declined in recent years; they were 2,385 in 1994, 1,800 in 1995, 634 in 1996, and 876 in 1997 (Lebon 1998).

23. Amselle (2003) points out that among the officers of France's Arab Bureaux, many were indeed Berberophiles, but that many others were Arabophiles, and some made little distinction between the groups.

24. Some Kabyles did vote for the FIS in 1991, and one of the most important leaders of the GIA is of Kabyle origin (Stone 1997). Others aligned themselves with Islamists' armed struggle against the government during protests in Kabylia in 2001, but by this time, Islamists' political power had dwindled (Volpi 2003).

25. Although the spoken Berber language is increasingly being referred to in general as Tamazight (*Amazigh* is the indigenous word for Berber), different Berber groups speak different dialects, and the only spoken form of Berber traditionally known as Tamazight is that spoken in central Morocco (Arkoun 2004).

26. The seven other legal candidates had withdrawn before the election in response to irregularities designed to ensure Bouteflika's win.

27. Socioeconomic and urban/rural distinctions, however, remain important. See

Platt (1986) on sex-role socialization of girls and boys on Tunisia's Kerkennah islands for conservative rural views of sex differences and the potential of girls and women.

28. However, even in Algeria and Morocco, polygamous marriages are rare (Rude-Antoine 1997).

29. According to the census, the most numerous group of immigrants in France in 1999 was Algerians, closely followed by Portuguese, then Moroccans, Italians, Spaniards, and Tunisians. The number of Algerian immigrants surpassed those from Portugal between 1990 and 1999.

30. *Beur* is derived from *Arab* said backward in slang known as *verlan*. It became popular in the 1980s as the term for the children of North African immigrants, but it is a more accepted term in Paris than in other regions of the country. Thus some members of the second generation refer to themselves as Beurs/Beurettes, and some eschew this term (Begag 1990).

31. It is possible that in answering surveys, people may claim a different background, given the history of French and Algerian attitudes toward Berbers and Arabs. Thus, among immigrants, an Arab may claim to be Kabyle because of a perception of preference for Kabyles in France (as Yasmine does in Chapter 4), and a Berber may claim to be Arab because she speaks Arabic and views Berbers as less modern. I thank Paul Silverstein for pointing this out.

32. This does not mean cutting all ties with the home country. The vast majority of Algerian immigrants have visited Algeria at least once since their installation in France (Tribalat 1996).

33. The French government provided financial incentives for North African immigrants to leave France beginning in the 1970s. In the 1980s they added reinsertion programs. Between 1984 and 1997, however, only 37,865 Maghrebins left with the help of these programs (Lebon 1998).

34. More than 33 percent of immigrants in France live in Paris and its suburbs (INSEE 1997).

35. Tribalat (1995, 1996) and her team of researchers surveyed over 3,000 Algerian and Moroccan immigrants between the ages of 20 and 59. Although this study represents some of the best statistical data about various immigrant populations (and is cited by well-known scholars such as Rude-Antoine 1997; Weil 2001; and Kastoryano 2002), it has been widely criticized in France because of its use of ethnicity, origin, and religious variables — variables that are specifically not included in the French census. Given France's tradition of assimilation and the loss of ethnic identity, combined with the residual fear from the Holocaust of recording data tied to religion and ethnicity, Tribalat's work is seen by some, as Martiniello (2000:119) describes it, as breaking a taboo and challenging the idealized view "of a single and indivisible republican citizenship." This despite the fact that "from a strictly methodological point of view" the study "was almost faultless" (Martiniello 2000:119). Interestingly, despite Tribalat's (1995, 1996) original conclusions that French fears about nonwhite immigrants being unassimilable are unfounded and her March 27, 1997, statements to *L'Humanité* reporter Jean-Paul Monferran in favor of more acceptance of cultural dif-

ference, in the last few years, she has become increasingly wary of Islam in France (Geisser 2003). For a French critique of the use of ethnicity statistics in social science research, see Noiriel (2001).

36. See Sayad (2004) on Algerian men's working conditions, particularly in the automobile industry, between World War II and the mid-1980s. In addition to racial discrimination, he catalogs numerous industrial accidents and their effects on the mental health of workers.

37. Quiminal (1997) points out that in an attempt to slow the number of women entering the country under family reunification laws in the 1970s, the French government tried to make it illegal for these wives to seek employment. She also notes that the women who join their husbands in France by coming with tourist visas may not work legally and thus are forced to work under the table, usually doing babysitting or cleaning work.

38. Eight percent of Maghrebins migrated to France to pursue their education (Gourévitch 1998).

39. In 1997, the figures were 12,221 Algerians, 10,297 Moroccans, and 3,601 Tunisians, for a total of 26,119 Maghrebin arrivals (Lebon 1998).

40. Another 13,769 of these immigrants were reexamined cases who had won admittance under a new 1997 law. The others came in various different categories, such as temporary workers or students (INSEE 2000b).

41. The definition of *unemployed* here is looking for work, so these figures do not include women who choose not to work.

42. In France, the poor do not live downtown, in the inner city, as in the United States. The centers of French cities are the most expensive places to live, and thus immigrants usually live on the outskirts or even in the suburbs (*banlieues*) of major cities where public housing was built by the government. Certain suburbs around Paris have an almost notorious reputation for their large concentrations of poor, immigrant families living in public housing and for their high crime rates. Kastoryano (2002) discusses the ellipses in popular discourse from "suburban youth" to "youth of immigrant origin" and the fear of "Muslim ghettos," even though these neighborhoods house immigrants from various countries as a result of French policies that sought to disperse immigrant groups and generally contain high concentrations of people of French origin (Gaspard 1998; Silverstein 2004; Weil 2005). See Kepel (1987) and Césari (1997, 1998, 2000) on Islam in these suburbs. See also Body-Gendrot and Martiniello (2000).

43. The riots were finally quelled, in part as a result of the implementation of emergency powers, including a curfew, invoked under a 1955 law designed to curb violence in Algeria during the war for independence. This law has been used only one other time since then, during independence agitation in the French territory of New Caledonia in the South Pacific; it has never before been implemented in metropolitan France.

44. In one earlier case, the bombers were Arab Christians, and yet the media and politicians denounced Muslim fundamentalism (Khellil 1991).

45. "Level of activity" is defined as employed or seeking work.

46. The birthrate in the Maghreb has continued to drop dramatically in the past ten years (LaCoste-Dujardin 2004a), and thus will probably continue to decrease among North Africans in France.

47. Another study, however, presents different numbers. Of immigrants arriving after age 15, 41 percent of Algerians and 55 percent of Moroccans speak their native language with their spouse, 42 percent of Algerians and 29 percent of Moroccans alternate between French and Arab/Berber, and 18 percent of Algerians and 16 percent of Moroccans only speak to their spouse in French (Tribalat 1996). Of those immigrants arriving after age 15 who have children living in France, 19 percent of Algerians and 26 percent of Moroccans exclusively speak their native language with their children, 46 percent of Algerians and Moroccans alternate between French and Arab/Berber, and 35 percent of Algerians and 28 percent of Moroccans speak only in French to their children (Tribalat 1996).

48. Total naturalizations have increased for all three nationalities since 1990: approximately 26 percent of Moroccans, 27 percent of Algerians, and 40 percent of Tunisians had become French citizens by 1999 (INSEE 2000a).

49. Joumana, who had been attending school in Morocco and who came to France at age 13, was enrolled in school for approximately six months, but during this time she did not learn to speak French and consequently dropped out. Chafiqa, who arrived at age 14 near the end of Algerian war for independence, was never enrolled in school either in Algeria or in France.

50. The high number of respondents who were university educated was partially the result of more successful recruitment among certain social networks and partially by design. Well-educated women were more likely to accept to participate in the study and to help me find other participants. At the same time, having similar numbers of well-educated and poorly educated women allows me to make comparisons between the groups. Patterns among the respondents were tied more to these factors than to country of origin or being Arab or Berber.

51. Only one woman who did not eat pork and who fasted during Ramadan did drink alcohol. Previous authors (Venel 1999; Bowen 2004) use daily prayer to separate "practicing Muslims" from "believing Muslims" and thus would classify women who practice food restrictions and fast as "believers" but not as "practicing Muslims" if they do not also pray regularly. I found that even women who did not practice at all still called themselves "believers," and therefore I designate the other two groups as religious for those who do all but pray and very religious for those who also pray daily.

CHAPTER 2. GENDERED LIVES FROM THE MAGHREB TO FRANCE

1. Marginalization includes focusing only on disconnected, distorted, and often inaccurate representations of Muslim women in France. For example, articles on immigrants in France frequently show women dressed in black *hidjab* that covers their entire bodies, even though most Muslim women in France do not veil, and of

those who do, the majority simply wear a scarf of various colors tied over their hair. In my interviews, even among the illiterate women who spoke French poorly, those who wore head coverings were in the minority. These common depictions feed into the collective process of othering and the fear of difference, a fear that has historically (and as currently seen in the headscarf affair) been played out on women's bodies. Uproars about clitoral excision, forced marriages, and polygamy also relate to ideas about protecting women and children from barbaric men. See Raissiguier (2003:12) for a discussion of how in these kinds of reductive representations, "it is women who, while often robbed of any real agency, are conjured up to capture the cultural distance between the French and their post-colonial others."

2. See the discussion of Amina's daughter born out of wedlock and Tunisian attitudes toward unmarried mothers who keep their babies in Chapter 5.

3. Charrad (2001) asserts that traditionally, men are more concerned with the behavior of their female blood relatives than with the behavior of their wives, and thus control over daughters and sisters can extend beyond marriage to the point that in some regions, fathers or brothers, rather than husbands, are expected to avenge the shame of adultery.

4. Weibel (2000:101) explains the importance of marriage in Islam: "[M]arriage is defined by the three axes around which it is articulated, sexual satisfaction, control over procreation, and the establishment of a home . . . [R]efusing to marry is an irresponsible act: irresponsible given the natural functions of one's body which equals a lack of respect towards the creator, and irresponsibility towards society. In this context, the establishment of a matrimonial bond becomes conditional to the socialization of the subject and his/her integration into the collectivity. Supreme rite of passage, marriage definitively binds the individual to the group and confers a well defined status on him/her" (translation mine). LaCoste-Dujardin (2004a) and Turki (1998) also discuss the disapproval of unmarried adults stemming both from Islamic views of celibacy and sexual relations outside of marriage and from the value placed on patriarchal lineage.

5. The preferred marriage is to someone from the same region, ideally the same town, and, traditionally, marrying a relative, especially a paternal cousin, is encouraged (Rude-Antoine 1997; Charrad 2001). Marrying one's cousin can be advantageous because it affords some protection from abusive in-laws (Joseph 1996).

6. Interestingly, only 38 percent of children of Algerian immigrants between the ages of 25 and 29 are married, compared with 48 percent of French people (Tribalat 1995:60; Weibel 2000:154).

7. Eleven women in the sample had never been married. Of the 34 who were or had been married, only five met their husbands in France. Amel's husband was Muslim but not of North African origin. Warda's Algerian husband and Fatima's Senegalese husband, both met and married more than 30 years ago, were traditional to varying extents. Although Warda was happy with her spouse, Fatima eventually divorced. Two younger women — Besma, whose husband had since died, and Rym — married Maghrebin men with western attitudes whom they met in France.

8. Andezian (1986) asserts that among Algerians in France, women become largely responsible for assuring the symbolic system needed to maintain identity and organize daily life, in part by taking on greater and more overt responsibility for religious acts and teaching than they were allowed in North Africa. They increasingly take on the primary role in actions in which before they were only assistants, such as tenants of public baths and singers at rites like circumcisions. In some rituals, the role of men has disappeared entirely. Women who are knowledgeable about Islam also meet in groups to discuss the validity of traditional practices, thus becoming responsible for deciding which norms and behaviors will change and which will remain.

9. Of the women interviewed, approximately one-third worked full time, one-third worked part time, and the other third were not employed. Of the nonworking group, 11 were housewives, two were actively seeking full-time employment and considered themselves unemployed, and one had retired early.

10. Non-European female immigrants had an unemployment rate of 38.4 percent in 1990 (INSEE 1990).

11. Both Hagan (1998) and Freedman and Tarr (2000) argue that immigrant women's precarious situation in the labor market makes them dependent on men for financial resources and often also for residence papers. Quiminal (1997), Rude-Antoine (1997), Gaspard (1998), and Raissiguier (1999, 2003) all point out that in general, immigrant women in France who arrived under family reunification laws are dependent on men because their legal position is determined by their relationship as spouse or daughter.

12. Divorce is also becoming more prevalent in the Maghreb. Almost one-fourth of Moroccans, especially those who live in big cities, will face divorce (LaCoste-Dujardin 2004a). The number of women over 35 who are widowed or divorced and living alone in poor conditions is also increasing (LaCoste-Dujardin 2004a).

13. Women's work outside the home can upset family dynamics. Women's work has led to an increase in divorce in Mexican and Vietnamese populations in the United States (Fernandez-Kelly and Garcia 1990; Kibria 1994). The findings on divorce point to the stress that women's work puts on immigrant families despite their economic need. Many men object to their wives' employment and feel, often correctly, that her earning power translates into more power within the household.

14. One of Sayad's (2004:156) respondents, who immigrated to France in 1953 and was interviewed in 1985 at the age of 51, explained that although he had briefly considered bringing his wife, he thought it was wrong because in France, "she would lose her freedom. It would only make her unhappy, lonely; she would be imprisoned in one room, dirty, dark, damp. That's all there is for her. She would long for the sun, the sky; she would miss the sky."

15. This is a particularly interesting finding given arguments that race and gender must not be viewed as separate, additive components (Collins 2000; Glenn 1992; Espiritu 1997). Here we see unexpected positive effects of French people separating out these various components of identity for Maghrebin immigrant women and weighing one, gender, more heavily than another, race.

16. Of course, many women in North Africa do gender the same way as many French women, by wearing revealing clothing and flirting with men. Thus calling this the "French way" is not entirely accurate and downplays the variation and changes in gender norms in the Maghreb. It does, however, represent most French people's perceptions that this behavior is French and not Maghrebin.

17. Kibria (1994) argues that visible immigrant women depend on their families and communities for protection against racism and anti-immigrant prejudice in society. Thus, the family is at the same time both a locus of patriarchal oppression and a haven from other forms of oppression.

18. This should be contrasted to African American women in the United States who have had to fight to be seen as women at all, given the history of slavery (see Collins 2000).

CHAPTER 3 CULTURAL CHOICES

1. One of the characteristics of tightly bounded societies is the level of distance in interpersonal relationships (Lamont 1989).

2. As Simmel (1950:119) argues, "[t]he feeling of isolation is rarely as decisive and intense when one actually finds oneself physically alone, as when one is a stranger, without relations, among many physically close persons, at a 'party,' on a train, or in the traffic of a large city."

3. One of Lamont's (2000) male respondents also recounted a story in which an elderly French man thanked him for his help when French people passed him by after he had fallen.

4. A few of the other respondents had at least all of their immediate family members in France, including parents, and thus did not face these issues to the same extent.

5. See Lamont (1992, 2000) on views of money as demarcations of boundaries between groups.

6. The other is the child of Amina's French ex-boyfriend.

7. Of course, these cultures have been living in interaction since colonization. Although Besma argues that cultural mixing is more about time than about immigration, immigration does bring into especially sharp focus the patterns of behavior, whatever they may be, that members of a particular group confront when they move to a foreign country.

8. Only one participant, Hiba, has a regional tattoo that is visible on the inside of her wrist

9. Rude-Antoine (1997) also reminds us that only a century ago in France, women were expected to cover their heads and most of their bodies while in public and that it was a norm for a long time for women to wear a hat with a small veil to church.

10. For contrasting patterns among religious groups in a secular society, see Ammerman (1987) and Davidman (1991). Ammerman (1987) studied fundamental-

ist Christians in the United States for whom accommodation is anathema. Davidman (1991) studied two groups of Orthodox Jews in the United States. She found that one group, Lubavitch Jews, practiced resistance, whereas the other, members of an Orthodox synagogue in New York, were more open to accommodation and did not seek separation from other groups in society.

11. Muslims believe that Jesus was a prophet. Christmas, however, is not typically celebrated by Muslims.

12. Only one woman who did not eat pork and who fasted during Ramadan did drink alcohol.

13. In her study of fundamentalist Christians in the United States, Ammerman (1987) found that even these strict resisters of secular life were forced to make compromises in the world of work. Although they were supposed to "bear witness," talking about their religion in an effort to save others, many felt uncomfortable doing this at work on someone else's time clock. In addition, despite believing that a woman's primary role should be as wife and mother, many women chose to work in order to be able to buy a house, a decision that privileged their material needs over absolute adherence to their faith.

14. These assertions are responses to questions that would not have arisen for some of the older women had they remained in North Africa. As in the case of fundamentalists confronting modernity, it is encounters with cultural pluralism and a secular society that force these women to rethink taken-for-granted cultural and religious behaviors (Ammerman 1987).

15. These assertions echo the findings of Read and Bartkowski (2000) among Muslim immigrant women who choose to veil in Austin, Texas. These similar statements are interesting given that these women live in the United States and are of higher socioeconomic status than those who say this in France. In addition, in their case study, it is women who do veil in public who make these statements.

16. For more on North African women's reactions to the "headscarf affair," including the reactions of several well-educated women who disagree with banning the veil in school, see Killian (2003).

17. See Sayad's (2004) analysis of early generations of Algerian men who self-segregated as a way to protect themselves from racism. They tended to spend almost all of their time at work or in housing built for Algerian workers, and thus were seldom visible in public spaces frequented by French people.

18. Their position as immigrants very probably affects their choice to accommodate rather than resist. It is increasingly members of the second generation who choose to resist and who criticize the compromises and adaptation of their parents. See, for example, Gaspard and Khosrokhavar (1995) and Weibel (2000) for explanations of the reclaiming of the veil by second-generation women. Weibel's study of women of Maghrebin and Turkish origin in France and Germany who have adopted Islamic dress as a form of identity resistance and subscribe to a more encompassing philosophy of "Islam action" highlights the differences between these young women and older immigrants. Her respondents believe that the veil is a requirement of Islam

and think that all Muslim women should aspire to wear it. They take issue with the statement that Islam is an affair "of the heart," arguing instead that actions reveal what is in the heart (Weibel 2000:158).

19. LaFromboise et al. (1993) use the term *alternation* to refer to individuals who can navigate back and forth between behaviors from the country of origin and the country of residence according to what is more culturally appropriate with a certain group of people or in a certain situation. See also discussions of time and space in Nippert-Eng's (1996) study of the different degrees of boundary work Americans use to segment or integrate home and work.

CHAPTER 4. IDENTITY NEGOTIATION

1. Surprisingly, education and social class did not have an impact on how women identified. Of the seven women who categorized themselves as more French, one left school at age 11, another at age 13, and two more at the end of high school. All four of these poorly educated women worked in domestic service positions. The other three women were well educated and well employed.

2. I use the term *Maghrebin* in this section as a matter of linguistic convenience so that I can speak of women from all three countries. The women I interviewed do not generally think of themselves as Maghrebin (unless they are being referred to as such by French people); rather, they identify by their country of origin.

3. All Algerians born between 1947 and Algeria's independence from France in 1962 were automatically given French citizenship at birth.

4. Writing about Algerians in the first decades after Algeria's independence, Sayad (2004:117) explains that "in many respects, the emigrant looks in a way like someone who was colonized at the last moment, like a *colonisé* who has outlived a colonization from which he cannot liberate himself, like a postcolonial *colonisé* and therefore someone who wants to be colonized (because he wants to remain an emigrant)." Whereas men had the excuse of having to leave to find work to support their families back home, women who emigrated in the 1950s and 1960s were particularly criticized (Sayad 2004).

5. Nationality is more problematic for Algerians than for other Maghrebins because although previously French, after independence, Algerians in France were called upon to individually choose whether or not to be French at a time when taking French nationality was seen by Algerians as choosing the enemy's side (Sayad 2004). As the memories of the war for independence have faded, taking French nationality has become less loaded and consequently accepted by more and more Algerians, especially by younger people.

6. See Sayad's (2004) poignant discussion of why generations of Algerian men felt they had to lie about conditions in France and their true standard of living to friends and family members in Algeria who could not or did not want to understand the truth.

7. Bowen (2004:52) writes that "[a]n entire ethnography of cross-cultural per-

ceptions could be built on the ways in which some non-Muslim French people use their bodies, grimaces, and speech in describing the social orientations they impute to women wearing different styles of head coverings."

8. Among these nine, there was no pattern in regard to feeling more North African or more French. Four self-identified by country of origin, four stated that they were both, and one viewed herself as French. These responses are consistent with the breakdown in self-perceptions in the sample as a whole.

9. Pyke and Dang (2003) and Pyke and Johnson (2003) give examples of second-generation Vietnamese and Korean Americans who distance themselves from stigmatized identities ("fresh off the boat" or "whitewashed," Pyke and Dang 2003) or quiet, subservient Asian women (Pyke and Johnson 2003) by denigrating coethnics, yet in doing so end up contributing to negative stereotypes of what it means to be Asian.

10. Pyke and Johnson (2003) also point out that when Asian women speak out or stand up for themselves, they become transracialized ("whitewashed" if not actually white), but that white women who are quiet or submissive do not become Asian. Similarly, Lina and Rym are willing to extend the immigrant label to the children of North African immigrants born in France, but they do not stretch the definition to include white French people who are lower class or struggling with an oppositional identity. Thus the term *immigrant* remains fundamentally racialized.

CHAPTER 5. COPING WITH PROBLEMS IN FRANCE

1. As Quiminal (1997) argues, residing in an inadequate apartment is a particular hardship on women who are seen as responsible for organizing and running their living space. As a result of lower rates of employment, child-care expectations, and cultural norms limiting women's use of public space, women are also more likely to spend significantly more of their time in the home than men.

2. In a survey conducted in 1988, 34.5 percent of the French admitted that they would be unhappy having a North African supervisor at work (Jackson 1992, in Lamont et al. 2002).

3. See Turki (1998:134) for a discussion of the plight of unmarried, pregnant women in Tunisia pressured to give up their children for adoption in a cultural context that "prefers to have children abandoned without a mother" rather than "unmarried mothers with children" (translation mine). According to Turki, single women who keep their children have committed the ultimate sin in their society's eyes by not only having a sexual relationship before marriage, but also by endangering the social order by resisting the norms that define family through marriage and identity in relation to the father. The small numbers of unmarried Tunisian women who do keep their babies often hide their pregnancies and cut ties with their families by moving to a big city (Turki 1998). Amina's residence in France thus probably helped enable her to keep her daughter.

4. Silverstein (2004:11) points out that even areas viewed as "Arab quarters," like

the Goutte d'Or in Paris or the suburb of Saint Denis, are ethnically mixed. According to Gaspard (1998), the only real examples of immigrant ghettos are the Chinatown in Paris's 13th arrondissement and a few projects built expressly for fleeing *harkis* and their families after Algeria's independence. See Silverstein (2004) and Weil (2005) on the history of French housing policies.

5. Sayad (2004) also highlights the first Gulf war as a critical moment for young Maghrebins in France who were confronted with a wave of negative perceptions about Arabs, which included Arabs born and raised in France.

6. In Feagin's (1991) study of middle-class black Americans' responses to racism, he found that respondents carefully evaluated the actions of others before judging a situation as discriminatory. He notes that this hesitation to recognize acts of racism may be a result of a fear of being hypersensitive and also "reflects the hope that white behavior is not based on race, because an act not based on race is easier to endure" (103).

7. Likewise, writing about male Algerian immigrants, Sayad (2004:290) argues that "[f]or the dominated . . . reassuring the dominant is without doubt the price that has to be paid to ensure their own security (which is purely relative). As this self-assurance depends upon a security that has to be won from the other or in the face of the other, certain immigrants prefer to withdraw . . . and choose (or chose, in an earlier state of immigration) to opt for the greatest possible discretion or, in other words, to become as invisible as they can. They are helped here by the social and spatial relegation of which they are also the victims." Although a similar dynamic of "reassuring the dominant" is at work among women who believe that they can prevent racism by dressing nicely and behaving politely, this marks a change from the time when the belief was that racism could only be prevented through segregation and invisibility.

8. Lamont et al. (2002) found the same response among male Maghrebin immigrants.

CHAPTER 6. CHILDREN AND THE FUTURE

1. The phrase "socially expected durations" is borrowed from Merton (1984).

2. These boarding houses served over 120,000 immigrant workers and retirees, mainly North and sub-Saharan Africans, in the late 1980s (Diop and Michalak 1996).

3. In his study of self-identification by immigrant children in the United States, Rumbaut (1994:779) found that the effect of the mother's perceived identity choice was stronger than that of the father's, "pointing to the possibly stronger effect of mothers in ethnic (and other) socialization processes, along with the actual absence of fathers in a substantial number of these families." Mothers were indeed found to have a stronger effect than fathers on the retention of cultural behaviors among the children of Vietnamese immigrants in the United States (Killian and Hegtvedt 2003).

4. Amina's boyfriend left her, and Cherifa's husband died. Currently, she is dating another French man.

Bibliography

Ahmed, Leila. 1992. *Women and Gender in Islam*. New Haven, CT: Yale University Press.

Alba, Richard, and Victor Nee. 1997. "Rethinking Assimilation Theory for a New Era of Immigration." *International Migration Review* 31, no. 4: 826–74.

———. 2003. *Remaking the American Mainstream: Assimilation and Contemporary Immigration*. Cambridge, MA: Harvard University Press.

Altorki, Soraya, and Camillia Fawzi El-Sohl. 1988. *Arab Women in the Field: Studying Your Own Society*. Syrcause: Syracuse University Press.

Amiraux, Valérie. 2004. "Le Foulard en République: Quinze Ans Déjà." *Les Cahiers de l'Orient* 76, no. 4: 73–88.

Ammerman, Nancy Tatom. 1987. *Bible Believers: Fundamentalists in the Modern World*. New Brunswick, NJ: Rutgers University Press.

Amselle, Jean-Loup. 2003. *Affirmative Exclusion: Cultural Pluralism and the Rule of Custom in France*. Translated by Jane Marie Todd. Ithaca, NY: Cornell University Press.

Andezian, Sossie. 1986. "Women's Roles in Organizing Symbolic Life: Algerian Female Immigrants in France." In *International Migration: The Female Experience*, edited by Rita James Simon and Caroline B. Brettell, 254–65. Totowa, NJ: Rowman and Allanheld.

Arkoun, Mohammed. 2004 [1995]. "Aux Origines des Cultures Maghrébines." In Lacoste and Lacoste, *Maghreb, Peuples et Civilisations*, 85–91.

Auslander, Leora. 2000. "Bavarian Crucifixes and French Headscarves: Religious Signs and the Postmodern European State." *Cultural Dynamics* 12, no. 3: 283–309.

Babès, Leïla. 2000. *L'Islam Intérieur: Passion et Desenchantement*. Beyrouth: Editions Al Bouraq.

Bancel, Nicolas, Pascal Blanchard, and Françoise Vergès. 2003. *La République Coloniale: Essai sur une Utopie*. Paris: Albin Michel.

Bhachu, Parminder K. 1986. "Work, Dowry, and Marriage Among East African Sikh Women in the United Kingdom." In *International Migration: The Female*

Experience, edited by Rita James Simon and Caroline B. Brettell, 229–40. Totowa, NJ: Rowman and Allanheld.

Bhatnagar, Joti. 1981. *Educating Immigrants*. New York: St. Martin's Press.

Blumer, Herbert. 1969. *Symbolic Interactionsim: Perspective Method*. Englewood Cliffs, NJ: Prentice-Hall.

Begag, Azouz. 1990. "The 'Beurs,' Children of North-African Immigrants in France: The Issue of Integration." *Journal of Ethnic Studies* 18, no. 1: 1–14.

Begag, Azouz, and Abdellatif Chaouite. 1990. *Ecarts d'Identité*. Paris: Editions du Seuil.

Benedict, Ruth. 1961 [1934]. *Patterns of Culture*. Boston: Houghton Mifflin.

Berry, J. W. 1986. "Multiculturalism and Psychology in Plural Societies." In Ekstrand, *Ethnic Minorities and Immigrants*, 35–51.

Berry, J. W., and R. C. Annis. 1974. "Acculturative Stress: The Role of Ecology, Culture and Differentiation." *Journal of Cross-Cultural Psychology* 5: 382–406.

Body-Gendrot, Sophie. 2000. "Urban Violence and Community Mobilizations." In *Minorities in European Cities: The Dynamics of Social Integration and Social Exclusion at the Neighborhood Level*, edited by Sophie Body-Gendrot and Marco Martiniello, 75–87. New York: St. Martin's Press.

Body-Gendrot, Sophie, and Marco Martiniello, eds. 2000. *Minorities in European Cities: The Dynamics of Social Integration and Social Exclusion at the Neighborhood Level*. New York: St. Martin's Press.

Bowen, John R. 2004. "Does French Islam Have Borders? Dilemmas of Domestication in a Global Religious Field." *American Anthropologist* 106, no. 1: 43–55.

Bozorgmehr, Mehdi. 1997. "Internal Ethnicity: Iranians in Los Angeles." *Sociological Perspectives* 40, no. 3: 387–404.

Bourdieu, Pierre. 1977. *Outline of a Theory of Practice*. Cambridge: Cambridge University Press.

Burke, Peter. 1991. "Identity Processes and Social Stress." *American Sociological Review* 56: 836–49.

Caplan, Nathan, Marcella H. Choy, and John K. Whitmore. 1991. *Children of the Boat People: A Study of Educational Success*. Ann Arbor: University of Michigan Press.

Césari, Jocelyne. 1994. *Etre Musulman en France, Associations, Militants, et Mosquées*. Paris: Karthala-IREMAM.

———. 1997. *Faut-il Avoir Peur de l'Islam?* Paris: Presses de Sciences Po.

———. 1998. *Musulman et Républicains: Les Jeunes, l'Islam, et la France*. Brussels: Complexe.

———. 2000. "Islam in European Cities." In *Minorities in European Cities: The Dynamics of Social Integration and Social Exclusion at the Neighborhood Level*, edited by Sophie Body-Gendrot and Marco Martiniello, 88–99. New York: St. Martin's Press.

Charrad, Mounira M. 2001. *States and Women's Rights: The Making of Postcolonial Tunisia, Algeria, and Morocco*. Berkeley: University of California Press.

CNCDH. 2004. *Rapport Annuel 2003 sur la Lutte Contre le Racisme et la Xénophobie.* Commission Nationale Consultative des Droits de l'Homme. Paris.

Collins, Patricia Hill. 2000 [1991]. *Black Feminist Thought: Knowledge, Consciousness, and the Politics of Empowerment.* New York: Routledge.

Couvreur, Gilles. 1998. *Musulmanes de France: Diversité, Mutations et Perspectives de l'Islam Français.* Paris: Les Editions de l'Atelier.

Crenshaw, Kimberlé. 1989. "Demarginalizing the Intersection of Race and Sex: A Black Feminist Critique of Antidiscrimination Doctrine, Feminist Theory, and Antiracist Politics." *University of Chicago Legal Forum* 139.

Davidman, Lynn. 1991. *Tradition in a Rootless World: Women Turn to Orthodox Judaism.* Berkeley: University of California Press.

Deutsch, Sarah. 1987. "Women and Intercultural Relations: The Case of Hispanic New Mexico and Colorado." *Signs* 12: 719–40.

Diop, Moustapha, and Laurence Michalak. 1996. "'Refuge' and 'Prison': Islam, Ethnicity, and the Adaptation of Space in Workers' Housing in France." In *Making Muslim Space in North America and Europe*, edited by Barbara Daly Metcalf, 74–91. Berkeley: University of California Press.

Dominguez, Virginia R. 1989. *People as Subject, People as Object: Selfhood and Peoplehood in Contemporary Israel.* Madison: University of Wisconsin Press.

Ekstrand, Lars H. 1985. *Ethnic Minorities and Immigrants in a Cross-Cultural Perspective.* Lisse, Netherlands: Swets & Zeitlinger.

Espiritu, Yen L. 1997. "Race, Gender, Class in the Lives of Asian Americans." *Race, Gender & Class* 4, no. 3: 12–19.

Etienne, Bruno. 1990. *La France et l'Islam.* Paris: Hachette.

Fassin, Didier, Alain Morice, and Catherine Quiminal, eds. 1997. *Les Lois de l'Inhospitalité: Les Politiques de l'Immigration à l'Epreuve des Sans-papiers.* Paris: La Découverte.

Feagin, J. R. 1991. "The Continuing Significance of Race — Antiblack Discrimination in Public Places." *American Sociological Review* 56, no. 1: 101–16.

Fernandez-Kelly, Maria P., and Anna Garcia. 1990. "Power Surrendered, Power Restored: The Politics of Work and Family Among Hispanic Garment Workers in California and Florida." In *Women, Politics and Change*, edited by L. Tilly and P. Gurin, 130–49. New York: Russell Sage.

Fernea, Elizabeth Warnock, and Basima Qattan Bezirgan. 1978. *Middle Eastern Muslim Women Speak.* Austin: University of Texas Press.

Fiske, Susan T., and Shelley E. Taylor. 1991. *Social Cognition.* New York: McGraw-Hill.

Foner, Nancy. 1986. "Sex Roles and Sensibilities: Jamaican Women in New York and London." In *International Migration: The Female Experience*, edited by Rita James Simon and Caroline B. Brettell, 133–51. Totowa, NJ: Rowman and Allanheld.

Freedman, Jane. 2000. "Women and Immigration: Nationality and Citizenship." In *Women, Immigration and Identities in France*, edited by Jane Freedman and Carrie Tarr, 13–28. Oxford, UK: Berg.

Freedman, Jane, and Carrie Tarr, eds. 2000. *Women, Immigration and Identities in France*. Oxford, UK: Berg.

Gabaccia, Donna. 1989. *Immigrant Women in the United States: A Selectively Annotated Multidisciplinary Bibliography*. Westport, CT: Greenwood Press.

Gans, Herbert J. 1992. "Comment: Ethnic Invention and Acculturation: A Bumpy-Line Approach." *Journal of American Ethnic History* 11, no. 1: 42–52.

———. 1999. "Toward a Reconciliation of 'Assimilation' and 'Pluralism': The Interplay of Acculturation and Ethnic Retention." In *The Handbook of International Migration: The American Experience*, edited by Charles Hirschman, Philip Kasinitz, and Josh DeWind, 161–71. New York: Russell Sage Foundation.

Gaspard, Françoise. 1998. "Femmes de la Méditerranée, Femmes des Banlieues Française." In *La Méditerranée des Femmes*, edited by Nabil el Haggar, 159–72. Paris: L'Harmattan.

Gaspard, Françoise, and Farhad Khosrokhavar. 1995. *Le Foulard et la République*. Paris: La Découverte.

Geisser, Vincent. 2003. *La Nouvelle Islamophobie*. Paris: Editions La Découverte.

Ghiles, Francis. 1994. "Mounting Slaughter Pushes Algeria to an Abyss." London *Sunday Times*, October 23.

Glaser, Barney G., and Anselm L. Strauss. 1967. *The Discovery of Grounded Theory: Strategies for Qualitative Research*. New York: Aldine De Gruyter.

Glenn, Evelyn Nakano. 1992. "From Servitude to Service Work: Historical Continuities in the Racial Division of Paid Reproductive Labor." *Signs* 18, no. 1: 1–43.

Goffman, Erving. 1963. *Stigma: Notes on the Management of Spoiled Identity*. Englewood Cliffs, NJ: Prentice-Hall.

Gold, Steven. 1997. "Transnationalism and Vocabularies of Motive in International Migration: The Case of Israelis in the United States." *Sociological Perspectives* 40, no. 3: 409–22.

Gordon, Milton. 1964. *Assimilation in American Life: The Role of Race, Religion and National Origins*. New York: Oxford University Press.

Gourévitch, Jean-Paul. 1998. *Immigration: La Fracture Légale*. Paris: Le Pré aux Clercs.

Graham-Brown, Sarah. 1988. *Images of Women: The Portrayal of Women in Photography of the Middle East, 1860–1950*. New York: Columbia University Press.

Grasmuck, Sherri, and Patricia Pessar. 1991. *Between Two Islands: Dominican International Migration*. Berkeley: University of California Press.

Hagan, Jacqueline Maria. 1998. "Social Networks, Gender, and Immigrant Incorporation: Resources and Constraints." *American Sociological Review* 63, no. 1: 55–67.

Harrison, Algea O., Melvin N. Wilson, Charles J. Pine, Samuel Q. Chan, and Raymond Buriel. 1990. "Family Ecologies of Ethnic Minority Children." *Child Development* 61: 347–62.

Hill, Hope M., Fernando I. Soriano, S. Andrew Chen, and Teresa LaFromboise. 1994. "Sociocultural Factors in the Etiology and Prevention of Violence Among Ethnic Minority Youth." In *A Reason to Hope: A Psychosocial Perspective on Violence and Youth*, edited by Leonard D. Eron, Jacqulyn H. Gentry, and Peggy Schlegel, 59–132. Washington, DC: American Psychological Association.

Hogg, Michael, and Dominic Abrams. 1988. *Social Identifications*. New York: Routledge.

Hondagneu-Sotelo, Pierette. 1994. *Gendered Transitions: Mexican Experiences of Immigration*. Berkley: University of California Press.

hooks, bell. 1990. *Yearning: Race, Gender, and Cultural Politics*. Boston: South End Press.

Horowitz, Donald L. 1998. "Immigration and Group Relations in France and America." In *The Immigration Reader: America in a Multidisciplinary Perspective*, edited by David Jacobson, 320–38. Malden, MA: Blackwell.

INSEE. 1990. *Recensement de la Population de 1990*. Paris: Institut National de la Statistique et des Etudes Economiques/Ministère de l'Economie des Finances et de l'Industrie.

———. 1997. *Les Immigrés en France*. Paris: Institut National de la Statistique et des Etudes Economiques.

———. 1999. *France, Portrait Social*. Paris: Institut National de la Statistique et des Etudes Economiques.

———. 2000a. Recensement de la Population de 1999 – La Proportion d'Immigrés est Stable Depuis 25 Ans. Julien Boeldieu and Catherine Borrel. No. 748, November 2000.

———. 2000b. *Annuaire Statistique de la France, Edition 2000*. Vol. 103, no. 45. Results from 1998. Paris: Institut National de la Statistique et des Etudes Economiques/Ministère de l'Economie des Finances et de l'Industrie.

Jayaratne, Toby Epstein, and Abigail Stewart. 1991. "Quantitative and Qualitative Methods in the Social Sciences: Current Feminist Issues and Practical Strategies." In *Beyond Methodology: Feminist Scholarship as Lived Research*, edited by Mary Margaret Fonow and Judith A. Cook, 85–106. Bloomington: Indiana University Press.

Johnson-Odim, Cheryl. 1991. "Common Themes, Different Contexts: Third World Women and Feminism." In *Third World Women and the Politics of Feminism*, edited by Chandra Talpade Mohanty, Ann Russo, and Lourdes Torres, 314–27. Bloomington: Indiana University Press.

Joppke, Christian. 1998. "Multiculturalism and Immigration: A Comparison of the United States, Germany, and Great Britain." In *The Immigration Reader: America in a Multidisciplinary Perspective*, edited by David Jacobson, 285–319. Malden, MA: Blackwell.

Joseph, Suad. 1996. "Gender and Family in the Arab World." In *Arab Women: Between Defiance and Restraint*, edited by Suha Sabbagh, 194–202. New York: Olive Branch Press.

Karakasidou, Anastasia. 1996. "Women of the Family, Women of the Nation: National Enculturation Among Slavic Speakers in Northwestern Greece." *Women's Studies International Forum* 19, no. 1/2: 99–109.

Kastoryano, Riva. 1996. *La France, l'Allemagne, et Leurs Immigrés: Négocier l'Identité.* Paris: Armand Colin.

———. 2002. *Negotiating Identities: States and Immigrants in France and Germany.* Translated by Barbara Harshav. Princeton, NJ: Princeton University Press.

Kennedy-Brenner, Carliene. 1979. *Foreign Workers and Immigration Policy: The Case of France.* Paris: Development Centre of the Organisation for Economic Co-operation and Development.

Kepel, Gilles. 1987. *Les Banlieues de l'Islam.* Paris: Le Seuil.

Khellil, Mohand. 1991. *L'Intégration des Maghrébins en France.* Paris: Presses Universitaires de France.

Khosrokhavar, Farhad. 1997. *L'Islam des Jeunes.* Paris: Flammarion.

Kibria, Nazli. 1993. *Family Tightrope: The Changing Lives of Vietnamese Americans.* Princeton, NJ: Princeton University Press.

———. 1994. "Migration and Vietnamese American Women: Remaking Ethnicity." In *Women of Color in U.S. Society,* edited by Maxine Baca Zinn and Bonnie Thorton Dill, 247–64. Philadelphia: Temple.

Killian, Caitlin. 2002. "Culture on the Weekend: Maghrebin Women's Adaptation in France." *International Journal of Sociology and Social Policy* 22, no. 1–3: 75–105.

———. 2003. "The Other Side of the Veil: North African Women in France Respond to the Headscarf Affair." *Gender & Society* 17, no. 4: 567–90.

Killian, Caitlin, and Karen A. Hegtvedt. 2003. "The Role of Parents in the Maintenance of Second Generation Vietnamese Cultural Behaviors." *Sociological Spectrum* 23, no. 2: 213–45.

Kim, Uichol, and J. W. Berry. 1986. "Predictors of Acculturative Stress: Korean Immigrants in Toronto, Canada." In Ekstrand, *Ethnic Minorities and Immigrants,* 159–70.

King, Deborah. 1989. "Multiple Jeopardy, Multiple Consciousness: The Context of a Black Feminist Ideology." *Signs* 14, no. 1: 42–72.

Lacoste, Yves. 2004 [1995]. "Peuplements et Organisation Sociale." In Lacoste and Lacoste, *Maghreb, Peuples et Civilisations,* 59–68.

Lacoste, Camille, and Yves Lacoste, eds. 2004 [1995]. *Maghreb, Peuples et Civilisations.* Paris: La Découverte.

Lacoste-Dujardin, Camille Lacoste. 1992. *Yasmina et les Autres de Nanterre et d'Ailleurs: Filles de Parents Maghrébins en France.* Paris: La Découverte.

———. 1996. *Des Mères Contre les Femmes: Maternité et Patriarcat au Maghreb.* 2nd ed. Paris: La Découverte.

———. 2000. "Maghrebi Families in France." In *Women, Immigration and Identities in France,* edited by Jane Freedman and Carrie Tarr, 57–68. Oxford, UK: Berg.

———. 2004a [1995]. "De la Grande Famille aux Nouvelles Familles." In Lacoste and Lacoste, *Maghreb, Peuples et Civilisations,* 119–25.

———. 2004b [1995]. "Les Codes du Statut Personnel ou l'Influence de la "Charia" dans le Droit Familial." In Lacoste and Lacoste, *Maghreb, Peuples et Civilisations,* 126–30.

LaFromboise, Teresa, Hardin L. K. Coleman, and Jennifer Gerton. 1993. "Psycho-logical Impact of Biculturalism: Evidence and Theory." *Psychological Bulletin* 114, no. 3: 395–412.

Lalonde, Richard, Donald Taylor, and Fathali Moghaddam. 1992. "The Process of Social Identification for Visible Immigrant Women in a Multicultural Context." *Journal of Cross-Cultural Psychology* 23, no. 1: 25–39.

Lamont, Michèle. 1989. "The Power-Culture Link in a Comparative Perspective." *Comparative Social Research* 11: 131–50.

———. 1992. *Money, Morals, and Manners: The Culture of the French and the American Upper-Middle Class.* Chicago: University of Chicago Press.

———. 2000. *The Dignity of Working Men: Morality and the Boundaries of Race, Class, and Immigration.* New York: Russell Sage Foundation.

Lamont, Michèle, Ann Morning, and Margarita Mooney. 2002. "Particular Universalisms: North-African Immigrants Respond to French Racism." *Ethnic and Racial Studies* 25, no. 3: 390–414.

Lebon, André. 1998. *Immigration et Presence Etrangère en France, 1997/1998.* Ministère de L'Emploi et de la Solidarité.

Lofland, John, and Lyn H. Lofland. 1995. *Analyzing Social Settings: A Guide to Qualitative Observation and Analysis.* 3rd ed. Belmont, CA: Wadsworth.

Mansell, Gerard. 1961. *Tragedy in Algeria.* New York: Oxford University Press.

Martinez, Luis. 2000. *The Algerian Civil War, 1990–1998.* Translated by Jonathan Derrick. London: Hurst.

Martiniello, Marco. 2000. "The Residential Concentration and Political Participation of Immigrants in European Cities." In *Minorities in European Cities: The Dynamics of Social Integration and Social Exclusion at the Neighborhood Level,* edited by Sophie Body-Gendrot and Marco Martiniello, 119–28. New York: St. Martin's Press.

McCall, George J. 2003. "The Me and the Not-Me: Positive and Negative Poles of Identity." In *Advances in Identity Theory and Research,* edited by Peter J. Burke, Timothy J. Owens, Richard T. Serpe, and Peggy A. Thoits, 11–25. New York: Kluwer Academic/Plenum Publishers.

———. 1996. "Muslim Women and Fundamentalism." In *Arab Women: Between Defiance and Restraint,* edited by Suha Sabbagh, 162–68. New York: Olive Branch Press.

Merton, Robert K. 1984. "Socially Expected Durations: A Case Study of Concept Formation in Sociology." In *Conflict and Consensus: A Festschrift for Lewis A. Coser,* edited by W. W. Powell and Richard Robbins. New York: The Free Press.

Moghadam, Valentine. 1993. *Modernizing Women: Gender and Social Change in the Middle East.* Boulder, Colo.: Lynne Rienner Publishers.

Mohanty, Chandra Talpade. 1991. "Cartographies of Struggle: Third World Women and the Politics of Feminism." In *Third World Women and the Politics of Feminism,* edited by Chandra Talpade Mohanty, Ann Russo, and Lourdes Torres, 1–47. Bloomington: Indiana University Press.

Murphy, H.B.M. 1973. "Low Rate of Mental Hospitalization Shown by Immigrants to Canada." In *Uprooting and After*, edited by Charles Zwingmann and Maria Pfister-Ammende, 221–31. New York: Springer-Verlag.

Naidoo, Josephine. 1986. "Value Conflicts for South Asian Women in Multicultural Canada." In Ekstrand, *Ethnic Minorities and Immigrants*, 132–46.

Nippert-Eng, Christena. 1996. *Home and Work: Negotiating Boundaries Through Everyday Life*. Chicago: University of Chicago Press.

Noiriel, Gérard. 1988. *Le Creuset Français*. Paris: Seuil.

———. 1998. *Réfugiés et Sans-Papiers: La République Face au Droit d'Asile, XIXe–XXe Siècle*. Paris: Hachette.

———. 2001. *Etat, Nation, et Immigration*. Paris: Gallimard.

Park, Robert E., and E. W. Burgess. 1969. *Introduction to the Science of Sociology*. 1921; reprint, Chicago: University of Chicago Press.

Patton, Michael Quinn. 1990. *Qualitative Evaluation and Research Methods*. 2nd ed. Newbury Park, CA: Sage Publications.

Platt, Katie. 1986. "Cognitive Development and Sex Roles on the Kerkennah Islands of Tunisia." In Ekstrand, *Ethnic Minorities and Immigrants*, 120–31.

Phinney, Jean S., and Mary Jane Rotherman. 1987. *Children's Ethnic Socialization*. Beverly Hills, CA: Sage Publications.

Portes, Alejandro, and Rubén G. Rumbaut. 1996. *Immigrant America: A Portrait*. 2nd ed. Berkeley: University of California Press.

Portes, Alejandro, and Richard Schauffler. 1994. "Language and the Second Generation: Bilingualism Yesterday and Today." *International Migration Review* 28, no. 4: 640–61.

Portes, Alejando, and Min Zhou. 1993. "The New Second Generation: Segmented Assimilation and Its Variants." *Annals of the American Academy of Political and Social Sciences* 530: 74–96.

Prieto, Yolanda. 1992. "Cuban Women in New Jersey: Gender Relations and Change." In *Seeking Common Ground: Multidisciplinary Studies of Immigrant Women in the United States*, edited by Donna Gabaccia, 185–201. Westport, CT: Greenwood Press.

Pyke, Karen, and Tran Dang. 2003. "'FOB' and 'Whitewashed': Intra-Ethnic Identities and Internalized Oppression Among Second Generation Asian Americans." *Qualitative Sociology* 26:147–72.

Pyke, Karen, and Denise L. Johnson. 2003. "Asian American Women and Racialized Femininities: 'Doing' Gender Across Cultural Worlds." *Gender & Society* 17:33–53.

Quiminal, Catherine. 1997. "Familles Immigrées entre Deux Espaces." In *Les Lois de l'Inhospitalité: Les Politiques de l'Immigration à l'Epreuve des Sans-papiers*, edited by Didier Fassin, Alain Morice, and Catherine Quiminal, 67–81. Paris: La Découverte.

Raissiguier, Catherine. 1994. *Becoming Women/Becoming Workers: Identity Formation in a French Vocational School*. Albany: State University of New York Press.

————. 1999. "Gender, Race and Exclusion: A New Look at the French Republican Tradition." *International Journal of Feminist Politics* 1, no. 3: 435–57.

————. 2003. "Troubling Mothers: Immigrant Women from Africa in France." *Jenda: A Journal of Culture and African Women Studies* 4, no. 1: 1–15.

Read, Jen'nan Ghazal, and John P. Bartkowski. 2000. "To Veil or Not to Veil? A Case Study of Identity Negotiation Among Muslim Women in Austin, Texas." *Gender & Society* 14, no. 3: 395–417.

Roberts, Bryan R. 1995. "Socially Expected Durations and the Economic Adjustment of Immigrants." In *The Economic Sociology of Immigration: Essays on Networks, Ethnicity, and Entrepreneurship*, edited by Alejandro Portes, 42–86. New York: Russell Sage Foundation.

Rude-Antoine, Edwige. 1997. *Des Vies et des Familles: Les Immigrés, la Loi et la Coutume*. Paris: Editions Odile Jacob.

Ruedy, John. 1992. *Modern Algeria*. Bloomington: Indiana University Press.

Rumbaut, Rubén. 1994. "The Crucible Within: Ethnic Identity, Self-Esteem, and Segmented Assimilation Among Children of Immigrants." *International Migration Review* 28, no. 4: 748–94.

Said, Edward. 1979. *Orientalism*. New York: Vintage Books.

Sayad, Abdelmalek. 2004. *The Suffering of the Immigrant*. Translated by David Macey. Cambridge, UK: Polity Press.

Sassen, Saskia. 1999. *Guests and Aliens*. New York: The New Press.

Schain, Martin A. 1988. "Immigration and Changes in the French Party System." *European Journal of Political Research* 16: 597–621.

Schem, Elisabeth. 1994. Information on Khalida Messaoudi in *Le Nouvel Observateur*, September 22–28.

Schulz, Amy J. 1998. "Navajo Women and the Politics of Identity." *Social Problems* 45, no. 3: 336–55.

Sciolino, Elaine. 2004. "Bobigny Journal: French Sikhs Defend Their Turbans and Find Their Voice." *New York Times*. January 12.

Silverstein, Paul A. 2002a. "An Excess of Truth: Violence, Conspiracy Theorizing and the Algerian Civil War." *Anthropological Quarterly* 75, no. 4: 643–74.

————. 2002b. "The Kabyle Myth: Colonization and the Production of Ethnicity." In *From the Margins: Historical Anthropology and Its Futures*, edited by Brian Keith Axel, 122–55. Durham, NC: Duke University Press.

————. 2004. *Algeria in France: Transpolitics, Race, and Nation*. Bloomington: Indiana University Press.

Simmel, Georg. 1950. *The Sociology of Georg Simmel*. Translated by Kurt H. Wolff. New York: The Free Press.

Simon, Catherine. 1994. "Les Kabyles Se Mobilisent Contre le Pouvoir et le FIS." *Le Monde*, September 23.

Snow, David A. 1980. "The Disengagement Process: A Neglected Problem in Participant Observation Research." *Qualitative Sociology* 3, no. 2: 100–122.

Snow, David, and Leon Anderson. 1987. "Identity Work Among the Homeless:

The Verbal Construction and Avowal of Personal Identities." *American Journal of Sociology* 92, no. 6: 1336–71.

Souilamas, Nacira Guénif. 1999. *Des "Beurettes" aux Descendants d'Immigrants Nord-Africans*. Paris: Grasset.

Srole, Leo, Thomas S. Langer, and Stanley Mitchell. 1962. *Mental Health in the Metropolis: The Midtown Manhattan Study*. Vol. 1. Rev. ed. New York: New York University Press.

Stebbins, Robert A. 1991. "Do We Ever Leave the Field? Notes on Secondary Fieldwork Involvements." In *Experiencing Fieldwork: An Inside View of Qualitative Research*, edited by William B. Shaffir and Robert A. Stebbins, 122–55. Newbury Park, CA: Sage Publications.

Stone, Martin. 1997. *The Agony of Algeria*. New York: Columbia University Press.

Stora, Benjamin. 2001. *Algeria, 1830–2000: A Short History*. Translated by Jane Marie Todd. Ithaca, NY: Cornell University Press.

———. 2005. "Les Aveux les Plus Durs: Le Retour des Souvenirs de la Guerre d'Algérie dans la Société Française." In *L'Esclavage, la Colonisation, et Apres . . . ,* edited by Patrick Weil and Stéphane Dufoix, 585–97. Paris: Presses Universitaires de France.

Stroobants, Jean-Pierre. 2003. "Le Foulard, Vu d'Ailleurs." *Le Monde*, December 19.

Swann, William B. Jr., J. J. Griffin, S. C. Predmore, and B. Gaines. 1987. "The Cognitive-Affective Crossfire: When Self-Consistency Confronts Self-Enhancement." *Journal of Personality and Social Psychology* 52: 881–89.

Swidler, Ann. 1986. "Culture in Action: Symbols and Strategies." *American Sociological Review* 51: 273–86.

Taïeb, Eric. 1998. *Immigrés: L'Effet Générations*. Paris: Editions de l'Atelier.

Tajfel, Henri. 1981. *Human Groups and Social Categories: Studies in Social Psychology*. Cambridge: Cambridge University Press.

Taylor, Steven J. 1991. "Leaving the Field: Research, Relationships, and Responsibilities." In *Experiencing Fieldwork: An Inside View of Qualitative Research*, edited by William B. Shaffir and Robert A. Stebbins, 238–47. Newbury Park, CA: Sage Publications.

Tribalat, Michèle. 1995. *Faire France: Une Enquête sur les Immigrés et Leurs Enfants*. Paris: La Découverte/Essais.

———. 1996. *De l'Immigration à l'Assimilation: Enquête sur les Populations d'Origine Etrangère en France*. Paris: La Découverte/INED.

Turki, Rim. 1998. "Le Tabou de la Maternité Célibataire dans les Sociétés Arabo-Musulmanes (Exemple de la Tunisie)." In *La Méditerranée des Femmes*, edited by Nabil el Haggar, 133–55. Paris: L'Harmattan.

Turner, John. 1985. "Social Categorization and the Self-Concept: A Social Cognitive Theory of Group Behavior." In *Advances in Group Processes: Theory and Research*, vol. 2, edited by E. J. Lawler, 77–121. Greenwich, CT: JAI Press.

UNESCO. 1984. *Social Science Research and Women in the Arab World*. London: Frances Pinter.

Venel, Nancy. 1999. *Musulmanes Françaises: Des Pratiquantes Voilées a l'Université.* Paris: L'Harmattan.

Volpi, Frédéric. 2003. *Islam and Democracy: The Failure of Dialogue in Algeria.* London: Pluto Press.

Warner, R. Stephen, and Judith G. Wittner. 1998. *Gatherings in Diaspora: Religious Communities and the New Immigration.* Philadelphia: Temple University Press.

Waters, Mary C. 1990. *Ethnic Options: Choosing Identities in America.* Berkeley: University of California Press.

Weibel, Nadine B. 2000. *Par-Delà le Voile: Femmes d'Islam en Europe.* Editions Complexe.

Weil, Patrick. 1991. *La France et ses Etrangers, l'Aventure d'une Politique de l'Immigration de 1938 à Nos Jours.* Paris: Calmann-Lévy.

———. 2001. "The History of French Nationality: A Lesson for Europe." In *Towards a European Nationality: Citizenship, Immigration and Nationality Law in the EU,* edited by Randall Hansen and Patrick Weil, 52–68. New York: Palgrave.

———. 2002. *Qu'est-ce Qu'un Français? Histoire de la Nationalité Française Depuis la Revolution.* Paris: Grasset.

———. 2005. *La République et Sa Diversité: Immigration, Intégration, Discriminations.* Paris: Seuil.

West, Candace, and Don Zimmerman. 1987. "Doing Gender." *Gender & Society* 1: 125–51.

Wieviorka, Michel. 1996. *Une Société Fragmentée — Le Multiculturalisme en Débat.* Paris: La Découverte.

Wihtol de Wenden, Catherine. 1984. "The Evolution of French Immigration Policy After May 1981." *International Migration* 22: 199–213.

———. 1988. *Les Immigrés et la Politique.* Paris: Presses de la Fondation Nationale des Sciences Politiques.

Yinger, J. M. 1981. "Toward a Theory of Assimilation and Dissimilation." *Ethnic and Racial Studies* 4, no. 3: 249–64.

Zappi, Sylvia. 2004. "Les Chiffres de la CNCDH pour 2003: Le Nombre des Agressions Racistes et Antisémites Diminue Mais Demeure Elevé." *Le Monde,* April 2.

———. 2005. "Selon un Sondage, 56% des Français Pensent que le Nombre d'Etrangers Est Trop Important." *Le Monde,* December 18.

Zhou, Min, and Carl L. Bankston. 1998. *Growing Up American: How Vietnamese Children Adapt to Life in the United States.* New York: Russell Sage Foundation.

Zhou, Min, and John Logan. 1989. "Returns on Human Capital in Ethnic Enclaves: New York City's Chinatown." *American Sociological Review* 54, no. 5: 809–20.

Index

The authorized representative in the EU for product safety and compliance is:
Mare Nostrum Group
B.V Doelen 72
4831 GR Breda
The Netherlands

www.ingramcontent.com/pod-product-compliance
Lightning Source LLC
Chambersburg PA
CBHW020657270326
41928CB00005B/170